WAGNER AND SUICIDE

Wagner and Suicide

by
John Louis DiGaetani

McFarland & Company, Inc., Publishers
Jefferson, North Carolina, and London

ALSO BY JOHN LOUIS DIGAETANI
AND FROM MCFARLAND

*Carlo Gozzi: A Life in the 18th Century Venetian
Theater, an Afterlife in Opera* (2000)

Frontispiece: Engraving of Richard Wagner by Lazar Binenbaum,
from a photograph by Franz Hanfstaengl.

All photographs depicting productions of the Metropolitan Opera
are by Winnie Klotz, Metropolitan Opera, and are used by permission.

LIBRARY OF CONGRESS CATALOGUING-IN-PUBLICATION DATA

DiGaetani, John Louis, 1943–
    Wagner and suicide / by John Louis DiGaetani.
      p.   cm.
    Includes bibliographical references and index.

    ISBN 0-7864-1477-4 (softcover : 50# alkaline paper) ∞

    1. Wagner, Richard, 1813–1883 — Mental health.   2. Wagner,
Richard, 1813–1883. Operas.   3. Composers — Mental health.
4. Suicide.   I. Title.
ML410.W13D45   2003
782.1′092—dc21   2003001404

British Library cataloguing data are available

©2003 John Louis DiGaetani. All rights reserved

*No part of this book may be reproduced or transmitted in any form
or by any means, electronic or mechanical, including photocopying
or recording, or by any information storage and retrieval system,
without permission in writing from the publisher.*

On the cover: detail (flopped) of photograph of Richard Wagner
by Franz Hanfstaengl. Music framing ©2003 Art Today.

Manufactured in the United States of America

McFarland & Company, Inc., Publishers
   Box 611, Jefferson, North Carolina 28640
      www.mcfarlandpub.com

For Audre and Carol

Contents

Acknowledgments	viii
Introduction	1
1 Wagner's Bipolar Life: Mania and Depression	7
2 *Die Fliegender Holländer*: The Isolated Personality	21
3 *Tannhäuser*: The Artistic Personality and Suicide	37
4 *Lohengrin*: The Dream Persona from Another World	55
5 *Tristan und Isolde*: Suicide as the Best Alternative	73
6 *Die Meistersinger von Nürnberg*: Mania and Reconciliation	94
7 The *Ring* Cycle: Suicide as Threat and Triumph	111
8 *Parsifal*: Beyond Polarity	148
9 Suicide in Opera and Drama	165
10 Wagner, the Decadents, and the Modern British Novel	172
Conclusion	182
Bibliography	187
Index	193

Acknowledgments

I would like to thank Hofstra University for granting me a sabbatical leave and travel funds to work on this project. I would also like to thank Earl Harbert, Christine Hofmann, Naomi Dicker, Elayne Horn, Mary Ann Spengler, Dorothy Olson, Audre Meltzer, and Carol Zitrin for their help and encouragement with this book.

Finally, I would like to thank Winnie Klotz of the Metropolitan Opera for the use of her wonderful photos.

Introduction

In his famous book *Beyond the Pleasure Principle*, Sigmund Freud suggested that most adults, and even many children, have at points in their lives considered suicide as a solution to their personal problems. Most psychiatrists and psychologists will tell you how often their patients talk about suicidal fantasies, and even about suicide attempts, but this topic remains in most circumstances taboo for general discussion. However, Richard Wagner's operas address this generally unspoken and often embarrassing human fantasy. The present work will investigate the suicide theme in Wagner's life and in his operas, especially in the librettos of the operas. While Wagner's operas are rarely analyzed from a literary point of view, Wagner himself took his texts very seriously and felt that the words were often more important than the music in his operas. This book will also look at suicide as a theatrical and operatic phenomenon and see how the suicide theme has occurred in other important works of the literary and performing arts.

I will also argue in this book that Wagner suffered from what we would now call bipolar illness—or manic-depressive behavior. His life was often governed by extreme mood swings that were bipolar in their nature and in their cyclical quality, and we will see cyclical themes used regularly in Wagnerian opera itself. Often these cyclical themes are most apparent as recurrent images in the librettos of the operas so this study will examine such literary techniques as image patterns and repetitions of key words in Wagner's texts. While Wagner's music has already been well-studied, Wagner the librettist and writer of operatic texts remains a largely neglected field, and evidence of bipolar illness does appear in many of Wagner's librettos.

The popular view of manic-depressive illness is that the manic part of the cycle is a wonderful experience of being able to do anything, and that only the depressive part of the cycle is painful. But medical experts on this illness indicate that there is both pleasure and real pain in both extremes of these cyclical mood swings. The manic phase can include nervous energy, spending binges, sleeplessness, and paranoid episodes in which the patient imagines individuals or groups trying to destroy him and all his important endeavors. The depressive part of the cycle can include an anticipation of a peaceful end of suffering, the vision of suicide as a wonderful escape fantasy—a place where the patient is finally safe and free from all his anguish. Neither the manic nor the depressive aspects of this illness remain completely free of pain or pleasure, but the patient remains a victim of cycles of extreme mood swings.

Of course, we all experience mood swings. There are times when we feel like successes and are happy with our lot in life, but there are also times when we feel like fools and total failures who have wasted our potential. But the bipolar patient suffers from much greater extremes than the average person ever experiences in his own mood swings. When that person feels like a success, he or she feels like one of the seminal minds of the time—with brilliant insights that can end wars and change the course of human events. When most of us have our blue periods, we don't feel that our single best option is suicide, a fate that would be welcomed not only by us but by everyone around us. In short, our mood swings, though they do exist, remain moderate in comparison to the extremes that the bipolar patient has to endure. Here, I will argue that Richard Wagner suffered from pronounced bipolar illness, which we can see both in his correspondence and in his operas.

Had Wagner lived today, he might have taken lithium or some other medication to control the cyclical nature of this extreme illness. But if Wagner had been put on lithium, would we have those ten wonderful operas? We can only speculate: Perhaps we would have those operas, but they would be very different operas—though certainly Wagner on modern medication would have suffered much less in his lifetime. Yet his medical history is not set in our time, and we must discuss the man and his work in a different historical frame.

Using primarily Wagner's voluminous correspondence as evidence, this book will first show how manic-depressive illness, especially the depressive part of the illness, showed itself in Wagner's life. The book will then look for evidence of this cyclical behavior in Wagner's operas and especially in the characters who dominate them. His illness will also be shown to be at the core of the composer's notorious anti-Semitism, a product of the paranoid quality of his manic phase.

Introduction

Thomas Mann's famous essay, "The Suffering and Greatness of Richard Wagner," tells only part of the suffering of this composer, and Mann realized how much suffering Wagner endured. It is certainly significant that in his final opera, *Parsifal*, one of the characters, Amfortas, has a wound that will not heal. Richard Wagner had such a wound himself: bipolar illness, which often drove him to plan to kill himself. That his many suicidal thoughts did not lead him to end his life indicates the force of Wagner's perseverance and the strength of his inner resources. But in Wagner's life and his operas, suicide appears so often that it becomes a central theme.

This is certainly not the first study that has connected Wagner with mental illness; other commentators on both the man and his operas have found many symptoms of neurosis. In his own lifetime, Wagner's manic spending sprees and constant problems with creditors soon came to general notice. Many of his friends feared that he would end his life in debtors' prison, which sometimes seemed a real possibility. When Wagner's letters to his Viennese seamstress were first published, with Wagner's elaborate designs for his dressing gowns, some readers and critics suspected that he was a transvestite. Later Robert Jacobs argued that Wagner had all the symptoms of an Oedipus Complex and suffered because of his excessive dependence on his mother.

As long as Friedrich Nietzsche remained a close friend of Wagner's, "genius" was the word that most often appeared in Nietzsche's descriptions of the composer. But after their abrupt break, Nietzsche often referred to Wagner as "une nevrose," or a neurotic, whose music remained essentially neurotic as well. The critic Nordau argued that Wagner suffered from persecution mania and pronounced paranoia. Fuchs and Panizza argued that Wagner was actually a repressed homosexual. Wulffen argued that Wagner was in reality a criminal, and many modern critics have discussed his neurotic anti–Semitism. Jean-Jacques Nattiez has argued more recently that Wagner's personality was essentially androgynous, and this is a major theme in his operas as well. Clearly, Wagner has not lacked for pathological approaches to his genius. But all of these theories do not contain sufficient evidence to be truly conclusive, and all fail to explain the totality of his personality and operatic achievement. The suicidal impulses and the cyclical nature of bipolar illness, on the other hand, provide a totality which can explain the fascinating enigma which is Richard Wagner.

Perhaps because of his own bipolar illness, many of Wagner's operas reflect the philosophical theories of Giambattista Vico, the 18th century Italian philosopher who argued that our lives and the world are controlled by the cycles of nature. In the 20th century, Vico's theories would become central to the late novels of James Joyce, especially *Ulysses* and *Finnegans Wake*. But even in the 19th century, closer to Vico's own time period, Vico's theories were part of the Zeitgeist. I suspect that Wagner absorbed the philosophical theories of Vico by reading the literature of his great German compatriot Johann Wolfgang von Goethe. Nicholas Boyle, in his wonderful and comprehensive biography of Goethe, indicates that the author knew of Vico and his theories (Boyle 463). These theories appear most clearly in Goethe's most famous work, *Faust*. That great work begins with a Prologue in Heaven and three archangels speaking:

RAPHAEL:
> Die Sonne tönt, nach alter Weise,
> In Brudersphären Wettgesang,
> Und ihre vorgeschriebne Reise
> Vollendet sie mit Donnergang.
> Ihr Anblick gift den Engeln Starke,
> Wenn keiner sie ergründen mag;
> Die unbegreiflich hohen Werke
> Sing herrlich wir am ersten Tag.

GABRIEL:
> Und schnell und unbegreiflich schnelle
> Dreht sich umher der Erde Pracht;
> Es wechselt Paradieseshelle
> Mit tiefer, Schauervoller Nacht;
> Es schäumt das Meer in breiten Flüssen
> am tiefen Grund der Felsen auf,
> Und Fels und Meer wird fortgerissen
> in ewig schnellem Sphärenlauf.

MICHAEL:
> Und Stürme brausen um die Wette
> Vom Meer aufs Land, vom Land aufs Meer,
> Und bilden wütend eine Kette
> Der tiefsten Wirkung rings umher.
> Da flammt ein blitzendes Verheeren
> Dem Pfade vor des Donnerschlags.
> Doch deine Boten, Herr, verehren
> Das sanfte Wandeln deines Tags.

THE THREE ARCHANGELS:
> Der Anblick gibt den Engeln Stärke,
> Da keiner dich ergrüden mag.
> Und alle deine hohen Werke
> Sing herrlich wie am ersten Tag.

Introduction

RAPHAEL:
> The sun sings, in ancient ways
> With his brother spheres, a different song;
> And his predestined journey,
> He ends with a thunderous sound.
> His sight, which none can understand,
> Gives some power to angels; the group
> of works, unquestionably wonderful,
> Is great as on the first day.

GABRIEL:
> Understandably swiftly speeding,
> Earth's pride revolves in swift flight,
> As Paradise's brightness is followed
> by deep and fearful night;
> In powerful torrents foams the oceans
> Against the cliffs with roaring song—
> In swiftly speeding spherical movement,
> Both rock and sea move forth.

MICHAEL:
> And different storms roar and damage
> From sea to land, from the land to the sea,
> And, swirling, create a mixture of savage
> and destructive energy.
> There burns a bright devastation
> to clear the lightning's roar;
> Yet, God, thy messenger admires
> the mildness of thy day.

THE THREE ARCHANGELS:
> The view, that none can understand,
> Gives power to thy angels;
> thy assortment of creations,
> wonderfully splendid,
> is as glorious as on the first day.*

Clearly these three archangels who begin *Faust*'s Prologue in Heaven are singing about Vico's cycles of nature—the cycle of the earth's revolutions around the sun which produces the cycle of day and night, and the cycle of the tides which results in the movement of the oceans on our planet. One can see the whole conflict between God and Mephistopheles as an essentially cyclical conflict between the optimistic and cynical or pessimistic points of view. Wagner also saw the natural world in terms

---

*All translations in this book are by the author unless otherwise noted.

of cycles, as we will see in the following chapters, and the cyclical nature of Wagner's vision of the world was certainly based upon the cyclical nature of his bipolar illness. Cycles, then, especially the cycle of enjoying life but then desiring death, will recur in Wagner's correspondence and, more importantly, in his operas.

Chapter 1

Wagner's Bipolar Life: Mania and Depression

Bipolar illness results in the patient's leading a painful and difficult life since he or she experiences alternating mood swings from neurotic mania to suicidal depression. Kay Redfield Jamison's book *Touched with Fire: Manic-Depressive Illness and the Artistic Temperament* persuasively argues that this illness often appears in artists and writers. Jamison points out in that perceptive book that the following composers certainly suffered from bipolar illness: Hector Berlioz, Anton Bruckner, John Dowland, Edward Elgar, Mikhail Glinka, George Frideric Handel, Gustav Holst, Charles Ives, Otto Klemperer, Gustav Mahler, Modest Moussorgsky, Sergey Rachmaninoff, Gioacchino Rossini, Robert Schumann, Alexander Scriabin, Peter Tchaikovsky, and Hugo Wolf. These composers experienced extreme mood swings which in some cases resulted in suicide attempts.

Throughout his life Richard Wagner suffered from such an illness, though the depressive part of the cycle manifested itself most clearly in his letters and in his works. But mania was there as well; Wagner at frequent periods in his life went on wild spending sprees when he would buy all sorts of gifts for himself and others, totally ignoring the costs. As a result, during his life he was frequently in debt, often to the point of being hounded by creditors. At times, he barely escaped being sent to debtors' prison, and he had to flee cities like Dresden, Riga, Paris, and Munich because of the hot pursuit of his creditors and their legal and judicial representatives.

Photograph of Richard Wagner by Franz Hanfstaengl

Wagner's manic pattern of handling money became clear very early in his career. Near the beginning of his four-volume biography of Wagner, Ernest Newman gives a typical example of Wagnerian financing, which took place just after a wealthy patron, Julie Ritter, agreed to give the composer a monthly stipend to enable him to compose:

It seems clear from all this that at any rate the basic necessities of existence were secured for him by Frau Ritter's subsidy. But Richard Wagner could never be satisfied with the mere basic necessities for long. When the German theatres began to take up *Tannhäuser* his inveterate optimism made him assume that the process would go on indefinitely, and that as soon as the four operas of his first period had gone the whole round he would be ready with the *Ring*. He accordingly launched out into an expenditure on his house in the Zeltweg 13 that of necessity left him with heavy debts on his hands when the demands from the theatres slowed down. And as landlords and tradespeople became more pressing in their requests for a sight of the colour of his money he had no recourse but to appeal to his friends for assistance. He was astonishingly successful; well might Bülow call him a "genius of finance," who in each fresh need found fresh sources to tap [Newman, Vol. 2, 406].

This pattern of manic spending would be repeated over and over again in Wagner's life. He would receive some good news—like the appearance of a wealthy patron or the performance of one of his operas—and that would generate in the composer a manic period when he spent wildly beyond his means, secure in the grand sense of entitlement his mania generated. What followed in most cases was a financial crash, with creditors pounding on his door and his euphoria transformed into suicidal depression.

It was during one of these most desperate moments, when Wagner felt hounded by creditors, that the young King Ludwig II of Bavaria first came to his rescue. Yet even the Bavarian monarch's generosity could not stop Wagner's spending binges, and he continued to run up enormous debts. One of the main reasons Wagner became so unpopular in Munich was certainly his spending excesses, which taxed Ludwig II's generosity as well as that of the Bavarian people. In fact, when Wagner died in 1883 he was deeply in debt, and his wife Cosima had to struggle to make her family solvent. Wagner defended his spending sprees by saying that the new items were necessary for his art, but those claims seem preposterous when one examines what he spent on his elaborate living quarters, the luxurious clothes he bought himself, the expensive gifts he bought family members and friends. Mania produces the narcissistic sense of great entitlement to all the luxuries of life, and his behavior surely indicated this manic narcissism. That mania also included Wagner's view of himself as the man who could regenerate German art and indeed Germany itself. His views on the power of operatic art, especially in his operas, also indicate a narcissistic mania.

But the part of his life that is most fully documented in his voluminous correspondence is his frequent depression—though here too he is frequently asking his friends for money to keep him out of trouble with the police. His friend the composer Franz Liszt was especially generous in sending him money, particularly during Wagner's years in Paris, to keep him out of debtors' prison. Many of these debts, one can argue, were the result of his manic cycles, when he would buy every luxury he could get his hands on. But his letters, when not asking friends for money to bail him out of debt, sometimes go further to record his horrible depressions—the depressive part of his bipolar illness.

Even as a young man of 21, Wagner was writing to his friend Theodor Apel:

> Best of friends, I have been on the point of writing to you on a number of occasions, though I should have preferred any other moment to the present one; although I now have an hour free, I am on the whole so depressed, empty-headed, dull-witted & uninspired that I simply do not know how I might appear before you with the requisite poise & dignity. God has created music purely to spite me, and I find it a real tonic to turn now & again to reading; pounding out music gives me no satisfaction, and when I have to do it, as was the case last week, then it must be the Creator's intentional aim to add to my sense of wretchedness [Spencer/Millington 22].

This letter clearly indicates a depressive period that Wagner is experiencing when he hates everything, especially music. Significantly, as well, he seems to suggest that God is purposely torturing him, a sadistic view of the divinity.

Bryan Magee, in his book *Wagner and Philosophy*, states:

> He felt unable to relate to other people; they did not understand him, he could not communicate with them. As a result, the world always seemed to him an alien place, both puzzling and hostile. He did not understand it, was not at home in it, did not like it. He wanted to escape from it. Until his fifties not a year of his adult life went by in which he did not seriously contemplate suicide. In the short section of his autobiography devoted to his childhood he tells how, as a small child, the uncontrollable vividness of his imagination had given him nightmares every night from which he would awake screaming, with the result that none of his brothers or sisters would sleep near him, and he was made to sleep by himself at the farthest end of the family's apartment, where his total cut-offness in the dark served only to increase his nightmares and worsen his screaming. All his life, until he began to share it with Cosima, he longed for an end to his psycho-emotional isolation; and because the erotic played such a powerful role in his life, what he wanted above all else was a woman who would love him without regard to whether she understood him or not; who would just accept him as he

was and devote herself to him unquestioningly, renouncing her own life for his, in effect [Magee 19–20].

A Freudian would suggest that Wagner spent his whole life, on one level, looking for a mother figure who would give him the unconditional love he did not receive from his own mother. When as a child he cried in the dark because of his nightmares, Wagner's mother simply put him in the furthest corner of her apartment to get away from him and his many needs. She clearly was not able to provide him with the unconditional love only a mother can provide. If one does not receive such unconditional love from a parent, one will never get it from anyone else—though Wagner was very lucky indeed to find his second wife Cosima, who was able to provide him with something close to unconditional love.

Some of Wagner's most poignant and death-ridden letters were those he wrote to Franz Liszt. In February of 1853, a week before Liszt was to conduct *The Flying Dutchman* in Weimar, Wagner wrote to him:

> Good luck with the "flying Dutchman"! I cannot get this melancholy hero out of my head!... For me there is no longer any possibility of redemption, except for—*death*. Oh, how happy I should be to die in a storm at sea,—but not on my sick-bed!!! Indeed—I should be glad to perish in the flames of *Valhalla*! Mark well my new poem—it contains the world's beginning and its end! [Spencer/Millington 280–281].

Clearly the suicidal Vanderdecken, the hero of *The Flying Dutchman*, was a man close to Wagner's heart, especially in terms of his desire to die.

Wagner wrote again to Liszt on March 30, 1853, and here again he talks about suicide.

> This cannot go on; I cannot bear life much longer.... Then I shall begin a different life. Then I shall get money how and where I can; I shall borrow and steal, if necessary, in order to *travel*. The beautiful parts of Italy are closed to me unless I am amnestied. So I shall go to Spain, to Andalusia, and make friends, and try once more to live as well as I can. I should like to fare round the world. If I can get no money, or if the journey does not help me to a new breath of life, there is an end of it, and I shall then seek death by my own hand rather than live on in *this manner* [Wagner/Liszt 271–272].

In this letter Wagner talks most directly about his depression, about his desperate desire to travel, and about his desire to commit suicide. On May 30, 1853, Wagner wrote to Liszt in a similar vein:

> Dearest friend, have you not yet had enough of Weimar? I must own that I frequently grieve to see how you waste your strength there. Was

"Liszt und Wagner" by Carl Roehling

there any truth in the recent rumor of your leaving Weimar? Have they given in? But all this is idle talk. My brain is a wilderness, and I thirst for a long, long, sleep, to awake only when my arms are around you. Write to me very precisely, also whether you are inclined, after a little stay at Zurich, to go with me to the solitude of the Grisons; St. Moritz might, after all, do you good, dearest friend; we shall there be five thousand feet high, and enjoy the most nerve-strengthening air, together with the mineral water, which is said to be of beneficial effect on the digestive organs. Think this over, consult your health and your circumstances, and let me know very soon what I may hope for. Farewell, best and dearest of friends. Have my eternal thanks for your divine friendship, and be assured of my steadfast and warmest love [Wagner/Liszt 289].

There is clearly a homoerotic element to this letter, but does it also suggest a joint suicide? Wagner writes that he longs to have his arms around his friend Liszt and that they have a long, long sleep together. Is Wagner suggesting that Liszt join him in the mountains of Switzerland to end their lives together? Perhaps. Years later Wagner will write to his friend Mathilde Wesendonck from Venice with a similar dream of union with the beloved and then death.

About six months later, on January 15, 1854, Wagner again wrote to Liszt:

Dearest friend, The *Rhinegold* is finished—: but I am finished as well!!! During recent weeks I have necessarily and intentionally rendered myself insensible by means of my work, and in so doing have suppressed every impulse to write to you until such time as I had completed it. This is the first morning that I can no longer find a pretext not to give vent to the wretchedness that I have nourished and restrained for so long! Let it breakforth then,—I can no longer contain it!...

But how shameful that in return to having sacrificed the most noble thing I own, I have not even received the reward which seemed to have been set aside for me! I still remain the beggar I was before! Dear Franz! not a year of my life has passed recently without my finding myself at least *once* on the very brink of a decision to end my life. Everything about it is so muddled and so hopeless!... I no longer have any faith, and only one hope remains: to *sleep*, to *sleep*, so deeply, so deeply—that all sensation of life's anguish fades. I ought after all to be able to achieve that sleep: it is not so difficult [Spencer/Millington 296-299].

Wagner seems to be stating here that in most years of his life he has thought of suicide, and that the very act of creation has exacerbated this wish to end his life. Surely the repeated desire to sleep, to sleep, is his temptation to that eternal sleep which is death. Here again, the suicidal fantasy mixes freely with the love that Wagner clearly feels for Liszt.

On December 16, 1854, Wagner wrote in a similar vein to his friend Liszt:

> When I think back on the storms that have buffeted my own better judgment—indeed, now that these storms have swelled so often to the fury of a tempest,—I have yet found a sedative which has finally helped me to sleep at night; it is the sincere and heartfelt yearning for death: total unconsciousness, complete annihilation, the end of all dreams—the only ultimate redemption!
>
> But since I have never in my life enjoyed the true happiness of love, I intend to erect a further monument to this most beautiful of dreams, a monument in which this love will be properly sated from beginning to end: I have planned in my head a *Tristan und Isolde*, the simplest, but most full-blooded musical conception; with the "black flag" which flutters at the end, I shall then cover myself over, in order—to die [Spencer/Millington 323–324].

It is strange to hear Wagner saying that he has never experienced love. He was then married to Minna, and had also participated in several love affairs. How could he not have experienced love? Surely this dejection is the result of a profound depression. And he ends the letter by telling Liszt that he plans to write *Tristan und Isolde*, a monument to love, and then to kill himself. These letters to Liszt were the most personal he had ever written, and clearly contain a homoerotic element, connecting love with suicide.

On June 7, 1855, Wagner again wrote to Liszt, and here again the subject was the connection between love and suicide. The immediate occasion for this letter was Wagner's reading of Dante.

> I have followed Dante through Hell and Purgatory with the deepest fellow-feeling; having emerged from the pit of hell, I washed myself with fervent emotion, together with the poem, at the foot of Mount Purgatory—in the waters of the sea, I then savoured the divine morn, the pure air, rose up from one cornice to the next, mortified one passion after another, struggled to subdue my wild instinct for survival, until I finally stood before the flames, abandoned my final wish to live and threw myself into the fiery glow in order that, sinking into rapt contemplation of Beatrice, I might cast aside my entire personality, devoid of will. But that I was roused once more from this ultimate self-liberation in order, basically, to revert to being what I had been before... [Spencer/Millington 343].

Wagner imagines a fiery and suicidal end here, exactly like Brünnhilde's death at the end of the *Ring* cycle. And once again Wagner dreams that he can find happiness only in suicide.

Other than Liszt, the person who triggered the same kinds of suicidal letters was Mathilde Wesendonck, especially in 1858 during Wagner's affair with her. On August 21, 1858, he wrote to her:

> On my last night in the Asyl I retired to bed after 11 o'clock: I was due to depart at 5 o'clock the next morning. Before I closed my eyes, the same thought flashed through my mind that had always done each time I wanted to lull myself to sleep with the idea that, one day, I would die here: this is how I would die when you came to me for the last time, when, openly and before the whole world, you enfolded my head in your arms, and received my soul with a final kiss! To die in this way was the fairest of my imaginings, and it had taken shape entirely within the locality of my bedroom: the door leading to the stairs was closed, you entered through the study curtains; thus you wrapped your arm around me; thus I died, gazing at you.—And what now? Has even this chance of dying been snatched away from me? Coldly, like some hunted animal, I left the house in which I had been entombed with a daemon which I could no longer exorcise except by flight.—Where—where now shall I die?—And so I fell asleep [Spencer/Millington 416].

Clearly Wagner's recurrent fantasy while having his affair with Mathilde Wesendonck was his wish to die with her. The image of the final kiss, the kiss of death, would be an image the composer would use in the second act of *Parsifal*. Even after Wagner was forced to leave her because of the discovery of the affair by his wife Minna and by Mathilde's husband Otto, Wagner's suicidal fantasies continued. Once Wagner arrived in Venice after leaving his wife and the Wesendoncks in Switzerland, he immediately wrote to Mathilde, specifically on November 1, 1858:

> Today is All Souls' Day! I have woken up from a brief, but deep, sleep after long and terrible sufferings such as I have never previously suffered. I stood on the balcony and gazed down into the black depths of the Canal; a strong wind was raging. Had I jumped and fallen in, no one would have heard me. I would have been free of all torment the moment I jumped. And I clenched my fist in order to lift myself up on to the parapet.—Could I—with my eyes upon you,—upon your children? Now All Souls's Day has dawned!—All Souls! May you rest in peace!—Now I know that it will yet be granted to me to die in your arms! [Spencer/Millington 427–428].

Clearly the ideation of love and suicide persisted in Wagner's relationship with Mathilde Wesendonck, and of course this very ideation would later form the core of his opera *Tristan und Isolde*. In this letter he describes his temptation to drown himself. In a similar vein, Wagner also wrote repeatedly from Venice to Franz Liszt—for example, on January 2, 1859, Wagner wrote:

> Let me come to the point. After living in exile for ten years, my amnesty has become of less importance to me than the guarantee of an existence free from care and secure from discomfort for the rest of my life. Do not be surprised. The return to Germany is of relative value to me. The only positive gain would be my seeing you often and living together with you.... Believe me implicitly when I tell you that the only reason for my continuing to live is the irresistible impulse of creating a number of works of art which have their vital force in me. I recognize beyond all doubt that this act of creating and completing alone satisfied me and fills me with a desire of life, which otherwise I should not understand [Wagner/Liszt 271].

Here too Wagner describes a suicidal depression, and here too his letters to Liszt have a homoerotic tone. Liszt and Mathilde Wesendonck were not the only persons to receive such letters. On February 21, 1859, Wagner wrote to his friend Eliza Wille:

> But the endless pain of this intermediate state, when desire stirs again and each time comes up against the same old obstacle, has a deeply depressing effect upon me. Then work is the only answer. But what work! I feel as though I shall never have done with it; as though I wanted to force death to catch me in the act! Never before have I worked so intimately; every stroke of my pen has the significance of an eternity for me; and I do not continue until I feel attacked by what I have written. It is a strange feeling to survey the thing as a whole and realize that never before have I written anything of such musical unity, of such inexhaustible fluency. Tristan will be beautiful! But it is eating into me. Who knows whether there will be any part of me left? [Spencer/Millington 448].

Here too Wagner writes of the connections between love and suicide, and especially the connection between the process of creating art, in this case his opera *Tristan und Isolde*, and his ideation about death and suicide. He indicates that only his creativity keeps him from committing suicide, yet the difficulty of using that creativity in the act of composing often makes him want to die. Wagner often wrote to friends and lovers of the agony of the composition process.

Wagner wrote again to Mathilde Wesendonck about his depression and his desire to die. On August 3, 1863, from Penzig, Wagner wrote:

> Meisterin, things are not good!—And I am heartily sickened of life. I recently discovered this quite clearly, thanks to an incident in which

my very life was in danger. It happened on the Danube in Pest, in the selfsame boat in which two young Hungarian cavalrymen had traveled from Rotterdam to Pest last summer. A charming and intelligent woman by the name of Countess Bethlen, the mother of six children, had taken control of the tiller. There was a violent squall, and she grew anxious and sprang her luff: the waves drove the vessel against a raft, so that it cracked apart. I was seized only by the sense of well-being which was so agreeably bracing that the young people around me could only marvel at my behavior, whereas they had thought that someone as excitable as I am could be counted on to get very worked up. When they applauded me,—for I played a small part in the rescue,—I could scarcely contain my laughter! But what is the use of it all! Death does not come so easily, especially when our time is not yet to hand [Spencer/Millington 568].

Clearly in a situation when Wagner could have drowned, he was delighted by the prospect—or so he wrote to Mathilde Wesendonck. The situation is eerily like that of the Dutchman Vanderdecken and Senta in *The Flying Dutchman*, when death by drowning comes to them both at the finale of the opera. Only in death by drowning do the Dutchman and Senta succeed in finding peace.

The next woman Wagner wrote to in such a vein was Franz Liszt's daughter Cosima, who would become his second wife. At the time she was married to Hans von Bülow. On April 10, 1864, Wagner wrote a desperate letter to her.

Dear Cosima, Would Hans be kind enough to write to me the moment he returns from Petersburg? I need the advice and the loyal assistance of all who love me, in order that I might reach and carry out certain decisions which, if at all possible, will cure my sick existence to the extent that I may yet be able to achieve something. Death eludes me, but life, too, is impossible, at least the sort of life I have been leading until now.—It is not peace which I have here, but only a refuge. I cannot entertain the thought of work: this says it all. I beg you: tell Hans to write; for the time being we must stick together. With a sad heart, sick and wretched ... RW [Spencer/Millington 583].

It is interesting that the erotic and suicidally depressive tone of Wagner's letters to Franz Liszt reappears in Wagner's letters to Liszt's daughter Cosima. This suicidal letter, suggesting as it does that only death can end Wagner's suffering, certainly would have fallen on a sympathetic ear. Already Cosima herself had entered a suicide pact with another friend, Karl Ritter, because of the unhappiness of her marriage to Hans von

Bülow. And her diaries, which she began once she became Wagner's lover, indicate that she too was often as suicidal as Wagner. In fact, their common feelings of depression provided a powerful bond between them and may have been the basis of their eventual marriage.

On January 10, 1869, Cosima wrote in her diary:

> Dear Loulou and dear Boni [her two daughters by Hans von Bülow], today is your father's birthday; I wish that he may spend it in a mood of peaceful reconciliation, though there is nothing I can contribute towards it. It was a great misunderstanding that bound us together in marriage; my feelings toward him are today still the same as 12 years ago: great sympathy with his destiny, pleasure in his qualities of mind and heart, genuine respect for his character, however completely different our temperaments. In the very first year of our marriage I was already in such despair over this confusion that I wished for death [Cosima 5].

Two days later, on January 10, 1869, Cosima used her diary to connect her "despair" with Wagner's kindred state of mind. As she wrote, "The King's silence is also curious and unkind. R's great depression in connection with his work, he really feels like abandoning the musical completion of his *Nibelungen* entirely" (Cosima 5–6). Here, Cosima refers to the great depression of Richard Wagner, a depression strong enough for him to devalue everything he does, including his current operatic project, the *Ring* cycle.

We can also see the suicidal quality of the love between Wagner and Cosima again in her diary entry of November 28, 1869.

> Six years ago today R. came through Berlin, and then it happened that we fell in love; at that time I thought I should never see him again, we wanted to die together.—R. remembers it, and we drink to this day. In the evening I reflected on how love works on us like a Plutonian eruption, it burst through everything, throws all strata into confusion, raises mountains, and there it is—utmost transformation and utmost law. In the morning R. told me he had always wanted to come to me; now, when he is working on his Brunnhilde, I am constantly before his eyes [Cosima 44].

But, despite these frequent references to suicide in his letters and Cosima's diaries, did Wagner ever actually attempt suicide? The evidence remains ambiguous. After he died in 1883, in Venice, following a series of painful heart attacks, his doctor wrote of the case. In it, he said that one of the frustrations of ministering to Wagner in his last weeks was that he would consume at one gulp all the medicine that the doctor had prescribed.

Could this action have been the suicidal attempts of Wagner to poison himself at a time when he knew he was dying? As the German doctor, Friedrich Keppler, wrote:

> It is self-evident that the innumerable psychical agitations to which Wagner was daily disposed by his peculiar mental constitution and disposition, his sharply defined attitude towards a number of burning questions of art, science, and politics, and his remarkable social position did much to hasten his unfortunate end.
> The actual attack that resulted in his so sudden death *must* have come from such cause, but I cannot venture any surmise as to that.
> The medical treatment I gave him consisted of massage of the abdomen and the fitting of a proper truss; I avoided medicinal treatment as much as possible, since Wagner had a bad habit of taking promiscuously, and in considerable quantities, many strong medicines that had been prescribed for him by physicians whom he had previously consulted [Newman, IV, 706].

Dr. Keppler may be suggesting here that Wagner's habitual use of medications may have been self-destructive, and for that reason the doctor avoided prescribing dangerous drugs. Dr. Keppler also refers to "innumerable psychical agitations to which Wagner was daily disposed by his peculiar mental constitution."

And what of Cosima? Did she ever attempt suicide? We know that at one point during her marriage to Hans she had entered a suicide pact with Wagner's friend Karl Ritter. Ernest Newman, in the third volume of his still definitive biography of Wagner, reports about this scene:

> There was a wild strain in Cosima which, in her earlier years, was liable to break through the restraints she had learned even by then to impose on her feelings.... At Geneva, it seems, there had been a passionate scene with Karl [Ritter], Cosima had asked him to kill her: he, who was unhappy in his own marriage, offered to die with her. She wanted to throw herself from a boat into the Lake, and desisted from her purpose only because he swore to follow her [Newman, III, 297–298].

It is also interesting to note that when Wagner died in Venice Cosima refused to leave his body. As Ernest Newman describes the scene:

> All that night Cosima sat alone with the body, murmuring incoherent words of love into the deaf ears. She refused all care, all nourishment: she had lived in him and for him, and now she wanted to die with him. It was not until the late afternoon of the following day, twenty-five

hours after he had died, that they succeeded in parting her from him [Newman, IV, 712].

While Cosima was in this desperate state with the body of Wagner, her former husband Hans von Bülow sent her a telegram which said: "Soeur, il faut vivre!"—Sister, one must live! Could Hans, who knew her so well after the years of their unhappy marriage, have feared that she would commit suicide because of her grief over the death of Wagner? That is clearly implied in his telegram to her in Venice in 1883 (Newman, IV, 714). And indeed her family feared for her life right after the death of the composer, though luckily she lived many more years and served to make the Bayreuth Festival the annual event it is now. At the time of Wagner's death most Wagnerians thought the festival would die with the death of the egomaniacal composer, but Cosima proved them wrong and established the festival as a yearly event. While Wagner had succeeded in staging only his *Ring* cycle and *Parsifal* on the Bayreuth stage, his widow's determination established the festival we know now as a yearly event which stages all ten of Wagner's mature operas, though not all in one summer. Cosima learned from her husband an ability to get substantial amounts of money from both wealthy patrons and governments in order to create Wagnerian art.

The letters and diaries clearly indicate a suicidal quality to the personality of both Cosima and Richard Wagner. Some cynics may argue that Wagner used the suicide threats as a ploy to get more money from his friends, but Wagner mentioned thoughts of suicide not only to people who might be able to lend him money but to many others as well. We have also seen a manic side to his personality, suggesting bipolar illness. We will see in Wagner's great comedy *Meistersinger* that the composer's vision of the artist totally unified with his country and his audience fails the test of realism but instead appears a wonderfully manic fantasy. Just as in his lunatic spending binges, Wagner was often the victim of the manic part of his bipolar illness, imagining he would unify all of Germany in its adoration of him and his art. While most operatic comedies end in a happy marriage, the traditional ending of comedies in spoken and sung drama, such a traditional ending was not enough for Richard Wagner. He wanted to reflect the manic high of art and artist unified with national and indeed universal happiness for all people. That such a vision was based on the manic-depressive quality of his cyclical illness will become clear in this study. That very illness, especially in its depressive phase, will appear over and over again in Wagner's operas. It helped to create some of the greatest art the world has ever seen, while leaving the creator of this very art often yearning for annihilation.

Chapter 2

Der Fliegende Holländer: The Isolated Personality

After writing juvenilia in his early years—*Die Feen* and *Das Liebesverbot*, plus his first early success, *Rienzi*, which succeeded not only at Dresden but in many other opera houses in Germany—Wagner moved ahead to create what he regarded as his first real opera, *Die Fliegende Holländer*. This, he felt, was his first serious composition, and he wanted this work performed at Bayreuth—unlike his first three operas. As Mueller and Wapnewski have said:

> In retrospect, Wagner regarded *Holländer* as his first fully valid work. "The period during which I worked in obedience to the dictates of my inner intuitions began with the Flying Dutchman," he wrote to August Rockel on 23 August 1856. And in a letter to King Ludwig II of 22 September 1864, he described *Holländer* as "that earlier, less ambitious work that was nonetheless already typical of my true style." The breakthrough of his "true style," which Wagner achieved in *Holländer*, is intimately related to the genesis of the work, or more precisely to the original and unique way in which the central stylistic features of Wagner's music were grasped and set into place [Mueller/Wapnewski 414–415].

Wagner's first completed opera, *Die Feen*, was based on Carlo Gozzi's play *La Donna Serpente*, which was a mythic fairy tale "fiabe," as Gozzi liked to call his unrealistic fairy-tale plays. Although *Die Feen* never achieved success, it is significant that Wagner's first attempt at opera took a mythic form, a form he would ultimately return to with *The Flying Dutchman*.

Wagner's next opera, *Das Liebesverbot*, was based on Shakespeare's *Measure for Measure*, and Wagner's attempt to compose music to Shakespearean comedy also failed. Only with *Rienzi* did Wagner meet with popular success. The opera, based on a novel by Bulwer Lytton, is about Roman history which, together with Carlo Gozzi's play, indicates Wagner's early fascination with Italy and Italian settings, something he probably picked up from Goethe, whose own Italian obsessions were legendary. In his book *Italienische Reise*, Goethe stated that the only time he was ever really happy was his time spent in Italy.

But with *Dutchman* Wagner revisited again his original attraction to operatic composition, the mythic opera. Part of what set the opera into his mind was undoubtedly Wagner's own horrendous experience of 1839 when he attempted to go from Germany to England by boat. He and his wife Minna (as well as the other passengers on board) almost drowned in a terrible storm, and then they were forced to spend several months in the fjords of Norway waiting for favorable weather before they could complete their journey. As Ernest Newman says of this trip:

> Normally the voyage to London, in the summer, was a rather pleasant affair of some eight days. For Richard and Minna it lasted at least three and a half weeks. Storms more than once drove them out of their course: on the 27th July the sea captain was forced to seek harbour on the Norwegian coast. As the boat made its way into the sheltering fjord the cries of the crew as they furled the sails came echoing from the rocks in a rhythm that Wagner was to remember later, when he was writing the seamen's chorus in the *Flying Dutchman*. The little village at which they had landed was Sandwike, a few miles from Arendal: "Sandwike it is; full well I know the bay," says Daland in the opera. On the 31st, in spite of the Norwegian pilot's warning, the captain of the *Thetis* insisted on leaving his shelter. The storm drove them towards a reef that seemed likely to split the vessel in two; but it struck it only a glancing blow, and, congratulating themselves on their escape, once more they turned her bow to the land. They set sail again on 1st August, were favoured with fine weather for four days, and then, on the 7th, ran into another storm that proved to be the worst they had yet experienced; to the terrors of the waves were added those of thunder and lightning. They all gave themselves up for lost: Minna, imploring heaven for the favour of a death by lightning rather than by drowning, begged Richard to bind him to her so that they might not be parted when they sank [Newman 249–250].

Wagner's own experience with the fearful and life-threatening power of the sea was augmented by his extensive reading as well. Barry Millington provides a fine summary of the literary sources of the opera in the following passage:

Wagner's main source for his opera on the tale of the Flying Dutchman was Heinrich Heine's telling of the legend in *Aus den Memoiren des Heeren von Schnabelewopski*, published in 1834; this was a German reworking of a French text published in the *Tableaux de voyages* the previous year (his original brief version had appeared in the *Reisebilder* of 1826). But Heine's developed version is mordantly ironic, with more than a touch of misogyny. It tells how the accursed sea captain is forced to roam the sea until Judgment Day unless he be saved by a woman's devotion. "The poor Dutchman! He is often only too glad to be rescued from his dear wife and return on board ship in order to recover from feminine loyalty." At the end, after "Mrs. Flying Dutchman" has made her redemptive leap from the cliff into the sea, Heine appends the cynical, anti–Romantic moral that women "should beware of marrying a Flying Dutchman; and we men should draw from it the lesson that women at best will be our undoing"—presumably by chaining the wanderer to a marriage he does not really want. Heine's own possible sources are to some extent a matter of speculation. The legend seems to have grown up during the period of Britain's naval supremacy in the 18th century: England had waged a series of three inconclusive naval and colonial wars against the Dutch republic between 1652 and 1674, and the skirmishes, arising out of trading disputes, which continued to occur in the following century, would have given rise to such sailors' tales, which were passed down from one generation to another....

Wagner never gave his Dutchman a name, but he was given one in an important Scottish source entitled *Vanderdecken's Message Home; Or, the Tenacity of Natural Affection*, printed in the May 1821 issue of Blackwood's *Edinburgh Magazine* [Millington 277].

Yet despite the popularity of such material, *The Flying Dutchman* remains another example of a now famous opera that suffered failure at its premiere. As Ernest Newman reports:

> The first performance of the new opera, on the 2nd of January, 1843, was a cold douche for Wagner. The Dresden audience was a little repelled by this cold and gloomy subject after the brilliance and *panache* of *Rienzi*; Laube, who was present at the first performance, probably expressed the general feeling when many years later, he described the operas as being "ghastly pallid." The phlegmatic Waechter carried no conviction as the Dutchman. The setting was unimaginative, and the handling of the sea and ships incompetent. Wagner became painfully conscious that his daemon was to drive him along a road on which the general public would have some difficulty in following him at first. It was not in his music that the trouble lay, but in the fact that to appreciate even his music to the full it would be necessary for the German public to acquire a new sense of drama in opera; and this, as he soon learned to his cost, was going to be made extremely difficult for them by reason of the intellectual

shortcomings of the interpreters on whom, unfortunately, the theatrical creator has to rely for the transmission of this thought to his hearers. Schroeder-Devrient had practically to carry the new opera on her own shoulders.

The comparative failure of the *Flying Dutchman* may have been due to the fact that just about that time the German public was beginning to be a little weary of operatic subjects of the romantic, and especially the gloomy romantic type [Newman 349–350].

The Flying Dutchman is certainly nothing if not gloomy—at times it seems like a Halloween pageant, with the Dutchman himself a Dracula figure, a haunted, ghost-like creature eager to suck the blood from humans and kill them. The audience is immediately presented with the isolated, deeply depressed personality of the Dutchman living under the curse of wandering, and he is relieved of this personality only with the eroticized joint suicide in the opera's finale, which ends the curse on the Dutchman but also results in the death of both the Dutchman and Seanta.

So why is Wagner attracted to this, of all myths? The opera's plot centers around a gloomy and isolated individual who can find relief only in death, and the suicide of a faithful woman. The Dutchman is torn between two emotional poles: either he is depressed and yearns for death or he dreams of redemption and eternal bliss. These elements are central to the story, and I feel this is why the depressed, suicidal Wagner was attracted to this story—a story that led him to compose some of his most wonderful music. The emotional extremes of the Dutchman reflect the emotional polarities of bipolar illness: mania and suicidal depression.

When we first see the main character, he is of course the cursed figure of the doomed Dutchman. We get to know about him through his initial monologue, where almost from his first words we can see the direction of his thought and the depression of the entire opera:

> Die Frist ist um ... und abermals verstrichen sind siebe Jahr':
> voll Überdruss wirft mich das Meer ans Land.
> Ha! Stolzer Ocean!
> In kurzer Frist sollst du mich wieder tragen!
> Dein Trotz ist beugsam, doch ewig meine Qual.
> Das Heil, das auf dem Land ich suche, nie werd' ich es finden!
> Euch, des Weltmeers Fluten, bleib' ich getreu,
> bis euer lezte Welle sich bricht,
> und euer letztes Nass versiegt!
> Wie oft in Meerest tiefsten Schlund'
> sturzt' ich voll Sehnsuch mich hinab:
> Doch ach! den Tod, ich fand ihn nicht!

The Flying Dutchman: James Morris as the Dutchman.

Da, wo der Schiffe furchtbar Grab,
trieb mein Schiff ich zum Klippengrund,
doch ach! Mein Grab, es schloss sich nicht!
Verhöhend droht' ich dem Piraten,
im wilden Kampfe hofft' ich Tod:
"Hier" rief ich, "zeige deine Taten!
Von Schätzen voll ist schiff und Boot!"
Doch ach! des Meers barber'scher Sohn
schlagt bang des Kreuz und flieht davon...
Nirgends ein Grab! Niemals der Tod!
Dies der Vandammnis Schreckgebot.
Dich frage ich, gepries'ner Engel Gottes
der meines Heil's Bedingung mir gewann!
War ich Unsel'ger Spielwerk deines Spottes,
als die Erlösung du mir ziegtest an?
Vergeb'ne Hoffnung! Furchtbar eitler Wahn!
Um ew'ge Treu' auf Erden—ist's getan!
Nur eine Hoffnung soll mir bleiben,
nur eine unerschuttert steh'n:—
So lang' der Erde Keim' auch treiben,
so muss sie doch zu Grunde gehn.
Tag des Gerichtes! Jüngster Tag!
Wann brichst du an in meine Nacht?
Wann drohnt er, der Vernichtungsschlag.
mit dem die Welt zusammenkracht?
Wann alle Todten aufersteh'n,
dann werde ich in Nichts vergeh'n!
Ihr Welten, endet euren Lauf!
Ew'ge Vernichtung, nimm mich auf!

The time is up, and again seven years have passed.
The sea, sated, throws me on the land.
Ha! Mighty Ocean!
Soon you must hold me again!
Your stubbornness may change, but my doom is eternal!
Never shall I find the redemption I want on the land!
To you, mighty ocean, I remain true
until your last wave breaks
and your last waters go dry!
How often into the ocean's deepest waves
I have plunged longingly;
but alas! I have not found death!
There on the reefs, fearful cemetery
of ships, I have driven my own ship;
but I have not found death!
I challenged the fearful pirates
and hoped for death in a fierce battle:

> "Here," I yelled, "prove your deeds!
> My ship is full of treasures."
> But the sea's barbarous son
> crossed himself in horror, and fled.
> Nowhere a grave! Death never arrives!
> This is the dread sentence of damnation.
> I ask thee, blessed angel from Heaven,
> who won for me the terms for my forgiveness:
> Was I the unhappy victim of your joke
> when you did show me the way of redemption?
> Futile hope! Dread, empty illusion!
> Constant faith is a thing of the past!
> One single hope remains to me,
> it alone shall stand unshaken:
> long though the earth may bloom,
> it yet must also perish.
> Day of Judgment! Day of Doom!
> When will you arrive and end my night?
> When will the blast of destruction come
> and crack the world apart?
> When all the dead rise again,
> only then shall I pass into emptiness!
> You stars above, stop your movement!
> Eternal destruction, fall on me!

Rarely have Wagner's words more clearly stated a desire to die. In this, his first mature opera, the main character's opening monologue reveals not only suicidal depression but also the suicide attempts which have (unfortunately) failed. Clearly, the Dutchman feels that his only hope for ending his painful fate is death; never does he imagine that he can live peacefully with a faithful woman and so defeat the curse imposed on him, forever wandering.

In the quotation, we notice that the meter of this poetry is generally rhymed iambic tetrameter—sometimes varied but usually regular—a line length of four (though sometimes five) stressed accents and usually ten syllables with some rhyme but rarely in couplets. This is a fairly standard meter for librettos of the period, but only rarely has a libretto been used to indicate depression, suicide attempts, and the death-wish. It is interesting as well that Wagner uses several times the word "Sehnsucht," or "longing," a concept that would find ultimate fulfillment in that other most suicidal of Wagner's operas, *Tristan und Isolde*. There again depression and the desire for an eroticized suicide pact will appear with even greater force.

And whom can the Dutchman hope to attract, given his current very needy condition? Only another suicidal personality like Senta. Senta's entrance in the opera, despite the chorus of spinning women, immediately sets her apart. While the chorus is singing their merry tune, her music has the stormy, watery force much like that of the Dutchman. Throughout the opera, in fact, the music for the Dutchman and Senta stands in marked contrast to the merry dance rhythms for most of the normal, life-centered characters. While their music is happy and set to dancing rhythms, the Dutchman and Senta move to a completely different sound which separates them from the rest of normal humanity. Their music matches the violent, watery music that first appears in the opera's tempestuous overture. Most of the characters are people of the earth who seem to dance through life, but the Dutchman and Senta lead the isolated, stormy lives of sea people. The overall image pattern of water vs. land remains dominate in the opera, and the watery imagery is usually connected with storms, winds, and death.

In her first scene, when Senta recounts in her famous ballad the old story of the curse of the Flying Dutchman, she feels immediately drawn to this gloomy character who repels the rest of the people in the fishing village in Norway, where she was born and lives with her father. As she sings at the climax of her ballad:

> Ach! wo weilt sie, die dir Gottes Engel einst könne zeigen?
> Wo triffst du sie, die bis in den Tod dein bliebe treu eigen?
> Ich sei's, die dich durch ihre Treu' erlöset!
> Mög' Gottes Engel mich dir zeigen!
> Durch mich sollst du das Heil erreichen.
>
> ---
>
> Ah! Where is the woman who God's Angel might be able to show you some day?
> Where will you meet her, the woman who might remain true to you until death?
> Let me be the woman who will redeem you by her faithfulness!
> May God's angel bring me to you!
> Through me, you shall be redeemed!

While the rest of the women are horrified by what she is saying and disgusted by the whole story of the Dutchman, Senta alone responds sympathetically to him. She is even willing to die with him. Clearly we have a pairing here of two suicidal people in an eroticized suicide pact, something which seems to have haunted Wagner and which would reappear in many of his operas—especially *Tristan und Isolde*. Neither the Dutchman nor Senta can imagine living happily ever after; instead, both feel drawn to prove their love and fidelity through death. For both these characters, reality lies in the emotional extremes of either death or redemption, not living happily ever after.

2—Der Fliegende Holländer

The Flying Dutchman is one of the most nautical of Wagner's operas—from the overture onward Wagner uses the force of the sea to create watery-sounding, undulating music. The conductor Franz Lachner once said that the winds of the North Sea blow out at you from the score when you conduct this opera. Clearly in both the libretto and the music, wind and water remain important symbols in this opera. Water is a paradoxical symbol because it includes a totality which encompasses both life and death. While water is the source of all life—after all, our bodies are composed primarily of water—it is also a fearful symbol, since we can easily drown if we spend too much time under the water. Does Wagner use this symbol of life, water, to suggest as well the other side of the symbol, death by drowning? This is precisely what happens to Senta, the Dutchman, and his crew by the end of the opera.

Water remains one of the most recurrent of Wagner's symbols, occurring not only in the librettos but also in the watery-sounding music which Wagner created for many of his operas. *The Flying Dutchman* is about a nautical myth, the sea captain who is doomed to wander the seas of the world, and the first scene take place on board a ship. Similarly, the first act of *Tristan und Isolde* takes place on a ship going from Ireland to Cornwall, and Wagner's famous *Ring* cycle opens and closes with the river Rhine—the first scene of *Das Rheingold* takes place in the Rhine, and the river overflows its banks and is again onstage near the end of the final scene of *Götterdämmerung*. In addition, *Lohengrin* begins on the banks of the river Scheldt, where the opera also ends. And in *Parsifal* the first act is set just off a lake where Gurnemanz goes for his bath. In the first act of *Tannhäuser*, in the Venusberg, there are supposed to be fountains in the caves, according to Wagner's stage directions. Wagnerian opera seems obsessed with water, clearly one of Wagner's major and recurrent symbols, and that symbol creates a wonderful contrast in *The Flying Dutchman* between two major male characters: the Dutchman and Erik. While in the stage directions of the opera the Dutchman is a captain of a doomed ship, Erik is identified as a man of the land, a hunter.

Both characters love Senta, though each has a very different vision of his future with her. Erik recounts a dream in which Senta leaves him for a strange man, with whom she runs into the sea. Senta responds:

> Er such mich auf! Ich muss ihn seh'n!
> Mit ihm muss ich zu Grunde geh'n!
> ---
> He's looking for me! I must look for him!
> With him must I go into the ground!

Erik's dream and Senta's response clearly prefigure the suicidal ending of the opera. Dreams, as well as sleeping and waking, recur often in this opera and also appear in other Wagnerian operas. In *Lohengrin* Elsa recounts her dream, and *Tristan und Isolde* ends with Isolde recounting her dream of Tristan still alive. Cosima Wagner's diaries indicate that Wagner often liked to discuss and analyze his own dreams, and one could say that the mythological, unrealistic story of the *Dutchman* suggests that the whole opera reflects somebody's dreaming mind, perhaps Wagner's. Several modern directors have in fact staged the opera using this approach.

The man of the land, the hunter Erik, symbolizes the earth and all that the land can offer Senta. He offers her life, marriage, children—in other words, a normal life. But the man of the land contrasts with the man of the sea, the Dutchman, and Senta prefers death with the man of the sea. Why? Clearly, Wagner suggests, both characters have suicidal personalities and have found either alternative, the life of the land or the cursed life of the sea, too painful. In his correspondence, Wagner wrote of his desire to drown himself, as we have seen in Chapter 1. Death by water clearly attracted Wagner the man, and Wagner the composer as a result created *The Flying Dutchman*, in which his desire for a death by drowning is fulfilled in the end. As Senta sings in the final lines in the opera:

> Preis deinen Engel und sein Gebot!
> Hier steh' ich, treu dir bis zum Tod!
>
> ---
>
> Praise your angel and her statement!
> Here I stand, true to you unto Death!

"Tod," or death, is the final word in the opera, sung as Senta commits suicide and brings to an end the painful lives of both herself and the Dutchman. Erik and Daland, Senta's father, try to stop Senta from committing suicide, but they fail. Again, such eroticized joint suicide recurs in Wagner's operas, especially in the *Ring* and *Tristan*. And "Tod" is the word that also ends another Wagnerian opera, *Siegfried*, there serving to foreshadow the end of the *Ring* itself.

Perhaps the most mysterious character in *The Flying Dutchman* remains Senta's father, Daland, who suggests his daughter to the Dutchman as the woman who could be faithful to him unto death. Is Daland a total innocent who has no real apprehension of what the Dutchman is asking for in his quest for a faithful woman: a suicide pact? Or is he perfectly willing to sacrifice his daughter to the Dutchman's curse for the right price? Daland seems a very greedy character who is impressed enough with

The Flying Dutchman: James Morris as the Dutchman, Paul Plishka as Daland, Mechthild Gessendorf as Senta.

the Dutchman's immense wealth to sacrifice his daughter to the Dutchman's curse—though he may not foresee that Senta will die as a result of this bargain.

Already Wagner has established the contrast between the greedy landsman, Daland, and the generous landsman, Erik, to show the pros and cons of the life of the earth, or the material life. The Dutchman and Senta know both aspects of the material world, and both prefer death. Such a decision can only be the product of a profound depression. In fact, the curse theme running through the opera might well be seen as a metaphor for the curse of depression. If both these characters are seen as suffering from depression, suicide provides an ultimate cure—a cure that becomes all the more tempting as the depression continues. For some religious people, death also suggests the possibility of an afterlife, though most religions judge suicide to be a grave sin which will result in hell for the sinner.

This depression-suicide theme will continue to occur in Wagner's operas, as it continued to occur to Wagner's life. That Wagner suffered from depression and suicidal fantasies we know already—these facts are clearly indicated in his correspondence and memoirs. It is hardly surprising that this theme would continue to appear in his operas. Yet some would argue that Wagner uses this theme simply because it was a characteristic theme of Romanticism, a dominant artistic movement of his period. Certainly Goethe's *Werther* used this theme notably (though Goethe would not have used the term "Romantic" for it) and certainly other Romantic heroes like Heathcliff and the Byronic hero have a suicidal streak in their personalities, but no Romantic composer or writer uses suicide so often and so obsessively as Richard Wagner.

One of the continuing fascinations of Wagner's operas for many viewers is exactly these ideas. Suicide, after all, is a common human fantasy—not only for people suffering from depression, manic-depressive illness, or a period of intense grief and mourning. Suicide is a common fantasy when life becomes too stressful, especially when one's problems seem insurmountable.

In his first great opera, *The Flying Dutchman*, Wagner has clearly centered on a problem that would occur throughout his operas: the conflicts between mania and depression, between life and death. In addition, the dominant theme of the attraction to suicide will recur. Especially dominating and recurring will be the fantasy of the eroticized suicide pact, which first appears here in *The Flying Dutchman*. To fall in love and then die—not to fall in love, marry, and have children, but to fall in love and then commit suicide—together becomes an obsessive theme in this opera and will reappear in many of Wagner's works. Of course Wagner himself did not do that: he did marry—twice in fact—and did have children. But for much of his life he was like the Dutchman, wandering around Europe, cursed under a threat of arrest because of his involvement with the Dresden revolution of 1848/49. It is interesting that the wandering, accursed existence Wagner would endure for much of his adult life is predicted so early in *The Flying Dutchman*. Given such a difficult and wandering life, suicide must have often seemed to Wagner much sweeter, especially a suicide with someone he loved.

Another part of this equation is the cyclical nature of bipolar illness—mania and depression. This cycle we will often find appearing in Wagner's operas—the contrasting pairs that have so much in common they often seem to be complementary rather than the contrasting. Mania and depression become the yin and yang of Wagner's life—just as they become the yin and yang of Wagner's operas. The attraction to life versus the desire to end life and seek solace in death—sometimes contrasting but often very similar. As experts on bi-polar illness have indicated, the mania is not completely wonderful and the depression is not completely terrible since both have advantages and disadvantages to them. And mania and depression are particularly prevalent among artists. As Kay Redfield Jamison has said:

> Recent research strongly suggests that, compared with the general population, writers and artists show a vastly disproportionate rate of manic-depressive or depressive illness; clearly, however, not all (not even most) writers and artists suffer from major mood disorders. There remains skepticism and resistance to the idea of *any* such association, however—some of it stemming understandably from the excesses of psychobiography alluded to earlier (especially those of a highly speculative and interpretive nature), but much of it arising from lack of understanding of the nature of manic-depressive illness itself. Many are unaware of the milder, temperamental expressions of the disease or do not know that most people who have manic-depressive illness are, in fact, without symptoms (that is, they are psychologically normal) most of the time [Jamison, *Touched with Fire*, 5].

The connection, then, between bi-polar illness and artists and writers has been clearly established. But what is the exact nature of the disease? Here again Dr. Jamison is helpful is describing the specifics of bi-polar illness:

> Manic-depressive, or bipolar, illness encompasses a wide range of mood disorders and temperaments. These vary in severity from cyclothmia—characterized by pronounced but not totally debilitating changes

in mood, behavior, thinking, sleep, and energy levels—to extremely severe, life-threatening, and psychotic forms of the disease. Manic-depressive illness is closely related to major depressive, or unipolar, illness; in fact, the same criteria ... are used for the diagnosis of major depression as for the depressive phase of manic-depressive illness. These depressive symptoms include apathy, lethargy, hopelessness, sleep disturbance (sleeping far too much or too little), slowed physical movement, slowed thinking, impaired memory and concentration, and a loss of pleasure in normally pleasurable events. Additional diagnostic criteria include suicidal thinking, self-blame, inappropriate guilt, recurrent thoughts of death, a minimum duration of the depressive symptoms (two to four weeks), and significant interference with the normal functioning of life. Unlike individuals with unipolar depression, those suffering from manic-depressive illness also experience episodes of mania or hypomania (mild mania). These episodes are characterized by symptoms that are, in many ways, the opposite of those seen in depression. Thus, during hypomania and mania, mood is generally elevated and expansive (or, not infrequently, paranoid and irritable); activity and energy levels are greatly increased; the need for sleep is decreased; speech is often rapid, excitable, and intrusive; and thinking is fast, moving quickly from topic to topic. Hypomanic or manic individuals usually have an inflated self-esteem, as well as a certainty of conviction about the correctness and importance of their ideas. This grandiosity can contribute to poor judgment, which, in turn, often results in chaotic patterns of personal and professional relationships. Other common features of hypomania and mania include spending excessive amounts of money, impulsive involvement in questionable endeavors, reckless driving, extreme impatience, intense and impulsive romantic or sexual liaisons, and volatility. In its extreme forms mania is characterized by violent agitation, bizarre behavior, delusional thinking, and visual and auditory hallucinations. In its milder variants the increased energy, expansiveness, risk taking, and fluency of thought associated with hypomania can result in highly productive periods [Jamison, *An Unquiet Mind*, 13–14].

How does all this connect with Wagner's personality and especially with his first major work, *The Flying Dutchman*? In Chapter 1 we have already seen the bi-polar quality of much of Wagner's thought; in this chapter we can see that this opera presents classic patterns of extreme depression, especially in its suicidal ideation. The eroticized suicide pact with a beloved person becomes the grand finale of the opera, as the Dutchman and Senta fall in love and then prove their love by dying together. Their hope for redemption can be seen as symbolic of the manic half of bipolar illness. These two characters never seem to dream of getting married, having a family, and living happily together; instead, they both yearn for a manic "redemption" which lies beyond the possibilities of normal human life.

Given the evidence of suicidal depression in this opera and bipolar illness in Wagner's life, it is amazing that Wagner lived as long as he did. As a victim of both suicidal depressions and violent mood swings, he must have suffered. At one extreme he was spending money in manic fits and at the other extreme he was searching for someone to join him in a suicide pact—in just the way another Romantic writer, Heinrich von Kleist, died. Goethe's most popular work, the novel *Werther*, also ends in suicide. Clearly Wagner had some literary examples around him to help him conceive his suicidal fantasies.

The Flying Dutchman, Wagner's first mature work, contains the seeds of all the operas he would compose later in his career. In many significant ways, *The Flying Dutchman* remains Wagner's Ur-opera, for all of his later operas will develop out of this first of his mature operas. Water imagery occurs here, and will recur in most of his operas. The word "Erlösung," or redemption, especially redemption through a woman, occurs here, and this word will also appear often in *Parsifal*. Later, *Tristan und Isolde* will use the eroticized suicide pact plus water imagery. *Lohengrin* and *Tannhäuser* will use imagery of cycles, suggesting Gianbattista Vico's cyclical theories of nature. Even the comic *Meistersinger* will include water and boats in its final scene. Again, sleeping, waking, and dreaming will occur in the *Ring*, *Lohengrin*, *Tristan und Isolde*, and *Die Meistersinger von Nürnberg*. Clearly, in *The Flying Dutchman* Wagner introduced themes and images which he would vary and then use over and over again in all his later operas.

It is interesting as well to examine the final stage direction in *The Flying Dutchman*, after Senta promises to be faithful unto death.

"Sie stürz sich in das Meer; sogleich versinkt das Schiff das Holländers mit aller Mannschaft. Das Meer schwillt hoch auf und sinkt dann in einem Wirbel wieder zurück. Im Glühroth der aufgehenden Sonne sieht man über den Trümmern des Schiffes die verklärten Gestalten Senata's und das Holländer's sich unschlungen haltend den Meere entsiegen und aufwärts schweben. Eine blendende Gloria erleuchtet die Gruppe in Hintergrunde: Senta erhebt den Holländer, druckt ihn an die Brust und deutet mit der Hand wie mit ihrem Blicke himmelwärts. Das leise immer höher gerückte Felsenriff nimmt unmerklich die Gestalt einer Wolke an."

"She throws herself into the sea; instantly the Dutchman's ship sinks with all peoples onboard. The sea surges up and sinks back down in a whirl. In the glow of the setting sun, the transfigured images of Senta and the Dutchman in an embrace can be seen rising from the sea from among the parts of the ship and floating upwards. A dazzling light illuminates the group; Senta lifts the Dutchman, holds him to her breast, and indicates heaven with her hands and her eyes. The cliff, moving slowly by degrees, assumes imperceptibly the shape of a cloud."

Certainly if Wagner were alive today he would be creating movies rather than operas, since stage directions such as the above indicate that he wanted the stage to do what only film could do. The kind of visual realism and specificity which this stage direction calls for could not be done realistically on any stage—in Wagner's time or in our own. But it is certainly significant that the final image that Wagner wanted on stage was the image of a cloud—the cliffs that Senta jumps from become transformed into a cloud. We have already noted how frequently Wagner uses water imagery in his operas, especially in this opera, and the final image of a cloud suggests the cyclical nature of water itself. The water cycle of nature involves clouds producing rain and water for the earth, but then, through the heat of the sun and evaporation, that very water becomes transformed back into clouds. Wagner reminds us of the cyclical nature of water with that final image of a cloud floating onstage. Perhaps Wagner is suggesting here that the lovers have achieved a kind of immorality by being connected with one of the eternal cycles of nature, the cycle of rain, water, heat, evaporation, and clouds that then produce even more rain and water. Wagner will use this imagery of light and water again in his *Ring* cycle and *Tristan und Isolde*. Perhaps the cyclical nature of the extreme moods he experienced made him particularly sensitive to the eternal cycles of nature.

Chapter 3

Tannhäuser: The Artistic Personality and Suicide

We have seen in the previous chapter the bipolar nature of manic-depressive illness, with the victim often trapped in cycles between two polar extremes. We have also seen that artists are particularly prone to this illness and that, for the victim, neither is the manic phase totally pleasant nor is the depressive phase totally unpleasant—in other words, there is pleasure and pain in both halves of the cycle of this complex illness.

The complex nature of bipolarity can easily be illustrated in an analysis of Wagner's *Tannhäuser*, the story of a famous minstrel and poet of the Middle Ages named Tannhäuser who performed in the Wartburg and in other parts of Germany. Most of Tannhäuser's story is legendary, based on the medieval genre of the miracle play. Miracle plays and stories were very much a part of medieval literature, depicting the lives of saints, whose miracles demonstrated God's power on earth. Wagner uses this genre to explore the miracle of the artist and the complexity of his own personality and especially the complexity of the artistic personality. But even on a more basic level, the opera uses the medieval miracle play form to indicate the power of God's forgiveness, which will be given to mankind even if God's clergy, in this case the Pope himself, rejects the sinner. Forgiveness is available to all sinners, despite what the Pope or his clergy declare, and this is clearly one of the lessons of Wagner's *Tannhäuser*. But the opera functions on another level as well—as an allegory of bipolar illness.

For that very reason, *Tannhäuser* remained the opera which seems to have agonized Wagner the most. As Werner Brieg comments:

More than any other of Wagner's works, *Tannhäuser* was for its creator what would nowadays be termed a work in progress, a piece whose shape was continually changing in the course of its performance history. Wagner always regarded the most recent version as the only valid one, superseding all the others. Today we are more inclined to regard at least the two main phases of the work as equally valid; in performance practice these are known as the Dresden and the Paris versions....

Wagner worked on the libretto of *Tannhäuser* from June 1842 to April 1843 (at the time it was still called *Der Venusberg*). In the summer of 1843, while on holiday in Teplitz-Schoenau, he devised the first part of the composition, the Venusberg music, which he had been "carrying around" in his head for some time. In November of that year he resumed work on the composition, and on 17 January 1844 completed the draft of the first act. After a long interruption owing to unforeseen circumstances, he resumed work on the composition in September 1844, completing the draft of the second act by 15 October and that of the third act by 29 December. The score of the entire opera was finished on 13 April 1845 [Brieg in Muller/Wagnewski 422].

Susan Webb has also commented on the prolonged and agonizing production history of this opera:

Tannhäuser, Richard Wagner's fifth opera, was extensively revised during his lifetime, and, in a sense, was *never* finished to his satisfaction. He seemed to tinker endlessly with a supposedly finished work, one which had already been produced before an audience. It was not just a cut here or a transposition there; substantial scenes were rewritten, especially for the 1861 performances in Paris. The process began eight days after the Dresden premiere (October 19, 1845); yet in a diary entry from 1883, his wife Cosima describes Wagner as saying that he still owed the world *Tannhäuser*.

Perhaps part of his dissatisfaction stemmed from new awareness, as he was beginning to experiment seriously with the great themes that would occupy him for the rest of his life: the power of Nature and the numinous, and the great psychological conundrums—spirit vs. flesh, the problem of forgiveness, Love as a redemptive force, etc. He was beginning to plunder myth and the medieval for metaphors and situations [Webb/Wagner 8].

I contend, however, that another reason for Wagner's being haunted with this opera throughout his career, and even when he was close to death, derived from its similarity to Wagner's own mental conundrum: his manic-depressive illness. Wagner's experiences in life remained very close to those of his hero in this opera in terms of moods swings and of never being satisfied with what he had achieved. Wagner's great biographer Ernest Newman makes a relevant point on this topic:

> Like every other great dramatist, he never described anyone or anything but himself in his art, his own experiences, actual or potential. Shakespeare may never have committed a murder, but he must have had it in him to commit a thousand murders, and to know how each murderer would feel after his particular crime. Every character, every mood, in Wagner is potential Wagner, just as every character and every mood in Shakespeare was potential Shakespeare [Newman, I, 418].

Newman also points out the extreme polarity which characterizes Wagner's own life:

> In Wagner's life everything tended to the extreme. His music deals with problems of organization and of architecture to which there is no parallel elsewhere. His dramas cover an area of action and psychology that makes that of the ordinary opera seem small.... In no other composer's life does the pendulum, again and again, swing so far first to one side, and then to the other. From the depths of poverty and neglect he was suddenly lifted, in the winter of 1842-43, to what must have seemed to his friends and other contemporaries the very height of good fortune. He left Dresden in 1849 apparently ruined for ever. In the next few years, in spite of all the handicaps his exile imposed on him, he became the leading figure in not only German but European music [Newman, I, 429].

This very pattern of polar extremes which Newman describes in Wagner's life occurs as well in the operas. Certainly Wagner used cycles as well as foils extensively in *Tannhäuser*. The opera opens in the spring with Tannhäuser in the Venusberg longing for nature and springtime, and the opera ends in autumn. The cycle of the seasons implies the recurrent pattern of the experiences presented in the opera, with the implication that no solutions to this cyclical movement would ever be found—just as the cycle of the seasons is permanently part of nature.

Dramatic foils and foiling also dominate this opera. The pagan world is represented by the Roman goddess Venus while the Christian world is represented by the saintly Elisabeth. The sex-obsessed Tannhäuser, first seen living with the goddess Venus, makes an interesting foil with the celibate Wolfram, who seems to desire purity and celestial or Platonic love rather than physical love. But the foils themselves often become cyclical because they are often connected: Venus has a spiritual interest in the art of Tannhäuser, while Elisabeth clearly has a sexual interest and attraction to the minstrel. Just as the seasons recur in cyclical repetitions, so these characters, which first seem like opposites or foils, connect through cycles.

Tannhäuser is presented early in Act I, specifically in the opening Venusberg scene, as an artist. It is interesting to note that Wagner initially wanted to title the opera "The Venusberg," but friends pointed out that this would lead to comic and smutty puns so Wagner wisely changed the title. The Venusberg can be seen as representing the depressive phase of bipolar illness, as a symbol of the land of darkness and excessive, lawless sexuality. Here the sexuality is always touched by death, and in fact Tannhäuser mentions death and suicide as a means of getting out of the grotto of Venus. As he tells Venus, even if it costs him his life he must leave. It is interesting as well that in Wagner's stage directions he refers to several Roman and Greek myths about couplings between the gods and human beings—specifically, the stories of Europa and the Bull and Leda and the Swan. Of course these Roman myths reflect the coupling of a human and a goddess in this opera, Venus and the minstrel Tannhäuser.

But the goddess Venus is not merely a brothel owner or brothel madame, since there are many very pleasant qualities about her. For one thing, she remains very concerned about Tannhäuser's art and keeps asking him to sing and compose poetry to his songs. She clearly is one of the great appreciators of his art, and probably one of the main sources of his creativity. That creativity is connected with lawless sexual excess, and even death does not in any way diminish the beauty that results from the art.

As Venus pleads with Tannhäuser, she says:

> Ha! Du kehrtest nie zurück!
> Wie sagt ich? Ha! wie sagte er?
> Nie mir zurück? Wie soll' ich's denken?
> Wie es erfassen?
> Mein Geliebter ewig mich fliehn?
> Wie hätt' ich das erworben,
> wie traf mich solch Verschulden,
> da mir die Lust geraubt,
> dem Trauten zu verzeihn?
> Der Königin der Liebe,
> der Göttin, aller Hulden
> wär' einzig dies versagt,
> Trost dem Freunde zu weihn?
> Wie einst, lachelnd unter Tränen,
> ich sehnsuchtsvoll dir lauschte,
> den stolzen Sang zu hören,
> der rings so lang mir verstummt.

> Ah! You will never come back!
> What did I say? What did he say?
> Never come back to me! How could I think it!

> How comprehend this?
> My beloved leave me forever?
> How could I have deserved that?
> How could I do so much wrong,
> that the hope of forgiving my lover
> has been robbed from me?
> Were only this denied
> to the Queen of Love,
> the all-forgiving goddess,
> can devote herself to the solace of her love?
> How could I listen to you,
> I longing for you,
> longing to hear your song
> grown silent around here for so long!

Clearly Venus would miss the music and poetry of Tannhäuser since she is not just his lover but also a connoisseur of music and poetry—the arts of the minstrel. This spiritual aspect of Venus is reflected in the rhythms of some of her music, which often sounds like a mother's lullaby. The erotic but all-forgiving mother figure, which Venus represents here, will recur over and over again in Wagner's operas—in Isolde, Kundry, Brünnhilde. Sexuality and the figure of the mother generally combine in Wagner's opera—long before Freud wrote about the Oedipus conflict. Wagner's relationship with his own mother must have been strained, since the longing for the sexual usually combines with a longing for mother, and Wagner himself was attracted to mother figures in the women he fell in love with. Minna was older than Wagner when he married her, Mathilde Wesendonck and Cosima von Bülow were both mothers, surrounded with small children when Wagner first met them and subsequently fell in love with them.

For *Tannhäuser*, Wagner uses a basic meter for this libretto, iambic pentameter, though often varied. He rarely uses rhyme in this libretto, except when the minstrels are supposed to be singing during the singer's contest of Act II—a situation Wagner would use again for the singer's contest in Act III of *Meistersinger*. Wagner sought a conversational quality for the poetry of this libretto, and a conversational quality would preclude much rhyme. As a result, he often uses what we would call blank verse, or unrhymed iambic pentameter. This meter is, of course, the great meter of Shakespearean drama. This libretto also calls for much conflict between the characters, something which Wagner was always good at incorporating in his operas. By the end of the first scene of Act I, the conflict between Tannhäuser and Venus becomes central to the scene, and central to the opera.

But of course by the end of the Venusberg scene Tannhäuser finally calls upon the name of Maria, whose name he invokes to be released from enslavement to the Roman goddess Venus. In many ways, then, Venus represents the depressive cycle of manic-depressive illness: depressed, dark, without light, intensely sexual, essentially pagan, and yearning for death.

It is certainly significant as well that Wagner uses light and dark symbolism extensively in this opera, also suggesting cyclical rather than progressive movement. The darkness becomes repeatedly connected with the Roman goddess Venus while the light repeatedly remains connected with Elisabeth. Light and darkness are created, of course, by the spinning of the earth as it makes its way around the sun; both light and darkness remain linked as part of the recurrent and cyclical movement of the earth. Light and darkness can be seen as the polar extremes of life and death, linked through cycles.

It is certainly significant that the death-wish enters near the end of this first scene of Act I when Tannhäuser sings:

> Doch hin muss ich zur Welt der Erden:
> bei dir kann ich nur Sklave werden!
> Nach Freiheit doch verlangt es mich,
> nach Freiheit, Freiheit dürste ich!
> Zu Kampf und Streite will ich stehn,
> sei's auch auf Tod und Untergehen!
> drum muss aus deinem Reich ich fliehn!
> O Königin! Göttin! Lass mich zeihn!
>
> ---
>
> But I must go into the earthly world;
> I can only be a slave with you!
> I want my freedom,
> for freedom, I want my freedom!
> In combat and conflict shall I stand firm,
> be it unto death and destruction!
> But I must leave your kingdom!
> O Queen! Goddess! Let me go!

What Tannhäuser is saying here is that, even if it results in his destruction, he must leave the Venusberg. Doesn't this suggest a suicidal impulse as well? Will leaving the Venusberg mean the destruction of Tannhäuser? That is what the text states here, and that is precisely what happens by the end of the opera. At the very end of this scene, Tannhäuser says:

> Mein Sehnen drängt zum Kampfe,
> nicht such' ich Wonn' und Lust

> Ach, mägest du es fassen, Göttin!
> Hin zum Tod, den ich suche
> zum Tode drängt es mich!
>
> ---
>
> My desire urges me to battle,
> I am not seeking happiness and pleasure!
> Ah, If only you could understand, goddess!
> To death, which I seek,
> to death it compels me!

Here too Tannhäuser sounds like a suicidal person who says he is seeking death. He does not want pleasure but death, which certainly sounds like profound, suicidal depression. Venus' response to him at this point is most generous:

> Kehr zurück, wenn der Tod selbst dich flieht,
> wenn vor dir das Grab selbst sich schliesst!
>
> ---
>
> Return when death itself flees from you,
> when even the grave is closed to you.

And Tannhäuser's response again asserts his suicidal mentality:

> Den Tod, das Grab, hier im Herzen ich trag.
> durch Buss und Sühne wohl find' ich Ruh fur mich!
>
> ---
>
> Death and the grave I carry here in my heart,
> through atonement and suffering I will surely find rest!

These lines clearly indicate the suicidal quality of Tannhäuser's personality, since he insists on leaving the Venusberg even though he sees his departure as leading him directly to death. These passages indicate that not only is Tannhäuser consciously suicidal, but those suicidal thoughts occur more frequently when he is with Venus. Clearly she and the Venusberg can be seen as representing the most depressed and suicidal side of Tannhäuser, though also mixed with intense sexual pleasure as well as artistic creation.

The passage above also indicates a guilty aspect to the minstrel's personality, indicating that his existence with Venus has generated real guilt which needs to be atoned for. Does the sexual pleasure which Venus offers inevitably lead to guilt for the Christian minstrel, unlike for the citizens of ancient Rome? Wagner clearly indicates here the complexity of the medieval mind and the complexity of the Christian Church's relationship to human sexuality. It is surely significant as well that while Tannhäuser desperately wants to leave Venus, he still tells her that she alone will be the center of his art. As he says:

> Stets soll mir dir, nur dir mein Lied entönen,
> gesungen laut sei nur dein Pries von mir!
> Dein süsser Reiz ist Quelle alles Schönen,
> und jedes holde Wunder stammt von dir.
> Die Glut, die du mir in das Herz gegossen.
> Als Flamme lodre hell sie dir allein!
> Ja, gegen alle Welt will unverdrossen
> fortan ich nun dein kühner Streiter sein!

> Always, my song will be sung only to you,
> only your priase will I loudly sing!
> Your sweet charm is the source of all that's wonderful,
> and every wonder stems from you.
> The love that you put into my heart,
> like a flame, may it blaze brightly for you alone!
> Yes, against the whole world will I go undaunted
> now and forever I will be your bold champion.

It is interesting how cleverly Wagner uses the literary technique of foreshadowing in this first scene, for in the opening scene of the opera Wagner predicts its ending. Tannhäuser will leave Venus, and though he will ultimately die in the process of leaving her, he will never stop singing her praises. It is while singing the praises of Venus that Tannhäuser upsets everyone present in the Wartburg in the second act, but here he must leave her before he can continue his adventures.

The next scene of the opera, after Tannhäuser has escaped the Venusberg, begins with the little shepherd boy singing the praises of the lovely May (though the boy begins his song by praising "Frau Holda," or Venus). Without the sexuality that Venus symbolizes there can not be the new life which spring represents. Once again, cyclical imagery remains at the core of Wagner's opera. The shepherd boy's song also suggests the innate irony and futility of the minstrel's quest since the very new life he seeks will demand the sexual expression which he is seeking to avoid.

Once Tannhäuser is free of Venus, he escapes her seductive cave and finds the noblemen, knights, and minstrels of Thuringia, who by the end of the first act tell him that they will take him to the Wartburg and the "holy Elizabeth." But of course, as Venus herself predicts, he will find no happiness there either. Tannhäuser seems a man doomed to waver between two extreme moods, one represented by the Roman goddess Venus, the other represented by the Christian Saint Elisabeth—figures who symbolize the two poles of Wagner's own bipolar illness.

Act II begins with the wonderful aria "Dich teure Halle," in which Elisabeth sings about her excitement at being back in the wonderful minstrel's hall of the Wartburg, and also about her excitement at seeing the minstrel and knight Tannhäuser again. His entrance results in a famous duet between them. In her monologue and in her duet, Elizabeth makes clear that though she represents light, goodness, and other Christian virtues, she also yearns for the sexual delights provided by the Christian sacrament of marriage. While there is undoubtedly a virginal quality about Elisabeth, unlike the sensuous Venus, she makes clear that she is also very sexually interested to Tannhäuser and clearly wants to marry him. As Elisabeth sings in this scene:

> Verzeiht, wenn ich nicht weiss, was ich beginne!
> Im Traum bin ich, und tör'ger als ein Kind,
> Machtlos der Macht der Wunder preisgegeben.
> Fast kenn' ich micht nicht mehr; o, helfet mir,
> dass ich das Rätsel meines Herzens löse!
> Der Sänger klugen Weisen
> lauscht' ich sonst gern und viel;
> ihr Singen und ihr Preisen
> schien mir ein holdes Spiel.
> Doch welch ein seltsam neues Leben
> rief Euer Lied mir in die Brust!
> Bald wollt' es mich wie Schmerz durchbeben,
> bald drang's in mich wie jähe Lust:
> Gefühle, die ich nie empfunden!
> Verlangen, das ich nie gekannt!
> Was einst mir lieblich, was verschwunden
> von Wonnen, die noch nie genannt!
> Und als Ihr nun von uns gegangen,
> war Frieden mir und Lust dahin;
> die Weisen, die die Sänger sangen,
> erschienen matt mir, trüb ihr Sinn;
> im Traume fühlt' ich dumpfe Schmerzen,
> mein Wachen ward trübsel'ger Wahn;
> die Freude zog aus meinem Herzen:
> Heinrich! Heinrich!
> Was tatet Ihr mir an?

> Forgive me if I don't understand what I am doing!
> I seem in a dream, and more silly than a child,
> helpless, yielding to the power of a miracle.
> I hardly know my own mind anymore. Oh help me

>   to understand the mystery of my heart!
>   I used to listen with pleasure
>   to the wonderful melodies of the singers;
>   their singing and prizes
>   seemed a wonderful sport to me.
>   But what a strange new life
>   your song stirred in my breast!
>   One second it quivered through me like pain,
>   the next it pierced me like a great pleasure.
>   Feelings which I have never experienced before!
>   Longings which I had never known!
>   What once was beautiful to me vanished
>   before pleasures never before experienced!
>   And then when you left us,
>   gone were peace and joy from me;
>   the tunes which the singers sang
>   seemed dull to me, their sense meaningless;
>   in dreams I felt dull pain,
>   my waking became sad lunacy;
>   joy disappeared from my heart.
>   Henry! Henry!
>   What have you done to me?

The erotic music which Wagner wrote for this monologue clearly indicates the sexual awakening which the saintly, virginal Elisabeth is experiencing through her attraction to Heinrich and his sexual songs. The very sexuality which the minstrel sought to avoid by leaving Venus he is now confronted with in the awakening sexuality of Elisabeth. Her attraction to him is hardly virginal, and its intensity is also indicated by her mentioning that she feels she is often in a dream-like state—dreams also indicating in Wagner the central importance of emotions. Freud would say that the dreams indicate that her attraction to the minstrel has clearly entered into her subconscious mind.

So Elisabeth seems to represents the light of day, unlike the darkness of Venus, but also legal sexuality and the wonders of Tannhäuser's art, for she too yearns for his poetry and his music. She then can be seen as the manic part of the manic-depressive cycle, since she has a happiness and excitement about her which contrast significantly with the languid tempos connected with Venus. But both Elisabeth and Venus contain amazing similarities as well, for both are attracted to Tannhäuser's art but also to his body—both are clearly linked as are the very cycles of day and night and mania and depression. Exactly what the minstrel seeks to avoid by leaving Venus he is now confronted with in the monologue of the virginal but sexually needy St. Elisabeth.

Tannhäuser: Jessye Norman as Elisabeth, Richard Cassilly as Tannhäuser.

    Tannhäuser, then, finds himself trapped between his attractions to both Venus and Elisabeth. While he is with Elisabeth, he yearns for Venus; but while he is with Venus, he yearns for freedom and Elisabeth. And both women, on a deeper level, represent the same thing to him: the cycle of mania and depression. Ultimately he finds death at the end, while the pilgrims hope for his salvation thanks to the miracle of the blooming of the Pope's old wooden cane. The search for salvation, or "Erlösung," another key and often repeated word in this opera, becomes the Christian miracle at the end of the opera. While the Pope in Rome has denied Tannhäuser forgiveness for his sins with Venus, the pilgrims, carrying the flowering staff of the Pope, sing that this miracle proves that Tannhäuser has been redeemed. That flowering staff can certainly be seen as a symbol of spring and the rebirth of life on earth, though this final scene of the opera occurs in the autumn of the year. Here too Wagner reminds us of one of Vico's most recurrent and powerful cycles, the cycle of the seasons.

Tannhäuser remains a man caught between two extremes: the depression represented by Venus and the mania and excitement represented by Elisabeth, and Wagner's music illustrates both: The music for Venus tends to be slow and languid, but Elisabeth's music uses fast, exciting rhythms—as in her opening monologue, "Dich teure Halle." And just as Tannhäuser remains in thrall to these two women—wanting one when in the arms of the other—so too Wagner remains for much of his life trapped between the two cycles that formed the totality of his manic-depressive illness and life. Cyclical movement is never progressive but always regressive, suggesting entrapment rather than movement forward, and also suggesting the essential tragedy of Tannhäuser's life despite his final forgiveness indicated by the appearance of the pilgrims with the pope's flowering staff at the end of the opera.

Tannhäuser stands as an opera full of complexities which have often confused stage directors and singers. The opera is often performed, of course, primarily because of the gorgeous music it contains, but the characters remain complex and often confusing for many singers and many viewers and listeners. Perhaps it is the very complexities and mysteries of this opera which encourage us to keep seeing and hearing it. If we can totally understand a work of art, it tends to become mechanical and dull.

Thus, Venus is supposed to be the Roman goddess of sexuality and as a result is alleged to represent the sexual and even bestial side of human love and sexuality. But there is a wonderful spirituality about her attraction as well. She is very concerned with Tannhäuser the poet and minstrel and the quality of his art. When she urges him to stay with her in the Venusberg, in the first scene of Act I, it is his art which she repeatedly refers to, which gives her character a wonderful maternal spirituality and complexity.

And Elisabeth is alleged to be the Gothic symbol of purity, virginity, and chastity in the opera, but her music indicates a sexual attraction to Tannhäuser the man in addition to her artistic attraction to Tannhäuser the poet and composer. She clearly wants to marry and have a sexual relationship with Tannhäuser, despite her alleged symbolism of virginity and saintliness. In the second and third acts of the opera she even offers her life to save Tannhäuser, suggesting that she as well as the minstrel has a death-wish. This irony is made even more apparent in the final tribute to her in the opera, Wolfram's "Song to the Evening Star," the most famous aria in the opera. While Wolfram thinks he is singing a tribute to the "heilige Elisabeth," or "Saint Elisabeth," the audience is aware that in point of fact the evening star is the planet Venus—an additional and especially glaring irony in the opera.

In its place, the singing of Wolfram's "Song to the Evening Star" provides a wonderful example of situational irony, something which recurs often in this opera. Just before the pilgrims enter in the second scene of the first act of the opera, the little shepherd boy sings a song to "Frau Holda," which according to Wagner is another name for the goddess Venus. A closer look at the text of this little song of the shepherd boy indicates Wagner's deep commitment to irony in the opera:

> Frau Holda kam aus dem Berg hervor
> zu ziehn durch Fluren und Auen;
> gar süssen Klang vernahm da mein Ohr,
> mein Auge begehrte zu schauen.
> Da träumt' ich manchen holden Traum,
> und als mein Aug' erschlossen kaum,
> da strahlte warm die Sonnen,
> der Mai, der Mai war kommen.
> Nun spiel' ich lustig die Schalmei,
> Der Mai ist da, der liebe Mai!

Lady Venus comes down from the mountain
to cross plains and meadows;
my ear heard sounds so very sweet
that my eye wanted to look at her,
then I dreamed many happy dreams,
and soon my eyes opened,
when the sun shone warmly,
May, May has arrived.
Now I happily play the pipe:
May is here, happy May!

While the shepherd is supposing to be introducing the scene of the pilgrims, the antithesis of the Roman goddess Venus, it is situationally ironic that he first sings a praise to Venus coming from her mountain—and we have just left the cave in the mountain of Venus at the end of

Tannhäuser: Hakan Hagegard as Wolfram.

Scene 1 of this same act. The shepherd dreams (a common occurrence in Wagnerian opera) of the arrival of his beloved May. But what causes May and the renewed life of spring to occur but the sexuality that Venus represents? It is the sexual activities of both plants and animals that causes the spring and its new life. While Venus may represents death and depravity in the first scene, she becomes a fertility goddess here at the opening of the second scene of Act I. Thus, situational irony occurs yet again in this very ironic opera.

Again, the Thuringians who appear suddenly in this scene all claim to be devout Christians, yet they are quick to threaten Tannhäuser with death in the very next act when he disagrees with their Christian view of love. Their behavior becomes situationally ironic because while they defend their Christian beliefs, threatening to murder someone who disagrees with you hardly represents model Christian behavior. And the stage directions indicate that the Landgrave and his men are hunters, which gives them an ironic note as well. These knights seem more like predators of nature than Christian martyrs.

We have previously found that Wagner the librettist liked to use repetitions of key words and image patterns to communicate meaning to his audience. Among the repeated words in this opera are: Liebe (Love), Tod (death), Erlösung (Redemption), Wunder (miracle), and Traume (dream). This last word, dream, often occurs in this opera. Early in the first scene of the opera, Tannhäuser speaks of waking up from a dream, and other characters like the shepherd boy and Elisabeth talk about dreams and dream-like states. Given the fairy-tale quality of the opera, one can argue that it represents Wagner's dream of entrapment between conflicting cycles and his desire to die so as to be free of this entrapment and the unhappiness it has caused him. Even before the surrealist movement in the art of the 20th century, and even before Freud's famous *The Interpretation of Dreams*, Wagner sees that dreaming can be connected both to artistic creation and to the preconscious or subconscious mind of both his characters and people in general. But this dream, the dream of Tannhäuser, ends in death.

And why does Tannhäuser die so suddenly at the end of the opera? Why does he yearn for Elisabeth when he is with Venus, yet yearn for Venus during the song contest in the Wartburg when he is with Elisabeth? The confusion and complexity of the opera point to the need for a new interpretation of this work. The bipolar quality of the opera's two main female characters, Venus and Elisabeth, clearly suggests that they are representatives of the bipolar quality of Wagner's life and art. Venus represents the depressive part of the cycle, which includes Elisabeth as the manic half, with Tannhäuser (and Wagner) trapped between their varying attractions and repulsions. Just as Tannhäuser suffers (and ultimately dies) as a result of being entrapped by both of the women, so Wagner the man suffered from having to endure bouts of mania and depression, a cycle which produced great art and also produced great suffering for him.

Wagner clearly suggests here that the depressive part of his illness, while causing him much suffering, also remains the source of his creativity, just as Tannhäuser seems doomed to sing of the power of Venus, even when he is with Elisabeth.

The sudden, unexplained death of Tannhäuser at the end of the opera, as well as the equally sudden and unexplained death of Elisabeth, remain recurrent problems in Wagnerian opera. Elsa dies (or at least collapses) at the end of *Lohengrin*, as does Isolde at the end of her opera, without any clear reason. These sudden, unexplained deaths make for a dramatic resolution of the story of the opera, but that they are not clearly motivated and seem to have only emotional causes add to the unresolved questions these operas can raise in the viewer. These sudden deaths also add to the essentially anti-realistic quality of Wagner's art and connect his operas with dreams and even surrealism, though occurring before surrealism appeared in the 20th century.

The uniqueness and suffering of Wagner is exemplified as well in the uniqueness and suffering of Tannhäuser the character. While many people offer Tannhäuser friendship in the opera, especially the other minstrels at the Wartburg, and especially Wolfram, Tannhäuser remains an isolated figure who can not connect very long with either women or men in either friendship or love. Clearly Tannhäuser's isolation, and ultimately his death, can be seen as a result of the entrapment he experiences in his bi-polar life. As Tannhäuser tells Wolfram in the last act of the opera:

> Zurück von mir! Die Stätte, wo ich raste, ist verflucht!
> ------
> Away from me! The place where I rest is accursed.

Tannhäuser, by the end of the opera, feels isolated from, and accursed by, the rest of normal humanity, something other Wagnerian heroes also experience. Both Siegmund and Sieglinde feel like isolated, guilty creatures who destroy whoever comes near them, and Siegfried often complains of his isolation and loneliness.

While the isolated Dutchman finds his mate in Senta and her faithfulness at the end of the opera, Tannhäuser's isolation remains absolute at the end of his opera, though he is rewarded with a redemption in death by a wonderful and forgiving chorus in the finale. But Tannhäuser never experiences that kind of fulfillment, forgiveness, or redemption in life. He remains a doomed figure, and doomed by the bipolar nature of his experiences and his illness. Sieglinde in *Die Walküre* also feels like a cursed figure who should be avoided by the rest of humanity, as does her brother

Siegmund, who feels that he also is accursed; unhappiness follows him and he brings bad luck to others. The cursed, isolated figure certainly recurs in Wagnerian opera, and such repetition raises an obvious question: Did Wagner himself feel like an isolated, cursed human being who would bring only unhappiness to others? His letters indicate that he sometimes did feel that way. Especially in his correspondence to Franz Liszt, Wagner repeatedly complains of his loneliness, of his isolation from the rest of humanity.

Perhaps this Wagnerian theme of isolation is why Thomas Mann in his wonderful essay on the "The Suffering and Greatness of Richard Wagner" insisted on seeing Richard Wagner as an eternally suffering and isolated figure. Part of that suffering was undoubtedly doled out by a society which did not understand him, and another part was caused by his own monumental demands on that society. But an even greater part of his suffering was, I feel, caused by bipolar illness, which doomed him to suffer sudden attacks of mania or depression, but which also generated some of the greatest works of art in the Western canon.

And the bipolar nature of Wagner's mental illness generated in him an innate sense of the complex nature of contrast, since he himself was a victim of contrasting and extreme emotional states. The basis of so many of Wagner's operas remains sharp contrasts: the contrast between the land and the sea in *The Flying Dutchman*, the contrast between Venus and Elizabeth in *Tannhäuser*, the contrast between Wotan and Alberich in the *Ring* cycle, the contrast between Amfortas and Klingsor in *Parsifal*. A cliché in dramatic theory is that the basis of drama is conflict. Wagner understood dramatic conflict innately; it was something he experienced often in his own life as the victim of contrasting extremes of emotion. If it is the artist's lot to suffer more, it is also the artist's lot to have greater pleasure than most—often the pleasure of having created a successful and significant work of art and of being a uniquely gifted individual.

Mania and depression, the yang and yin of Wagner's life, represent an extreme form of what we all call "experience." Most people experience high points and low points in life—points when things are going well, points when things are going badly; moments when we feel like a success, moments in which we feel like a failure. Manic-depressive illness represents extremes of what most people feel in life. After all, we all have our optimistic moods and our pessimistic moods, and at times we are victims of them—though luckily not to the extent that the manic-depressive person is. While we can experience periods of exuberance, it is not mania; while we can experience depression, we are not suicidal. The basic cycles of life and swings of mood affect us all, and these repetitive cycles occur centrally in *Tannhäuser*.

Much of this analysis sounds like the theories of Giambattista Vico, the 18th century Neapolitan philosopher and scientist whose *Nuovo Scienzia* startled Europe during his time. Vico argued, as did his contemporary Sir Isaac Newton, that nature is controlled by cycles—day, night, the tides, the seasons—and that humanity, as a part of nature, remains also controlled by those cycles. The very progression of human life—from birth to maturity and death—represents one of the most basic cycles in all of living things. Mood swings are also cycles that we must endure, though they are not as extreme as those experienced by the bipolar personality. *Tannhäuser* remains, then, a uniquely fascinating and obsessive example of those very cyclical extremes. Goethe's *Faust*, as well as many of his poems, are also centrally concerned with cycles of behavior, cycles of seasons, cycles of nature, light and dark. Through Goethe, Wagner might well have absorbed the scientific theory of cycles of Giambattista Vico, and those cycles certainly appear in *Tannhäuser,* an opera about the cyclical experiences and death but ultimate redemption of a suicidal artist.

Chapter 4

Lohengrin: The Dream Persona from Another World

Dreams occur throughout Wagner's operas, as of course they did throughout his life. And in both Wagner's autobiography and especially in Cosima Wagner's diaries dreams figure prominently. Both works indicate that Richard Wagner took dreams very seriously and that they form one basis of his art. For example, the following passage from *Mein Leben* explains how Wagner, while on vacation in Italy, got the idea for the opening scene in *Das Rheingold*:

> For I was still driven to seek some sort of asylum which would afford me the soothing harmony I needed for artistic creation. But soon, as a consequence of over-indulgence in ice cream, I got an attack of dysentery, which produced a sudden and depressing lassitude after the initial exaltation. I wanted to get away from the horrendous noise of the harbor, beside which my hotel was situated, and seek the most extreme tranquility. For this purpose I believed an excursion to Spezia would be appropriate, and after a week I proceeded there by steamship. Even this voyage, which lasted only one night, turned into an arduous adventure as a result of violent head-winds. My dysentery was supplemented by seasickness, and by the time I reached Spezia I could hardly take a single step and went to the best hotel, which to my dismay was situated in a narrow and noisy alley. After a sleepless and feverish night, I forced myself to undertake a long walk the following day among the pine-covered hills of the surroundings. Everything seemed to be bleak and bare, and I asked myself why I had come. Returning that afternoon, I stretched out dead-tired on a hard couch, awaiting the long-desired onset of sleep.

It did not come; instead, I sank into a kind of somnambulistic state, in which I suddenly had the feeling of being immersed in rapidly flowing water. Its rushing soon resolved itself for me into the musical sound of the chord of E flat major, resounding in persistent broken chords; these in turn transformed themselves into melodic figurations of increasing motion, yet the E flat major triad never changed, and seemed by its continuance to impart infinite significance to the element in which I was sinking. I awoke in sudden terror from this trance, feeling as though the waves were crashing high above my head. I recognized at once that the orchestral prelude to *Das Rheingold*, long dormant within me but up to that moment inchoate, had at last been revealed; and I also saw immediately precisely how it was with me: the vital flood would come from within me, and not from without [Wagner, *My Life*, 498–499].

This passage suggests the close connection Wagner saw between his dream life and his artistic creations. His dream of rushing water, which came to him as he lay on a couch in Spezia, becomes the opening music for the first opera of the *Ring*, and we have already seen how often Wagner used water as a major symbol in his operas.

Here Wagner reacts like a typical Romantic, since the Romantic movement of the 19th century often reflects a major concern with dreams and dreaming. The English Romantic poets Coleridge and Keats were particularly fond of dreams, dreaming, and dream-like states while awake, and these states often appear in their poetry. Coleridge's "Kubla Khan," which first appeared in 1816, is given the subtitle of "A Vision in a Dream," and indeed the poem does present a dream-like view of the Orient.

John Keats begins his poem "The Fall of Hyperion: A Dream" with the following lines, which connect the art of poetry with the dreaming mind:

> Fanatics have their dreams, wherewith they weave
> A paradise for a sect; the savage too
> From forth the loftiest fashion of his sleep
> Guesses at heaven: pity these have not
> Trac'd upon vellum or wild Indian leaf
> The shadows of melodious utterance.
> But bare of laurel they live, dream, and die;
> For Poesy alone can tell her dreams
> With the final spell of words alone can save
> Imagination from the sable charm
> and dumb enchantment. Who alive can say
> "Thou art no poet; may'st not tell they dreams"?

Keats wrote these lines in 1819, and in that same year he wrote his more famous "Ode to a Nightingale," whose final stanza also emphasizes the connection between art and dreaming:

> Forlorn! the very word is like a bell
> To toll me back from thee to my sole self!
> Adieu! the fancy cannot cheat so well
> As she is fam'd to do, deceiving elf.
> Adieu! adieu! thy plaintive anthem fades
> Past the near meadows, over the still stream,
> Up the hill-side; and now 'tis buried deep
> In the next valley-glades:
> Was it a vision, or a waking dream?
> Fled is that music—Do I wake or sleep?

Here too the dreaming mind and the dreamlike state appear as necessary for the poetic vision, and by implication the artistic vision.

Wagner clearly agreed that dreams and dreaming are necessary for artistic creation since his dream life often became his art and since dreams occur so frequently in both his life and his art. He liked to talk about his dreams with his family and friends, and he also liked to write about dreams in his voluminous correspondence and in his autobiography. And some of Wagner's major theories of aesthetics come from his theories of dreams. Some of this he probably absorbed from Schopenhauer, who had also written about the connection between dreams and artistic creation. Even before Sigmund Freud wrote *The Interpretation of Dreams*, which started both psychology and psychoanalysis on its famous pursuit of the analysis of dreams, Wagner was insisting that dreams be taken seriously. And indeed he did take his dreams very seriously as they came to form the kernel of his vision for his music-dramas. But often dreams indicate something about the struggles of his life as well. For example, Cosima Wagner records one of her husband's dreams in her diary entry for January 6, 1876:

> R. dreamed that he had to conduct the Ninth Symphony, in Dresden or Munich, and passed beforehand through a railway station restaurant which had frankfurters; being very hungry, he ordered some; coming back to fetch them, he sees two men eating his portion, the assistant at the buffet maliciously insolent, also the manager, who refuses him not only the sausages, but beer as well; he is angry, then tries friendly words, all to no avail. In the end he leaves the restaurant, cursing, arrives at the concert hall, walks through the orchestra, is greeted with applause, but

has to climb, relies on his agility, but comes to a place which is too steep; when he cannot jump over it, he wakes up!... He says, "All one needs is bad experiences to stop the brain from carrying out the talk it is there to do, for demons of all kinds to take control and produce nothing but horrible images!" [Wagner, Cosima, 249–250].

Clearly Wagner's dreams not only influenced his operas, but they also revealed his problems in his ordinary life—such as trying to survive in an often hostile environment. This dream also suggests something about fears of not having enough food, and frankfurters do introduce phallic implications. We can never know the exact meaning of this one of Wagner's many dreams, but dreams remain connected with Wagner's artistic creation.

And what is the nature of those dreams? Well, clearly they vary with the opera, but Wagner wanted each of his operas to have a dream-like, anti-realistic quality, and that is perhaps one of the reasons why he set most of his operas in the medieval period—far enough away from the present and from reality to create a dream-like setting. Wagner was hardly a *verismo* opera composer, even though he lived to see the start of this movement in both literature and opera. Strict realism in opera was never one of Wagner's goals; instead, the subconscious and the dream-like in the distant past remained his hallmarks of operatic creation, and the mysterious and miracle-believing early medieval period he found particularly cordial.

Long before verismo and scientific dream interpretation, Wagner was involved in the composition of the libretto and the music for *Lohengrin*. As Barry Millington recounts:

> Departing from the method of composition he had employed in *Der fliegende Holländer* and *Tannhäuser,* Wagner made for *Lohengrin* a through-composed draft for the whole work, though it consisted of only two staves (one for the voice, one indicating harmonies, often just by a bass) and amounting to little more than "a very hasty outline," as he later described it. This work was done between May and July 1846, after which Wagner elaborated the instrumental and choral parts in a second complete draft, which he began on 9 September 1846 and finished, with the Prelude, on 29 August the following year.
>
> Various changes were made to the poem during the course of composition, especially in Act III, which probably accounts for the fact that the second complete draft for this act was made, unusually, before those of Acts I and II. This reversal of order has led to the oft-repeated, but incorrect, statement that the opera itself was composed in that order (i.e. beginning with Act III): the first complete draft, in which the work

was set down in a detailed outline, was written in conventional order. Wagner made his full score between 1 January and 28 April 1848....

Unlike *Tannhäuser*, with which he was never entirely satisfied, *Lohengrin* was not subjected to substantial revision by Wagner. He did, however, request Liszt, who conducted the premiere in Weimar in the absence of the composer (who was in exile in Switzerland), to make a significant excision in Lohengrin's Narration. The second part of that Narration, the cutting of which has been observed by tradition following Wagner's instructions, went on to explain that the knights in Monsalvat had heard Elsa's plea and taken the swan (spell-bound Gottfried) into service: one year's service for the Grail frees a victim from a magic curse. Thus the deleted passage explains Lohengrin's reference shortly after to "one year by your side," after which Elsa would have had Gottfried restored to her. There is some new and worthwhile music there, but the only commercial recording to restore the passage (that conducted by Erich Leinsdorf) rather confirms Wagner's judgment that its inclusion has an anti-climatic effect [Millington 284–285].

Though Wagner was not able to be present because of his political exile, Liszt did conduct the premiere of *Lohengrin* at Weimar in 1850, which, unlike the Paris premiere of *Tannhäuser*, was a tremendous success. Wagner did not get to hear a performance of his own work until eighteen years later, but despite Wagner's absence, *Lohengrin* succeeded with the public at Weimar and was soon performed in other theaters in Germany. It has remained Wagner's most popular work—and dreams and dreaming, waking and sleeping, are at its core. As Ernest Newman recounts in his famous four-volume biography of Wagner:

> *Rienzi* was given in Konigsberg in 1845, in 1847 in Berlin. *The Flying Dutchman* was given in Riga and in Cassel in June, 1845. These were the only productions of his early operas outside Dresden during the period of his Kapellmeistership. It was not until 1850, when Liszt gave *Lohengrin* in Weimar, that his real vogue in Germany as a whole began [Newman 413].

How does all this provide us with material for a new approach to the meaning of *Lohengrin*? Dreams connect with *Lohengrin* on many levels, as we will see. Dreams first occur during act 1, scene 1 of the opera when Friedrich von Telramund begins his horrible accusations against Elsa:

> O Herr, traumselig ist die eitle Magd,
> Die meine Hand voll Hochmut von sich stiess.
> Geheimer Buhlschaft klag' ich sie drum an:
> Sie wähnte wohl, wenn sie des Bruders ledig,

Dann könnte sie als Herrin von Brabant
Mit Recht dem Lehnsmann ihre Hand verwehren,
Und offen des geheimen Buhlen pflegen.

O King, this maid is dream-confused
who proudly withdrew her hand from mine.
I now accuse her of having a secret lover.
She dreams, perhaps, if she can remove her brother,
Then she could rule as Duchess of Branbant
and therefore rightly cast aside her promised man
to openly reign with her secret lover.

Here Friedrich accuses Elsa of living in a world of dreams, and of dreaming to marry some secret lover, which (he argues) is why she undoubtedly murdered her own brother, the rightful heir to the throne. It is interesting as well that Fredrich was originally intended to be her husband, thereby suggesting a reason for the intense rivalry between Elsa and Ortrud, since both were competitors for a marriage with Friedrich von Telramund.

It is significant, of course, that her first line when she finally enters in Act I is: "Mein armer Bruder!" (My poor brother!). Her sad concern for her lost brother cleverly foreshadows the ending of the opera when she will lose Lohengrin forever but regain her lost brother Gottfried von Brabant. Since the opera begins and ends with Elsa's lost brother Gottfried, we can see that Wagner once again uses cycles and cyclical movements in his work. When the King asks Elsa in the very first scene of the opera to defend herself, she sings her famous monologue:

Einsam in trüben Tagen
Hab'ich zu Gott geflecht,
Des Herzens tiefstes Klagen
Ergoss ich im Gebet.
Da drang aus meinen Stöhnen,
Ein Laut so klagevoll,
Der zu gewalt'gem Tönen
Weit in die Lüfte schwoll:
Ich hört ihn fern hin hallen,
Bis kaum mein Ohr er traf:
Mein Aug' ist zugefallen
Ich sank in sussen Schlaf.
....
In lichter Waffen Scheine
Ein Ritter nahte da,
So tugendlicher Reine

Lohengrin: Placido Domingo as Lohengrin, Anna Tomowa-Sintow as Elsa.

Ich keine noch ersah:
Ein golden Horn zur Hüften,
Gelehnet auf sein Schwert,
So trat er aus den Lüften
Zu mir, der Recke wert.
Mit züchtigem Gebaren
Gab Tröstung er mir ein:
Des Ritters will ich wahren,
Er soll mein Streiter sein!

Once when sad and depressed
I prayed to God.
My heart's deepest desire
Implored heaven's help.
Among my loud laments
was one whose grief was so rare
that it bore itself upward,
Far into haven's realm.
And I heard it resound
until it could not longer be heard.
My eyes became quite heavy,
and then I sank into sweet sleep.
....
I saw a knight arriving
with his armor gleaming bright;
His purity was blinding,
I never saw any like it.
A golden horn he carried,
He leaned upon his sword,
Thus, I suddenly saw him,
My radiant, hoped for Knight.
His tender, gentle manner
Released me from sorrow.
I now await his arrival,
He shall be my champion!

Elsa's monologue is neatly divided into two parts. In the first part Elsa describes herself as in need, due to the accusations against her, praying to God, and then falling asleep to escape her grief and suffering. The second stanza describes her dream once she has fallen into a deep slumber, and that dream contains the vision of a dream knight who will defend her honor and prove her innocence. Soon afterward the dream knight actually appears. It is certainly significant that the solution to all her problems should come to her in a dream, and then the dream itself materializes and becomes the reality of her faithful knight Lohengrin. Notice as well that Lohengrin arrives on a boat floating on the water; he is immediately connected with water and with all that it symbolizes, both renewed life and the possibility of death by drowning.

In this scene Wagner does interesting things with his poetry. Most of the libretto uses the iambic pentameter he had used earlier, but here he gives Elsa's dream a different verse-form, iambic tetrameter with frequent rhyming. Here, as in *Tannhäuser,* Wagner gives the aria (though he did not like this word) a more musical meter with shorter lines to emphasizes the rhymes. Longer lines with rhyme make the listener less aware of the rhymes because they come less frequently, and as a result the poetry sounds less musical. Wagner also repeatedly contrasts two important words in this opera: Wunder vs. Zauber—or miracle vs. magic, implying black magic. For Elsa and King Henry, Lohengrin is a miracle, but Ortrud in the second act argues that he is a product of Zauber, or black magic. This very conflict of two words and their implied meanings adds to the mysterious quality of Wagner's knight Lohengrin. Is he from God or from the devil? Should Elsa embrace his strange offer of protection provided she does not ask any questions about him or his past, or should she be suspicious? One of the wonderful things about Wagnerian characterization remains its frequent mystery. Who are the heroes? Who are the real villains? Each side of the argument has some merit in Wagnerian opera, and both sides add to the very mystery and the eternal fascination of his characters.

Out of Elsa's dream, a dream generated by her exhaustion and grief over the death of her brother and Friedrich's accusations against her, her vision of her savior and defender appears. Is she then dreaming of a dream-brother and knight who will save her? Is she dreaming the dream of most young women that a dreamboat will come along and rescue her from all the griefs of adolescence? After all, what we have here is an adolescent girl whose normal teenage griefs are compounded by the death of her parents and the loss of her brother. Partially Elsa's dream also indicates an erotic component, including as it does the dream of a savior, defender, and husband. For agreeing to Lohengrin's conditions not to ask about his name and ancestry, Elsa gets a husband but loses a brother.

As Charles Osborne has written:

> By asking the forbidden question, "Who are you? Where do you come from?" Elsa does indeed lose her savior Lohengrin, but with those same questions she regains her brother who is finally more real to her than the magical knight Lohengrin, because his only existence is in the real world. The visible world has its legitimate delights, and Wagner is not, after all, the only artistic genius. That is what, despite its author,

the libretto of *Lohengrin* appears at this point to be saying. The libretto, however, is not simply a peg for the music to hang on. Despite the fact that its philosophical meaning and validity are open to question, it works magnificently in purely dramatic terms. Upon a two-dimensional, medieval fear of the unknown world, Wagner has superimposed a drama which is modern in its psychology and unerring in its poetic instinct. Thus he retains the best not of two apparent worlds but of three: the spiritual, the psychological, and the aesthetic. It is the interplay between these three views of the world, in Wagner's music and his words, which makes *Lohengrin* a great opera [Osborne 48–49].

Clearly Osborne indicates here that Elsa does not lose everything when she loses Lohengrin, but the stage directions of the opera do say that she dies at the end of the opera as Ortrud collapses (but is still alive though her husband Friedrich von Telramund has died). Both Elsa and Ortrud waver in their meaning and function in this opera. This balanced, cyclical quality of the two major female characters is balanced by the cyclical nature of the two major male characters: when Gottfried disappears, Lohengrin appears; when Lohengrin leaves, Gottfried reappears.

Wagner again uses the format of the medieval miracle play—or *Wundertheater*—both to begin and to end his opera. The first act contains a miracle, the miraculous appearance of Elsa's savior Lohengrin, and the last act ends with another miracle, the sudden appearance of Gottfried, Elsa's brother. The opera opens with the King and chorus singing of the need for a leader for their lands, and the opera ends with the miraculous appearance of that leader—the young man Gottfried whose disappearance started the accusations of Friedrich against Elsa in the first act. Overall, there is a wonderful circularity about this opera, suggesting that the miracle of the first act is balanced by the miracle of the last act, and that though Elsa has lost her husband at the end of the opera, she has regained her beloved brother. The movement remains circular and indicates that cycles were again in Wagner's thinking for this opera.

And the source of that miracle is, of course, the first miracle: the sudden appearance of Elsa's mysterious defender. Only at the end of the last act do we hear his name, Lohengrin. As several critics have pointed out, Wagner's operas often contain references to each other. Peter Conrad has commented that "The casual links between Wagner's operas—Lohengrin's acknowledgment of Parsifal as his father, the projected meeting between Parsifal and Tristan—give them the cyclical shape of chivalric romance. But the political action which connected Verdi's most disparate operas resembles Shakespearean historical drama made over into a nineteenth-century novel" (Conrad 54–55). The medievalism and interconnectedness of Wagnerian opera adds to its dream-like quality. And this mysterious stranger who (as we will learn only at the end of the opera) is called Lohengrin, Elsa's dream knight, suggests the bipolar nature of the dream.

While Elsa represents a kind of a benign mania, with innocence, brightness, faithfulness, and new life, Ortrud represents the dark reverse of all these things, especially revenge, spite, and night. While Elsa can be connected with renewed life, she dies by the end of the opera; Ortrud can be connected with death since she is responsible for the death of her husband Fredrich von Telramund, yet she is still alive at the end of the opera. Both women collapse by the end of the final scene of the opera, but only one is dead, indicating the possibilities of some renewal for Ortrud, though not for Elsa. One functions as the yin and the other as the yang of the central dream in Wagner's opera. The two women also represent different religions, just as in *Tannhäuser* Venus represents the pagan beliefs of ancient Rome while Elisabeth represents chaste Christianity. So too in *Lohengrin* while Elsa represents medieval Christianity, Ortrud remains a stout believer in the old Germanic gods like Wotan and Fricka. When Ortrud appears as a penitent in front of Elsa in Act II, Elsa responds like a true Christian and forgives her enemies. But Ortrud says in the second act when Elsa foolishly lets her into the Kemenate:

> Entweihte Götter! Helft jetz meiner Rache!
> Bestraft die Schmach, die hier euch angetan!
> Stärkt mich im Dienst eurer heil'gen Sache!
> Vernichtet der Abtrünn'gen schnöden Wahn!
> Wodan! Dich Starken rufe ich!
> Freia! Erhab'ne, höre mich!
> Segnet mir Trug und Heuchelei,
> Dass glücklich meine Rache sei!
>
> ---
>
> Holy gods help me get my revenge!
> Repay the shame which you have suffered here!
> Strengthen me in your holy service!
> Destroy the dreams of the non-believer!
> Wotan! Great One, I call on you!
> Freia! Great One, hear my prayer!
> Help my deceit and treachery.
> Let my revenge be complete.

Here Ortrud pleads to the old Germanic gods for help in her plot, unlike Elsa whose prayers are always addressed to the Christian God. One aspect of the medieval world which clearly fascinated Wagner was its conflicts between Christianity and the older pre–Christian religions of Europe.

Lohengrin: Eva Marton as Ortrud.

Wagner, as a man of the theater, wanted conflict, wanted two equally weighty and interesting forces in a struggle to add to the dramatic excitement of his operas, and by the end we are not sure which side has won.

If the opera is a dream, one way of viewing it is as the dream of Lohengrin—and his dream contains a bipolar struggle between two women:

Elsa and Ortrud. This structure repeats a pattern we first saw in *Tannhäuser*, where another medieval knight is torn between two opposing women, Venus and Elisabeth. And the mysterious knight Lohengrin goes off alone by the end of the opera because of the bipolar nature of his dream of two women. According to Cosima Wagner's diaries, in 1883, a few months before his death, Wagner recalled the lonely Lohengrin and called the opera the saddest of his works (Wagner, Cosima, 505). If Lohengrin is the solitary dreamer, he remains alone at the end of the opera because he has been the victim of the bipolar realities that the benign Elsa and the malignant Ortrud represent, though each has some characteristics (both good and bad) of the other. While Elsa says how she loves Lohengrin, she does ask the forbidden questions; while Ortrud remains determined to destroy Lohengrin's power, her determination to find out the truth about his name and his heritage contains an element of nobility. Neither Elsa nor Ortrud is totally good or totally evil, just as neither mania nor depression has only one moral dimension. In any case, Lohengrin is alone at the end of the opera as he floats down the waters of the river Scheldt. If the opera is ultimately Lohengrin's dream, and that dreamer is really Richard Wagner, one can see why Wagner (according to Cosima) found this opera his saddest, since the dreamer (Wagner/Lohengrin) remains alone and disappearing at the end. One can surely argue that the opera represents Wagner's suicidal dream of leaving this world alone, abandoned by all.

Another way of looking at the opera is as Wagner's dream of unconditional love. Lohengrin, in demanding that no one ask him his name or about his parentage, is in a way demanding unconditional love of Elsa and the people of Brabant. Lohengrin seems to want to be loved totally and without any questions or demands. If the opera did indeed originate as one or Richard Wagner's dreams, then that dream can be seen as his wish for unconditional love. But unconditional love is only given to children, and only to children who are lucky in their relationship with their parents, for not all children get the unconditional love they need and deserve. That Wagner dreamed of demanding and getting unconditional love suggests that he did not get this kind of love as a child. Adults can never get unconditional love, though they will yearn for it if they did not receive this kind of love as children. As adults, we must live in a world of conditional love as the only possibility, though Lohengrin does not seem to want this kind of love.

Early in his autobiography, Wagner describes his earliest memories of his mother, and they are rather painful memories:

> By the time my recollection of her is first distinct she was already compelled by a head ailment to wear a cap continually, so that I have no remembrance of her as a young and pretty mother. The anxious and trying relations with a large family (of which I was the seventh surviving member), the difficulties in providing the necessities of life, and the fulfillment of a certain desire to keep up appearances even with very limited means, were not conducive to a comforting tone of motherly solicitude in her; I hardly remember ever being caressed by her, just as outpourings of affection did not take place in our family at all; on the contrary, quite naturally a certain impetuous, even loud and boisterous manner characterized our behavior. In these circumstances I remember it as epoch-making one night being taken to bed and looking up at her with tearful eyes when she gazed back at me fondly and spoke of me to a visitor with a certain amount of tenderness [Wagner, *My Life*, 11].

This passage suggests that Richard Wagner did not get much love, let alone unconditional love, from his mother, so naturally as an adult the composer would dream of receiving this unconditional love. Dream remains one of the central concerns in Wagnerian opera, appearing in every one of Wagner's ten mature operas. In *The Flying Dutchman* the Dutchman himself appears as if in a dream of Senta, and Erik also dreams about his loss of Senta. In *Tannhäuser* dream is mentioned frequently in terms of Tannhäuser's fluctuating existence between Venus and Elisabeth. We have already examined the dream-like qualities of Elsa and her love for Lohengrin in that opera. In *Die Meistersingers von Nürnberg* Walter's prize song describes his dream. Dream recurs often in Wagner's *Ring* cycle as well. Wagner says that he got the whole idea of the tetralogy as he was sleeping in Spezia, Italy; some of the specific scenes in the four operas can be interpreted as dreams. For example, when Brünnhilde appears before Siegmund for the "Todesverkundigungmusik" in Act II of *Die Walküre*, this can certainly be seen as Siegmund's dream. Or when Alberich appears to Hagen in the first scene of Act II of *Götterdämmerung*, the scene can certainly be understood as Hagen's dream of his demanding father Alberich.

Wagner theatrically suggests in these operas that art comes from dreams, and that characters often reveal themselves by means of their dreams. Just as enlightenment comes to Walter through a dream, just as the Shepherd dreams of "Frau Holda" in Act I of *Tannhäuser*, dreams and the influence of dreams permeate Wagnerian opera because dreams reveal characters and also serve to enlighten and inform characters, as well as dramatic situations.

We have seen that Freud must be considered the first scientist who took dreams seriously—not just as something to be discussed in the realm of the uneducated and by fortune tellers. As he argued in *The Interpretation of Dreams*, the act of analyzing a patient's dreams can help the doctor to understand and diagnose the patient's problems. In 1924, André Breton wrote his original manifesto of Surrealism, arguing that the great work of art should try to capture all the conscious and subconscious realities of dreams. And from this movement we have enjoyed the dream-like surreal paintings of Salvador Dalí, Tanguy, and Magritte. Yet the pages of the founder's declarations still retain great value as a key to interpretation.

> So strong is the belief in life, in what is most fragile in life—*real* life, I mean—that in the end this belief is lost. Man, that inveterate dreamer, daily more discontent with his destiny, has trouble assessing the objects he has been led to use, objects that his nonchalance has brought his way, or that he has earned through his own efforts, almost always through his own efforts, for he has agreed to work, at least he has not refused to try his luck (or what he calls his luck!).

As Breton continues several pages later:

> It was, apparently, by pure chance that a part of our mental world which we pretended not to be concerned with any longer—and, in my opinion by far the most important part—has been brought back to light. For this we must give thanks to the discoveries of Sigmund Freud. On the basis of these discoveries a current of opinion is finally forming by means of which the human explorer will be able to carry his investigations much further, authorized as he will henceforth be not to confine himself solely to the most summary realities....
>
> Freud very rightly brought his critical faculties to bear upon the dream. It is, in fact, inadmissible that this considerable portion of psychic activity (since, at least from man's birth until his death, thought offers no solution of continuity, the sum of the moments of dream, from the point of view of time, and taking into consideration only the time of pure dreaming, that is the dreams of sleep, is not inferior to the sum of all the moments of reality, or, to be more precisely limiting, the moments of waking) has still today been so grossly neglected. I have always been amazed at the way an ordinary observer lends so much more credence and attaches so much more importance to waking events than to those occurring in dreams. It is because man, when he ceases to sleep, is above all the plaything of his memory, and in its normal state memory takes pleasure in weakly retracing for him the circumstances of the dream, in stripping it of any real importance, and in dismissing the only determinant from the point where he thinks he has left it a few hours before: this firm hope, this concern [Breton 3–11].

Clearly Breton sees dream and dream analysis as the core of our humanity, and so it would become the core of the new art form called surrealism as well. In fact, both Freudian dream analysis and surrealism can be seen in Wagner's presentation of dreams in his operas. Wagner's extensive use of dreams in his music-dramas prefigured dream analysis and had an indirect influence on the Surrealist movement. And in writings from Wagner's personal life, as well, dreams are often presented and interpreted, especially in Cosima Wagner's *Diaries*, though many of the dreams are not presented in enough detail for modern analysis. Freud often stated that artists and creative writers had discovered the laws of psychoanalysis long before he did—he simply put them in a scientific context.

In any case, Wagner's *Lohengrin* provides us with an entire dream, and it is a dream containing a bipolar opposition; for while Elsa represents the forces of love and light, just as attractive is Ortrud, who represents the forces of knowledge and darkness. The ending of *Lohengrin* also suggests one of the great heresies of the medieval period, the Manichean heresy. In the final scene of the last act of the opera, just as Lohengrin is about to leave, Ortrud steps forward and announces:

> Fahr' heim! Fahr' heim, du stolzer Helde,
> Das jubelnd ich der Törin melde,
> Wer dich gezogen in dem Kahn!
> Am Kettlein, das ich um ihn wand,
> Ersah ich wohl, wer dieser Schwan!
> Es ist der Erbe von Brabant!

> Farewell, farewell, you proud hero!
> Happily I will tell that stupid virgin
> Who is the person who draws your boat.
> I put that chain around his neck,
> And so I know your swan!
> He is the ruler of Brabant!

That Ortrud would know something about the swan that Lohengrin does not know implies that her powers are equal to his. The Manichean heresy argued that the reason there was so much evil in the world is that Satan remains as powerful as God, that God is not the most powerful force in the universe. Instead, the Manicheans argued, the world involved the struggle of two equally powerful forces: God and Satan. The medieval heresy of Manicheism, then, provides yet another cycle in this dream-world full of cycles of varying types. Dreams would continue to appear in Wagnerian opera, just as they continued throughout Wagner's life. Whether daydreams or nightdreams, dreaming itself remains a central concern of human life—and Wagnerian opera.

It is significant as well that *Lohengrin* was the first opera of Wagner's to attract his patron King Ludwig II of Bavaria. Often called a dreamy, idealistic, and unrealistic person by his biographers, Ludwig II dreamed of helping Wagner once he became a king. As Geoffrey Skelton reports the events of May 2, 1864, arguably the most important day in Wagner's career:

> Wagner ... left Mariafeld for Stuttgart, with vague hopes of interesting the conductor there—Karl Eckert, a friend from his Vienna days—in a production of *Tristan und Isolde*, an emissary of the new King of Bavaria, Ludwig II, tracked him down and handed him a ring and a photograph of the king. This emissary, Franz von Pfistermeister, also conveyed a verbal message from the king which, according to August Roeckel, ran: "As this stone glows, so does the desire burn in him to meet the author and composer of *Lohengrin*" [Skelton 31].

Skelton goes on to report the special connection King Ludwig made with *Lohengrin*:

> Ludwig was fifteen years old when he saw his first opera. It was *Lohengrin*. "Bad as the production was," he wrote to Wagner later, "I was able to appreciate the essence of this divine work: in that performance was sown the seed of our love and friendship till death; the spark, which soon developed into a mighty flame for our sacred ideals, was at that time ignited within me." According to his contemporary biographer, Gottfried von Boehm, the young Prince had wept tears of ecstasy in the opera house and immediately set about learning the text of *Lohengrin* and Wagner's other music dramas by heart. He thought out ideas of his own for costumes and scenery to illustrate the legend of the Holy Grail and persuaded his art tutor to draw them for him. He also started to read Wagner's prose works, including the theoretical *Das Kunstwerk der Zukunft* (*The Artwork of the Future*). When in 1863 Wagner published the text of the *Ring*, Ludwig vowed on reading it that, when the time arrived, he would be the prince who would respond to Wagner's appeal for help in staging the work. His opportunity soon came, for on 10 March 1864 King Maximilian died, and Ludwig became King of Bavaria at the age of eighteen [Skelton 32].

It was *Lohengrin*, then, which first attracted King Ludwig II to Richard Wagner and his operas. This bi-polar dream opera entranced a man who would ultimately provide Wagner with the funds to live independently, finish his *Ring* operas, *Meistersinger*, and *Parsifal*, and build his festival theater at Bayreuth. Ludwig II facilitated the fulfillment of Wagner's greatest dreams, and those dreams involved his art works. Those Wagnerian dreams would also cost the Bavarian treasury millions of dollars and also indirectly cost King Ludwig II his throne. Wagner's dreams for his future and his future operas would ultimately become a nightmare of expenses and political complications for poor, mad Ludwig II. Wagner's manic demands for more and more money from the generous king certainly helped to make Wagner very unpopular in Bavaria, since these demands were ultimately paid for by the taxes of the Bavarian people.

In Munich, Wagner's political enemies called him "Lola Montez the Second," a nasty joke suggesting a homosexual connection between the king and the composer, a joke that was in fact prescient of future political complications for Ludwig II. His grandfather Ludwig I lost his throne in Bavaria because of his scandalous obsession with the Spanish dancer and prostitute Lola Montez (her real name with Eliza Gilbert and she ultimately died in New York and was buried in Brooklyn's Green Wood Cemetery). Ludwig II was forced to abdicate from the Bavarian throne in 1886, three years after the death of Wagner, in part because of the costs of his obsession with Wagner and Wagner's mania for more and more money. The composer said the money was for the productions of his operas but much of it also funded Wagner's increasingly lavish lifestyle in both Munich and Bayreuth. Poor Ludwig II was found drowned in Lake Starnberg in 1886, soon after his forced abdication, and he most probably committed suicide. If Ludwig II ultimately paid the cost of Wagner's dreams, in *Lohengrin* the dream vision became a totality which included bipolarity, cycles, and death and disappearance at the end.

Chapter 5

Tristan und Isolde: Suicide as the Best Alternative

Certainly Wagner's *Tristan und Isolde* is the opera that most reflects Wagner's own depression and suicidal thoughts, for this is Wagner's most suicidal opera. Many critics have already pointed out that the opera itself was the result of Wagner's thwarted love-affair with Mathilde von Wesendonck, in which her husband Otto played the unhappy role of King Marke. Whether Wagner and Mathilde ever actually had a love affair or whether the whole thing was Platonic today remains a mystery, but in any case it was during this emotional crisis of 1856–58 that Wagner felt that he no longer loved his wife Minna but instead loved Mathilde. This situation was the result of the Wesendonck's generous offer to the Wagners: they could live for free in the Asyl, a cottage on the Wesendonck property in Switzerland, near Lake Lucerne. To get away from the crisis caused when Minna, after reading one of her husband's letters to Mathilde, created a scene by accusing the pair of betraying Otto, Wagner moved to Venice. In fact he wrote most of the text and music of *Tristan und Isolde* in Venice, that wet but wonderful and unique city.

There certainly is a watery quality to much of the music, created by the undulating sounds of the chromatic key system Wagner used for this composition. The first act actually takes place on a boat sailing from Ireland to Cornwall, carrying the captive Irish princess Isolde to her new husband, King Marke. The person conducting her to meet her new husband is King Marke's most loyal knight, his nephew Tristan. This connection between King Marke and Tristan certainly adds an Oedipal element to their relationship. Is Tristan obsessed with Isolde, in part, because she is the wife of his father-figure and uncle? This is one of the many complex Freudian elements to this complex opera, yet the story is not alone in creating *Tristan*'s special effect. Peter Conrad has discussed the power of the music in this opera and the passive quality of its main characters:

> The chromaticism of Wagner's score, forever mutating motifs, won't rest until it has transformed and canceled everything, like Frau Minne who has—as Isolde tells Brangaene—changed death into love only to change it back again, at Tristan's bidding, into death. The duty of the characters is to sit still and wait for the music to extinguish them [Conrad 53].

This very passivity of the characters is explained in part by Wagner's interest in the philosophy of Schopenhauer. As Hartmut Reinhardt has written:

> If one wishes to trace Schopenhauer's influences in Wagner's musical-dramatic work, one thinks above all of *Tristan*, and not only for chronological reasons. The work was conceived in outline as early as 1854, the text was written by 1857, and the music was composed by 1859. The primary Schopenhauer source for this work is the treatise titled *Metaphysics of Sexual Love*.... For Schopenhauer, the Will inherent in all being is metaphysical. It does not manifest itself as a phenomenon, does not enter the world of "representation." Wagner's *Tristan* is, in the words of Nietzsche, an "opus metaphysicum": it is metaphysical precisely insofar as it grants the Will an overwhelming musical-dramatic presence. The preconscious promptings of the Will express themselves above all in the sexual drive, whose power and intimation of bliss Schopenhauer never tires of delineating in inspired phrases. In *Tristan* Wagner takes Schopenhauer at his word; the lovers are driven to the brink [Reinhardt 290–291].

One of the most fascinating things about this opera is the wonderful poetic text that Wagner wrote for it. Wagner was lucky enough to be able to write all his own librettos, a poetical ability that Puccini often envied when Puccini himself was struggling with his various and many librettists. Wagner begins *Tristan und Isolde* with the sailor's offstage song:

> Westwärts
> schweift der Blick:
> ostwärts
> streicht das Schiff.
> Frisch weht der Wind
> der Heimat zu:

mein irisch Kind,
wo weilest du?
sind's deiner Seufzer Wehen
die mir die Segel blähen?
Wehe, wehe, du Wind!
Weh, ach wehe, mein Kind!
Irische Maid,
du wilde, minnige Maid!

Westward goes my gaze:
eastward
goes the ship.
The wind blows freely
toward homeland:
my Irish child
where do you travel?
Is it the breath of your sigh
that keeps my ship moving?
Breezes, blow; breezes, blow!
Child, they bring only grief!
My Irish girl,
you wild, lovable girl!

Right at the beginning this song suggests that the opera will end tragically. The song also shows that the sailors onboard know of Isolde's grief at being forced to go to Cornwall, and they sympathize with her. It is significant that Isolde interprets this comment not as sympathy but as a mocking taunt. In her anger at her situation, she assumes that everybody is enjoying her suffering. It is significant as well that the sailor uses the word "minnige" to mean "loving" in the courtly sense. Minne—rather than Liebe—will be used frequently, thus connecting the fate of Tristan and Isolde with the courtly tradition of the medieval period. Of course this line of reference finally becomes ironic since Tristan and Isolde, in their sensuality, violate the medieval courtly codes of chaste love and marital fidelity.

The meter Wagner uses also suggests his literary purposes for this libretto. Wagner uses a very short line here, generally just four syllables, and sometimes even fewer. He uses iambic dimeter most often, though this meter is often varied. Such a short line would emphasize the rhymes and the musical quality of his poetry because the rhymes come much more quickly. Although the rhymes are often not regular, rhyming does appear often in the text of Wagner's libretto—as in the passage above. Both metrical length and rhyme patterns are varied rather than repeated exactly, but the short poetical line used for most of the opera makes for a very musical poetry. Yet the musical quality of the poetry does not disguise the seriousness of the themes in this work. In terms of image patterns, references to water and to night recur significantly in the libretto—reflecting the watery, nocturnal music of this opera (written in watery, dark Venice).

Suicide dominates this opera. In fact, each act of the opera ends with Tristan attempting suicide, and succeeding in his last attempt. In Act I, Isolde tries to kill Tristan by getting him to drink what she thinks is the death potion, though her maid Brangaene has switched the drink to the love potion, unbeknownst to Isolde. But when Tristan drinks the potion, he fully believes that it is the death potion. And even earlier in this first act, when Isolde accuses him of murdering her fiancé Morold, Tristan responds:

> War Morold dir so wert,
> nun wieder nimm das Schwert
> und führ es sicher und fest
> dass du nicht dir's entfallen lässt!
>
> ---
>
> If Morold was so important,
> then here take my sword,
> and surely and straight direct it,
> so it won't escape your purpose.

Given how angry we (and he) know Isolde to be at this point, Tristan's behavior in offering Isolde his sword seems suicidal. This suicidal behavior is also reflected in his drinking the potion which both of them think is poison. At the end of the second act Tristan drops his sword as Melot attacks him, which certainly demonstrates Tristan's suicidal behavior. In the end of the third act, he rips off his bandages as Isolde approaches, and so he succeeds finally in what he has been attempting throughout the opera, to kill himself. Perhaps subconscious Oedipal guilt causes Tristan to act so consistently in a suicidal manner throughout the opera. His uncle Marke took in and raised the orphaned boy Tristan, and how guilty that boy must now feel when he falls in love with Marke's lawful wife.

Just as Isolde is on her couch for analysis in Act I, in Act III of the opera Tristan is wounded and on his couch for analysis. The piping of the shepherd offstage causes Tristan to free associate about what that tune reminds him of:

> Muss ich dich so verstehn,
> du alte ernste Weise,
> mit deiner Klage Klang?
> Durch Abendwehen
> drang sie bang,

Tristan und Isolde: Hildegard Behrens as Isolde, Tatiana Troyanos as Brangaene.

Als einst dem Kind
des Vaterstod verkündet
Durch Morgengrauen
bang und bänger
als der Sohn
der Mutter Los vernahm.
Da er mich zeugt' und starb,
sie stervbend mich gebar.
Die alte Weise
sehnsuchtbang
zu ihnen wohl
auch klagend drang,
die einst mich frug
und jetzt mich frägt:
zu welchem Los erkoren
ich damals wohl begoren?
Zu welchem Los?
Die alte Weise
sagt mir's wieder:
mich sehnen—und sterben!
Nein! ach nein!
Sehnen! Sehnen!
Im Sterben mich zu sehnen
vor Sehnsuch nicht zu sterben!
Die nie erstirbt,
sehnend nun ruft
um sterbens Ruh
sie der fernen Ärztin su.

Must I understand you,
you tune so old and ancient,
with your so sad tone?
Through night air your
tone was fearful,
when I was a child
the tune marked my father's death;
through a gray dawn
still also fearful,
when the boy
was told of his mother's destiny.
He died before my birth,
she died when I was born;
the old tune of
eternal longing
creates the mourning song
they must have heard;
it asked me before

and it asks me now:
What was my destiny
the day my mother gave birth to me?
What is my destiny?
That song so old
again tells me:
of yearning and death!
No. Oh, no!
It says not that!
Yearning! Yearning.
Even as I die I must continue to yearn,
but can not die of yearning.
What never dies
calls yearningly for
the far-off healer
and asks for the repose of death.

The shepherd's sad piping reminds Tristan of the death of his parents—his father died before he was born and his mother died giving birth to him. Does this suggest another level of guilt in Tristan's psyche—the guilt of surviving the death of his parents, and perhaps the guilt of causing his own mother's death? And in his final vision of yearning, he imagines a healing woman (Isolde) who will not bring him health but will bring him the death he has been yearning for throughout the opera.

We see the suicidal quality of Tristan and his love of Isolde earlier in the opera, at the end of Act II, just before Tristan attempts suicide by challenging Melot to a fight and then dropping his sword as Melot attacks him. Tristan's final lines to Isolde in that act are:

Wo Tristans Haus und Heim,
da kehr' Isolde ein:
auf dem sie folge
treu und hold,
den Weg nun zeig Isold'!

Where Tristan has a home
there will Isolde come:
will she follow his way,
true and brave,
that way Isolde will see!

Tristan seems to be asking Isolde to follow him into death here, though whether she does or not remains debatable.

The opera has a fascinating symmetry about it, achieved through the wonderful words and situations that Wagner created in his libretto. As each act ends with Tristan's suicide attempt, so each act begins with an off-stage music. Act I begins with the sailor's song, heard though the sailor is not seen; in Act II, King Mark's hunters' horns are heard but not seen; in Act III the shepherd's piping is repeatedly heard (although the shepherd himself is rarely seen) by Tristan and Kurvenal, who remain onstage for the whole first scene. The very symmetry in the beginning and ending of each of the opera's three acts suggests a repeated pattern of behavior, and certainly cycles recur frequently in Wagner's operas, grounded in the bipolar cycles which governed much of Wagner's emotional life.

Just as we have seen that Tristan remains suicidal throughout the opera, so too does his beloved Isolde. She exemplifies a suicidal personality in many of her speeches and in her actions as well. Early in Act I she curses the ship taking her to Cornwall for her forced and politically-motivated marriage to King Marke. She curses the ship and all on board it to drowning—thus cursing herself to death by water as well. It is interesting that she fantasizes about death by water in her final monologue of the opera, the famous Liebestod. When she lures Tristan toward the end of the first act to drink what she thinks is the death potion, she demands half for herself. Clearly she wants both to kill Tristan and to kill herself. And her continuing adultery with Tristan—given what the penalties for adultery were in the Middle Ages—certainly constitutes suicidal behavior, despite King Marke's reaction in a painful forgiveness of her actions.

When Isolde recounts to Brangaene her fury at Tristan early in Act I, she says:

> Fluch dir, Verruchter!
> Fluch deinem Haupt!
> Rache! Tod!
> Tod uns beiden!
>
> ---
>
> Curse you, you betrayer!
> Curses on your head!
> Vengeance! Death!
> Death for both of us!

Here she makes very clear to Brangaene the force of her anger at Tristan, and her desire to kill first him and then herself. The Freudian connection between love and hatred becomes very clear here in Wagner's text. Often while Isolde sings of her rage at Tristan, the orchestra plays the love music—indicating to us that Isolde's very anger contains love rather than indifference to Tristan, which is the real opposite of love.

Just before Tristan drinks what he believes is the poison that will kill him, he says:

Ew'ger Trauer
einz'ger Trost:
Vergessens güt'ger Trank—
dich trink' ich sonder Wank!

Eternal grief's
only escape:
Forgetting's gracious drink—
I faithfully drink to you!

Isolde's response is significant as well:

Betrug auch hier?
mein die Hälfte!
Verräter! Ich trink sie dir!

Betrayed even here
Half is mine!
Betrayer! I drink to you!

Clearly both Tristan and Isolde want to die at this point in the opera, and both drink what they think is the death potion, though they later learn of course that Brangaene has instead given them the love potion. Certainly the same result would have occurred if Tristan and Isolde have been sharing a glass of water (as Thomas Mann has pointed out) since they both clearly love each other, and only when they both think they are about to die can they finally be honest with each other and admit to their love. The impossible nature of their adulterous love may have motivated this suicidal behavior on both their parts, but one suspects that a suicidal compulsion was a part of their personalities long before they fell in love.

The death-wish is clearly one of the things that both Tristan and Isolde display, and it obviously draws them together. Is this same quality what drew Wagner to Mathilde von Wesendonck? While Wagner was living in the Wesendonck Asyl, he wrote to Mathilde that his greatest wish was to die in her arms. A well developed death-wish was certainly part of what drew Wagner to Cosima Liszt. She undoubtedly told Wagner about her own thoughts of suicide, just as he undoubtedly told her of his. Cosima once made a suicidal pact with a friend, and as we have seen, Wagner's own correspondence is spotted with references to suicide. As George Marek reports in his fine biography of Cosima Wagner:

> Bülow then returned to the Asyl while Cosima and Marie went onto Geneva to see Blandine. There they ran into Karl Ritter. Cosima was

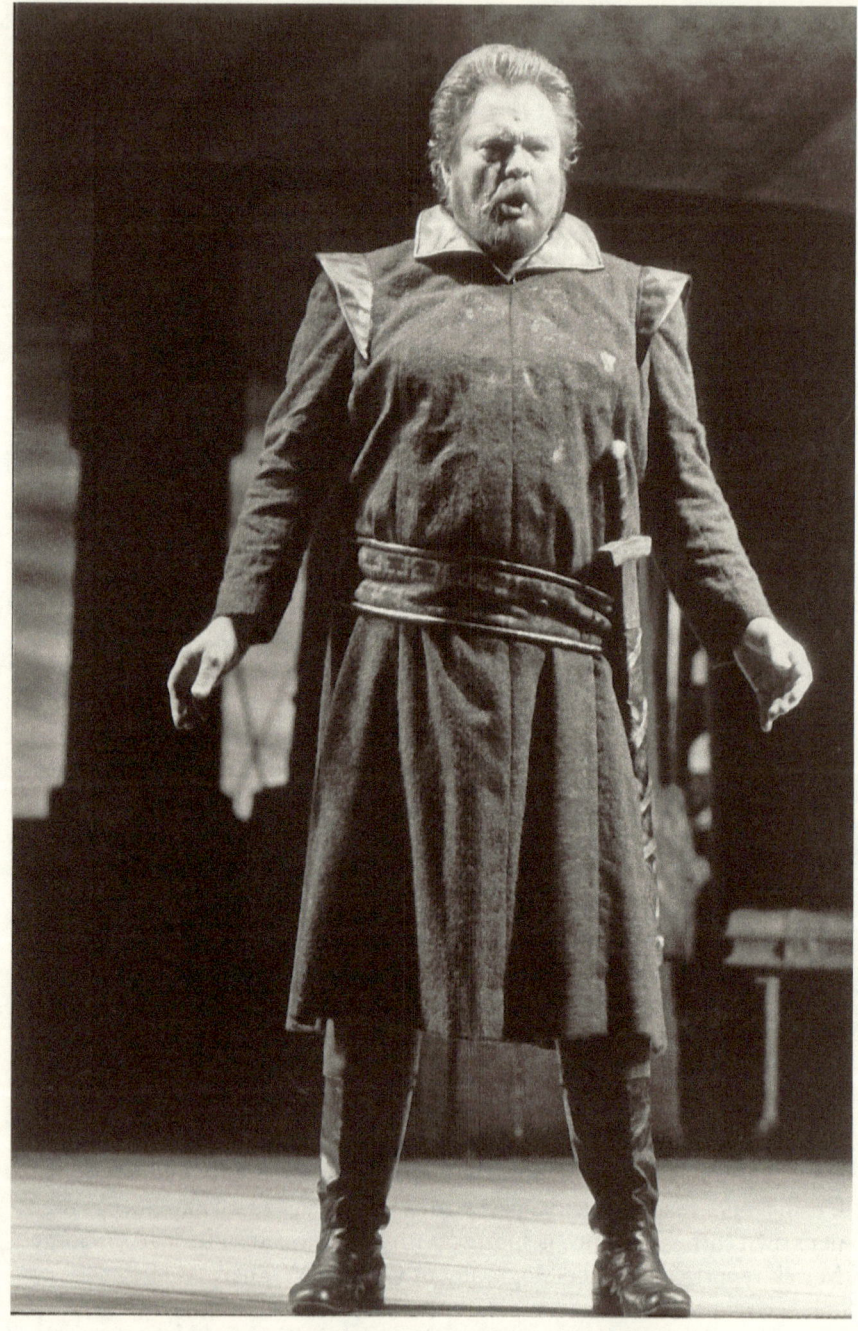
Tristan and Isolde: Richard Cassilly as Tristan.

5—Tristan und Isolde

attracted to this handsome and intellectual pupil of her husband's. She also realized that he was a deeply disturbed man. He told her that his marriage was a dismal failure, and she must have confessed to him her own unhappiness in a union with a man whom she could respect but never love, a being stunted and self-deprecatory who told her "having Wagner as a neighbor dwarfed him to impotence." Yes, she was as miserable as he. She no longer wanted to live. The wild streak in her broke through in Karl's presence, as another unhappiness often pushes one's own unhappiness to the surface. They took a little boat and went rowing on the lake. Suddenly Cosima begged him to push her overboard and drown her. Karl said he could do what she asked only if he himself could follow her. No—that was too horrible! So grim a pact she would not accept. Clinging to each other and weeping, they both determined to postpone the mortal decision for three weeks. They would then examine their minds once more and act accordingly. The danger, however seriously they meant it at the moment, passed; after three weeks Cosima wrote Karl that she deplored her impulsiveness, felt ashamed, thanked him for his sympathy, and urged him to keep the incident secret. He didn't; he told Wagner.

Cosima returned to the Asyl. Their time was up; Bülow had to return to Berlin. At the hour of farewell, indeed almost at the last moment, Cosima bent down, took Wagner's hand, and covered it with tears and kisses. He looked up, astonished. The sudden demonstrativeness of this reserved young girl made such an impression on him that he mentioned the incident later in the diary he was writing for Mathilde Wesendonck [Marek 34–35].

Cosima would again feel this suicidal when Wagner died in 1883. Hans von Bülow, who certainly knew her well, must have suspected that she would want to kill herself rather than continue living as Wagner's widow, since he immediately sent her a telegram, stating "Soeur il faut vivre" ("Sister, you must live!") (Marek 204). Marek also reported the reaction of Cosima's father Franz Liszt to her prolonged mourning: "'I'll tell you,' Liszt wrote in December 1883, 'that my daughter, hugging to herself the thought of death, is doing everything possible not to outlive Wagner.' More than nine months had passed" (Marek 207). Clearly during times of great stress Cosima repeatedly became suicidal.

Suicidal impulses also attracted King Ludwig II to Wagner, since the King's correspondence to Wagner is also spotted with references to suicide. The King often indicated that he would rather die than continue as King, especially if that meant that he could not be with Richard Wagner. Wagner repeatedly urged him not to abdicate, not to kill himself, but to live and continue serving as King of Bavaria. And indeed Ludwig's mysterious death in 1886 most probably was suicide (with his physician also drowned in a failed attempt to stop the depressed king's suicide). References to suicide by water appear frequently in Wagner's correspondence and in the incidents around and after his life. It is interesting that Ludwig II lived only three years after the death of his beloved composer Wagner.

In any case, suicidal impulses are clearly what drew Tristan to Isolde, as the techniques used throughout the opera powerfully demonstrate. Wagner does wonderful things with dramatic language as well as with dramatic situations. To indicate their total isolation from the other characters in the opera, Tristan and Isolde have their own special language which no one else fully understands. They often use oxymorons like "faithless friend" or "love-lost lover" to indicate the illogical and dangerous quality of their adulterous and illicit love. In King Marke's final monologue over the corpse of Tristan, he calls him a "faithless most faithful friend," (Du treulos treuster Freund!) which indicates that by using the language of Tristan, the oxymoron, he has finally understood the man and his tragic love.

Wagner includes in his libretto fascinating patterns of light and dark, in addition to water imagery. The first act occurs on a boat, the second act includes some water where Isolde puts out the torch, signaling Tristan to come to her, and in the third act Tristan looks out to the water for signs of Isolde's boat. The lovers come to see the world of darkness and water as their natural place. Isolde must kill the light—quench her torch—in Act II to signal to Tristan that it is safe to come to her. They find happiness and fulfillment in their own world of darkness and night. The Liebesnacht in the second act is the culmination of their night of love, and in it Tristan curses the day when he can not be with Isolde. As Isolde says to her maid Braengene in the second act:

> Die im Busen mir
> die Glut entfacht,
> die mir das Herze
> brennen macht,
> die mir als Tag
> der Seele lacht,
> Frau Minne will:
> es werde Nacht,
> dass hell sie dorten leuchte,
> wo sie dein Licht verscheuchte.
> Zur Warte du:
> dort wache treu!
> Die Lechte
> und war's meines Lebens Licht—

lachend
sie zu löschen zag' ich nicht!

She that warms the flow
within my breath,
she that has set my
heart afire,
who smiles as the sun
upon my soul,
Love's goddess wants
the night,
so brightly she glows,
So be careful:
and keep watch!
The brightness
though it were the light of my life
happily
without fear I would quench.

Here Isolde clearly connects her love for Tristan with darkness, and the light of her life she would happily quench just to be with him—indicating again the suicidal quality of their love. Tristan uses the contrasts of light and dark even more dramatically later in the act when he says to Isolde:

O, nun waren wir
Nacht-Geweihte!
Der tückische Tag,
der Neid-bereite,
trennen konnt' uns sein Trug,
doch nicht mehr täuschen sein Lug!
Seine eitle Pracht,
seinen prahlenden Schein
verlacht, wem die Nacht
den Blick geweiht:
seines flackernden Lichtes
flüchtige Blitze
blenden uns nicht mehr.
Wer des Todes Nacht
liebend erschaut,
wem sie ihr tief
Geheimnis vertraut:
des Tages Lugen
Ruhm und Ehr',
Macht und Gewinn
so schimmernd hehr,

wie eitler Staub der Sonnen
sind vor dem zersponnen!
in des Tages eitlem Wähnen
bleibt ihm ein einzig Sehnen—
das Sehnen hin
zur heil'gen Nacht,
wo ur-ewig,
einzig wahr
Liebeswonne ihm lacht!

Oh, now we are
night-enclosed!
The evil day
always envious,
though it separates us through fraud
can fool us no more by lies!
All its silly pomp,
its false show
is scorned by the person
with eyes night-blessed:
and the strange brightness
cast by its lightning
can fool our eyes no more.
He who finds death's might
sacred to his view,
he who has plumbed
the mysteries and depths,
will hold day foolish,
fame and honor
name and gain
—though very bright—
as idle specks in light,
which sway and vanish.
Mid the day's idle fancies
he has only one desire,
a desire for
the holy night,
where forever,
only faithful,
love and rapture bloom!

Clearly Tristan feels that only the night can make their love blossom, and that the light is inimical to that love. His love of night also of course suggests a love of that ultimate darkness, death. The light of day remains the light which Tristan most hates, while he yearns for death's ultimate darkness.

Goethe's *Faust* also repeatedly uses the imagery of light and dark—light of course for God and goodness and the darkness for Mephistopheles. Goethe repeatedly used this pattern of imagery in some of his other poetry. Goethe's "Singet nicht in Trauertonen" playfully defends the pleasures of the night and descries the burdens of the day. The poem ends with its famous refrain:

> Jeder Tag hat seine Plage,
> Und die Nacht hat ihre Lust.
>
> ---
>
> Each Day has its grief,
> and the night has its pleasure.

Schubert used this poem for one of his best examples of lieder music. While Schubert captures the playful quality of Goethe's poetry, Wagner's music in *Tristan* remains deadly serious.

The opera also has a wonderfully paradoxical ending. Clearly, Tristan is dead by the suicide he has been attempting throughout the opera. The opera of course ends with Isolde's famous Liebestod, but what does it mean?

> Mild und leise
> wie er lächelt,
> wie das Auge
> hold er öffnet
> seht ihr's, Freunde?
> Seht ihr's nicht?
> Immer lichter
> wie er leutet,
> stern-umstrahlet
> hoch sich hebt?
> Seht ihr's nicht?
> Wie das Herz ihm
> mutig schwillt,
> voll und hehr
> im Busen ihm quilt?
> Wie den Lippen
> wonnig mild,
> süsser Atem
> sanft entweht—
> Freunde! Seht!
> Fühlt und seht ihr's nicht?
> Hör' ich nur
> diese Weise

die so wunder-
voll und leise
Wonne klagend
alles sagend
mild versohnend
aus ihm tönend
in mich dringet
auf sich schwinget
hold erhallend
um mich klinget?
heller schallend,
mich umwallend,
sind es Wellen
sanfter Lüfte?
Sind es Wogen
wonniger Düfte?
Wie sie schwellen,
mich umrauschen
soll ich atmen
soll ich lauschen?
Soll ich schlurfen,
untertauchen?
Suss in Düften
mich verhauchen?
In dem wongenden Schwall,
in dem tönenden Schall,
in des Welt-Atems
wehendem All—
ertrinken
versinken—
umbewusst
höchste Lust!

Sweetly and gently
see him laughing,
see the eye
that is still open.
Don't you see, Friends?
Don't you see?
Ever lighter
how he's laughing
on the stars
highly he sits?
Can't you see?
How bravely his heart
still beats
full and clear!

5—Tristan und Isolde

How his lips
wonderfully mild
sweeter breath
that from him comes—
Friends! Look!
Don't you see him?
Do only I hear
these wonderful
and light
sounds,
all saying
wonderfully sounding
from him sounding
coming to me
rising upward
round me singing?
Always clearer
swelling around me,
are they waves
of gentle air?
Are they clouds
of wonderful air?
As they rise
and surround me,
Shall I breathe them?
Shall I listen?
Sweetly plunging
shall I drink them
and die in their swell?
In the sounding swell,
in the World Atom's
infinite All
To drown now
to sink
without thought
greatest bliss!

The Liebestod is the recounting of a daydream, consistently using the watery chromaticism of this opera. While the other characters onstage are mourning the death of Tristan, Isolde recounts her daydream or hallucination, which is that he is still alive, in water, and waving to her. She ends by saying that to sink and drown in that water with Tristan would be her greatest happiness, just as Wagner wrote to Mathilde Wesendonck that he wanted to drown with her. Isolde began the opera by wishing she could drown, and at the end of the opera she dreams that she does. But then what happens on stage? Wagner's stage directions say that she sinks down on Tristan's body as King Marke blesses the corpses on stage.

Does that mean that she too has died? If so, what has she died from? A broken heart? That seems laughably melodramatic and unrealistic, especially in one so young as Isolde. But of course we are dealing with dream-visions, and she can surely die in her own dream. Or perhaps the opera should end with her just looking entranced, still enjoying her own daydream of Tristan still alive—and the opera often does end this way when it is staged these days. This ending makes an interesting contrast to the ending of *The Flying Dutchman*, when the audience sees Senta commit suicide onstage, and then (at least according to Wagner's stage directions) the audience sees them both resurrected and floating into heaven. That ending clearly suggests a happy afterlife for both the Dutchman and Senta, but the ending of *Tristan* is much more enigmatic—allowing the director to choose many alternatives when staging the opera. Is Isolde dead at the end of the opera or alive and enjoying her hallucinatory death by water?

If we look at the final section of the Liebestod, we can see that Isolde dreams of Tristan alive and in water, clouds, and mists. She sees Tristan, then, as a part of the water cycle of nature—one of Vico's eternal cycles of nature. Just as sunshine on water causes evaporation, which then arises and causes clouds to be formed, which in turn will eventually form into rain drops and fall back on the earth, so Isolde sees Tristan as part of one of Vico's eternal cycles, the water cycle of nature. And she ends her Liebestod by saying how happy she would be to be with Tristan—dead and in nature's eternal water cycle.

While I have no evidence that Wagner ever read the English Romantic poet Percy Bysshe Shelly, the ending of the Liebestod does reflect the final stanza of Shelley's famous poem of 1820, "The Cloud," which is also about the eternal water cycle of nature:

> I am the daughter of Earth and Water,
> And the nursling of the Sky;
> I pass through the pores of the ocean and shores;
> I change, but I cannot die—
> For after the rain, when with never a stain
> The pavilion of Heaven is bare,
> And the winds and sunbeams, with their convex gleams,
> Build up the blue dome of Air—
> I silently laugh at my own cenotaph,
> And out of the caverns of rain,

> Like a child from the womb, like a ghost from the tomb,
> I arise, and unbuild it again.

Just as Shelley's wonderful "The Cloud" celebrates the water cycle of nature, which is eternal, so Wagner's Isolde at the end of the opera has a daydream in which she sees her Tristan as part of this cycle as well.

When it is discussed by the critics, the opera has often been connected with the philosophy of Schopenhauer. Newman, Reinhardt, and others have repeatedly suggested that Wagner had been reading Schopenhauer when he was working on the opera, but does the opera really reflect Schopenhauer? *Studies in Pessimism*, one of the philosopher's greatest works, clearly does reflect a pessimistic view of life, though he never advocates suicide as the best alternative. But Wagner clearly suggests that for Tristan and Isolde suicide really is the best alternative, implying a glorification of death as the only answer to their problems and the only refuge from their suffering. But does that death include the promise of an afterlife? Here Wagner remains very enigmatic. At the end of *The Flying Dutchman*, according to Wagner's stage directions, the Dutchman and Senta are seen going to heaven, clearly indicating an afterlife for them. The ending of *Tristan und Isolde* has no such reassurances, though the chromaticism of the music and Isolde's vision of Tristan in the eternal water cycle of nature does have positive suggestions. Clearly Wagner here suggests more than he asserts, which adds to the eternal fascination of this tragic opera.

Wagner throughout his life was anti-religious. His unfortunate anti-Semitism is already well-known, but also he often said very negative things about Christianity, and especially Roman Catholicism. Toward the end of his life he seemed to develop some sympathy with Buddhism, but that religion does not offer a personal afterlife. One of the wonderful things about Wagner is the eternal complexity and eternal doubt one senses in his best works. While Wagner's prose works often pontificate on matters of life and death, his operas remain wonderfully mysterious. Clearly Wagner spent most of his life raising questions he could not answer—like the rest of us. In *Parsifal*, it seems to me, Wagner suggests that his real religion is art rather than organized belief. Only art, Wagner suggests, can both create beauty and explore the complexity of human existence. That combination alone is worth worshipping in any organized way, or even in a unorganized way.

Such a worshipping of artistic beauty is evident in both the poetical text and the wonderful music that Wagner composed for this saddest of love stories, the sad tale of Tristan and Isolde. Yet the final effect of the opera on the audience remains triumphant rather than sad; Tristan's final and successful attempt at suicide seems to create happiness and fulfillment rather than sadness. Ultimately, Wagner has created a uniquely beautiful dream vision of the combination of love and suicide, beautifully summed up in the Liebestod which ends the opera. Is he suggesting that there is something uniquely attractive and beautiful about a love that ends in suicide? Or is he suggesting that some characters, like Tristan or Isolde, like some people, are best off committing suicide? Is the erotic suicide itself being glorified? That dream vision and those thoughts will appear repeatedly in his operas and they clearly must have haunted his life. Why would Wagner feel that love and suicide are so wonderful when they come together—a thought which most people find frankly repellent? Why did he feel that some characters, and people, need to commit suicide in the face of personal crisis?

Of course Freud would say that all these conflicts connect with one's relationship to one's mother. Could Wagner have sensed this combination of love and suicide from his mother? In *My Life* Wagner comments on his powerful reaction to seeing Titian's *Assumption of the Virgin* in Venice, and he later said to Cosima that this painting by Titian was how he envisioned Isolde's Liebestod, a kind of assumption of the eternal mother, Mary (667). How does all this connect with Wagner's relationship to his own mother, for sexuality is often combined with the maternal in Wagnerian opera, as we have seen in Tristan's monologue in Act III.

Well, Richard Wagner was certainly born in a time of crisis in his mother's life. Her first husband, Carl Friedrich Wagner, died in 1813, and within a year she married her second husband, Ludwig Geyer, as the Napoleonic wars were going on around her and Leipzig was being bombed. This chaos would hardly have been a convenient or auspicious time to have and nurture a child. As Ernest Newman reports:

> Apparently all that the widowed Johanna had at the moment on which to support herself and her eight children was some £40, being the current quarter's salary of her deceased husband, which would become payable on the 16th December. The "pension" of which some biographers speak is described by Mrs. Burrell as "a myth." But friends, Geyer among them, came quickly and energetically to the rescue. Mrs. Burrell tells us, on the authority of Anna Zocher, that Geyer at once made the journey to Leipzig, in spite of the difficulty and perhaps danger of it at that troubled time, to bring consolation and help. "It is certain," said Mrs. Burrell, "that she had no money, and what she owed for rent and war tax was wiped out, which proves her inability to give

it." Geyer's own position just then must have been an exceedingly anxious one. "You cannot have the smallest conception of the wretched state of Dresden," he writes to Johanna on the 22nd December. "People here have no spirit left to go on living, and yet are afraid of death, though they could not do anything more suitable than die" [Newman 19].

Could Johanna Wagner have often thought that her new child Richard would have been better off dead or unborn? Could his stepfather Ludwig Geyer have often felt that suicide was the best alternative in some critical situations? Could the young Richard himself have intuited strong feelings that he was a burden and that his mother wanted him dead and out of her way? From his mother's stress and suffering could he have first developed the connection between love and suicide? Or were all the suicides in his operas simply the result of the depression that Wagner had to endure as an adult, depression which his letters indicate often left him suicidal? We can not be sure, and all this remains hypothetical, but certainly the idea came to fruition in perhaps his most wonderful opera, *Tristan und Isolde*. In any case, the idea of suicide as a best and even triumphant alternative would haunt both him and his operas for the rest of his life.

Chapter 6

Die Meistersinger von Nürnberg: Mania and Reconciliation

Of the ten great Wagnerian operas, while some contain elements of comedy, the only one that should be regarded as a comedy in the standard sense is *Die Meistersinger von Nürnberg*. Here Wagner follows the typical pattern for comedy: boy meets girl, boy loses girl, boy gets girl. This opera ends in marriage, as do most of Shakespeare's comedies and many other comedies in Western theater, and there are even laughs along the way, though those laughs are clearly Wagnerian. Too often Wagner has been thought of as a composer and a man without a sense of humor, but this opera clearly proves that this is not the case.

One can see *Die Meistersinger* as a product of the mania in Wagner's personality, a mania which creates laughter and happiness—though not for all the characters. As in real life, there is a dark side to this opera as well, personified by the centrally important character of Sixtus Beckmesser.

Die Meistersinger is in many ways a foil to *Tristan und Isolde*, since the former can be seen as an product of Wagner's manic side while the latter remains the greatest example of Wagner's depressive side. While *Die Meistersinger* celebrates the combination of life and love, *Tristan* embodies the sad nexus of love and death. While the former opera is one of the great comedies of opera and ends in marriage, the latter remains one of opera's greatest tragedies and ends in death. The contrast of these two operas presents most clearly the bipolar nature of Wagner's dramatic and musical genius. Both operas have lovers, but one set of lovers exists in light and the other yearns for darkness.

Wagner worked on the libretto for this comic opera for over twenty years before its premiere in Munich in 1868, indicating that all those rhymes in the text did not come easily to him. As Newman summarizes:

> We possess three Prose Sketches by Wagner for the *Meistersinger*— (A) the original one of July 1845, (B) one that bears no date, but was evidently made in the autumn of 1861, at the time when he decided to take up again this old scheme of his for a comic opera, (C) one dated "Vienna, 18th November, 1861," a copy of which he sent to Schott on the 19th. B and C are virtually identical: at the end of the manuscript of B there are several pages of notes on the Meistersinger rules and practices, made after Wagner had become acquainted with old Wagenseil's so-called "Nuremberg Chronicle," in which the mastersingers and their art are discussed at some length. Not only do B and C differ considerably from A in matters of stage detail, but they breathe a somewhat different atmosphere. In his first form Wagner's Sachs was a rather cynical, ironic, embittered character, who, apart from his advocacy of the cause of the young Knight, reminds us comparatively little of the wise, kindly, mellow poet-philosopher he ultimately became in Wagner's treatment of him [Newman, III, 156–157].

Composition of the music went much more easily than the composition of the libretto for this opera. Wagner began writing the music in 1862 and completed it in 1867, the premiere occurring at the Konigliches Hof und National Theater in Munich on June 21, 1868—in fact on Johannistag (St. John's Day), as is celebrated in the opera itself (Millington 301).

Wagner was certainly fond of repetitions of key words, which often form literary leitmotifs that are equivalents in language for the musical leitmotivs of the opera's score. One of the literary leitmotifs in this opera is certainly the phrase "fanget an," which is repeated often in the text. Literally, this phrase means "let us begin," but it accrues symbolic significance as it is repeated. The concept of the necessity of beginning is clearly one of the things implied here. "Fanget an" becomes an inspiration for one of Walther's first monologues in the opera, at the end of the first act, but the phrase will be used repeatedly in the opera and slowly accrue more and more symbolic significance. It is the right beginning, and the need to begin, that mark the creative person, the opera implies. "Wahn," or illusion, also recurs in the opera, most significantly in Sach's sad monologue in the third act "Wahn, Wahn, uberall Wahn," where he laments a Nuremberg surrounded by dangerous illusions. This word has special meaning for Wagner since he named his house in Bayreuth "Wahnfried," or free from illusions.

In terms of poetic form, *Die Meistersinger* contains Wagner's most conventional poetry. It is the most highly rhymed of his many operatic texts, and it uses the most regular meters. Most of the lines contain four beats—four stressed syllables in a line of eight syllables—and most (but not all) of the lines are rhymed couplets. Wagner never again (and never before) uses such a regular meter and rhyme scheme, and clearly the conservative, old-fashioned poetic forms used here reflect the older period of the German late Medieval period in which the opera is set. For example, Walther starts a rhyme and Eva finishes it in the following passage:

WALTHER:
Verweilt! Ein Wort! Ein eizig Wort!

EVA:
Mein Brusttuch! Schau! Wohl liegt's in Ort.

MAGDALENE:
Vergesslich Kind! Nun heisst es: such!

WALTHER:
Fräulein! Verzeiht der Sitte Bruch.
Eines zu wissen, Eines zu fragen.
Was müsst' ich nicht zu brechen wagen?
Oh Leben oder Tod? Ob Segen oder Fluch?
Mit einem Worte sei mir's vertraut:
Mein Fräulein—sagt

WALTHER:
Wait! A word! Just a word!

EVA:
My handkerchief! Look! No doubt it's in my place.

MAGDALENE:
Forgetful child! Now I must go look for it!

WALTHER:
Miss! Forgive my etiquette.
I want to know one thing, to ask only one thing.
What will I not risk?
Even life or death ... blessing or curse.
Just one word, just tell me.
Miss....

Die Meistersinger von Nürnberg: Ben Heppner as Walter, Karita Mattila as Eva.

With this cleverly rhymed dialogue, Wagner clearly portrays the annoyance of Magdalene, the desperation of the ardent lover Walther, and the clever encouragement of Eva, and their intermeshed couplets indicate that they are on some level joined in their concern for Eva. For by the end of the opera, Magdalene will be happily married to David just as

Walther gets to marry the lovely Eva, whose rhyming indicates that this is what she wants from the beginning of the opera. The double marriage at the end of the opera—Walther and Eva, David and Magdalene—plus the whole town's praise of Hans Sachs makes for a very happy ending indeed.

In addition in the rhyming, this most comic of Wagner's operas contains much punning and other word play, as several critics have indicated. Like most Wagnerian operas, it also contains recurrent patterns of images which sometimes become symbolic. Certainly the images of spring and of Johannistag, or St. John's Day, the Summer Solstice, recur throughout the opera. The longest day of the year becomes in the opera a celebration of light, and the opera indeed moves from darkness to light—not only light, but the light of the longest day. On one level the opera is a pagan celebration of summer, sunlight, and the earth's fertility, as well as human fertility. There is even a pagan goat, and some goat music, in the parade in the beginning of the last scene of the opera, when the victory of summer over winter is celebrated. The goat is a popular image of rampant sexuality and fertility in European folklore, and the animal is also a symbol of the Greek god Pan, who is himself half goat. And the happy ending, typical of Shakespearean and other forms of comedy, celebrates marriage and the implied hope for new children and the continuity of fertility and of the human race.

The cycle of the seasons remains a central concern in this opera. We have seen how often Wagner thought in terms of cycles, and certainly the cycle of the seasons (one of the eternal natural cycles of Vico) is celebrated here. The entire cycle of the changing seasons, of course caused by the earth's orbit around the sun, becomes a cause for celebration at the end of the opera, but particularly the summer solstice, which indicates the victory of life over death, of sunlight over darkness, of warmth over frigidity.

We have seen earlier in this study that light and darkness recur often in Wagnerian opera, often becoming symbolic. In *Meistersinger* as well Wagner employs this pattern of images. The opera opens in interior darkness—the interior of St. Catherine's church—and ends in bright sunlight—the meadow outside Nuremberg on a sunny St. John's day, the longest day of the year. The movement from light to darkness is particularly clever in the second act, which opens with a cheerful summer evening ("Heitrer Sommerabend") and closes with the darkness of the riot scene at the end of the act. Act III opens with a sunny morning, but in the dark interior of Hans Sachs's workroom. Sachs's famous monologue, beginning "Wahn, Wahn, uberall Wahn" (illusions, illusions, everywhere illusions) is the darkest point in this act. This word remained particularly important to Wagner, having named his house "Wahnfried" when he finally built it in 1874, about six years after the premiere of this opera. But the second scene of the act occurs on a sunny meadow outside the city, where the sungod enters, Walter von Stolzing. With the arrival of the sungod and his eventual betrothal to Eva Pogner, the fertility of the earth and the triumph of light over darkness ends this comedy on a light note. The third act of the opera, a microcosm of the entire work, opens in interior darkness and ends in exterior sunlight. The heroine's name and the references to Eve in the Garden of Eden in Walther's Prize Song create a pattern of allusions to suggest Adam and Eve in the Garden of Eden in prelapsarian bliss. It is certainly significant as well that the opera moves from the darkness of a church interior to the bright sunlight of nature in the final scene.

Walther and Eva make an interesting contrast to Tristan and Isolde. While Tristan and Isolde can only be happy in the darkness and yearn for both darkness and death, Walther and Eva find happiness in the full light of day at the start of the summer solstice. While Tristan and Isolde's adulterous love is discovered with the dawn in Act II, Walther and Eva experience a riot and social madness in the darkness of their second act. While Tristan curses the sunlight in Act III, and is finally dead by his own hand by the end of this final act, Walther and Eva bless the sunlight which brings them mutual happiness and social approval. As Eva sings at the beginning of the famous quintet in the last act of the opera:

> Selig, wie die Sonne
> meines Glückes lacht,
> Morgen voller Wonne,
> selig mir erwacht;
> Traum der höchsten Hulden,
> himmlisch Morgenglühn:
> Deutung euch zu schulden,
> selig süss Bemühn!

> Joyfully, as the sun
> smiles at my good luck,
> morning full of joy
> happily awakens me;
> dream of the greatest happiness,
> heavenly morning light:
> happy, light burden
> to be obliged to you for understanding!

Notice how Eva begins the wonderful quintet by addressing the sun and connecting her love and her new-found happiness with Walther with the sunlight. This is a very different world from Tristan and Isolde's, where the lovers curse the sunlight and yearn for the darkness to hide their love. Where society can witness the love of Walther and Eva in the full light of day, Tristan and Isolde's adultery makes them happy only in the darkness of night. Notice that both sets of lovers connect their love with one of Vico's cycles, the cycle of day and night caused by the rotation of the earth.

Wagner cleverly quotes the music from *Tristan und Isolde* in Act III of this later opera when Eva suggests that she really loves Hans Sachs and should marry him. But Sachs says he knows the old story of Tristan and Isolde and does not want to become another King Marke to her Isolde. Sachs indicates in this scene that he knows she is already in love with Walther, and Sachs also indicates that he knows and wants to avoid the folly of old men marrying young women. It is interesting to note, however, that the real, historical Hans Sachs did marry a much younger woman when his first wife died, and Wagner himself of course married a second time the much younger Cosima von Bülow. She was of course the daughter of a man he also loved, Franz Liszt, and that may have been part of her attraction for Wagner.

The opera is certainly comic and happy, containing a thoroughly happy ending of marriage and the celebration of the whole town of Nurenberg. In addition, there is a light, cheerful quality to much of the music. While Wagner is best known for his genius in producing tragic operas, he also wrote the greatest single comic German opera. In Acts I and II there are charming dance tunes and a wonderful march at the beginning of Act III, Scene 2, plus more dance music for the delightful finale. But of course Verdi did the same things with his *Falstaff*, producing at the very end of his career a magnificent comedy. He too was famous for tragedy in opera, but then in his extreme old age produced perhaps the greatest Italian comic opera. Puccini's great comedy *Gianni Schichi*, though only one act, remains wonderfully drole, comic, and even cynical about social change.

Have there been any suggestions of comedy in any of Wagner's earlier works? Wagner's first opera, *Die Feen*, was based on Carlo Gozzi's comic *La Donna Serpente*, and is a comic fairy tale with a happy ending. Wagner's second opera, *Das Liebesverbot*, is another comic opera, based on Shakespeare's *Measure for Measure*, but these works remain juvenilia on Wagner's part and are not among the ten great Wagnerian operas. There are certainly moments of comedy in *The Flying Dutchman* (the maidens in the town, and the other townspeople) and in the *Ring* cycle (see Chapter 7), but nowhere else. Since Wagner tried comedy early in his career, clearly he remained interested in comedy in opera, and finally

6—*Die Meistersinger von Nürnberg*

Die Meistersinger von Nürnberg: **Bernd Weikl as Hans Sachs.**

he did create a successful comic opera in his maturity. *Die Meistersinger* was an instant success and for many years his most popular opera.

But does it reflect mania? In many respects it does reflect a kind of mania, a mania of happiness, but an unrealistic happiness combining artist and society in a happy and unified whole. In the prize song, Walther presents an image of the perfect woman in the perfect setting, Eve in the Garden of Eden. Such an image of perfection and happiness in a prelapsarian past is hardly realistic happiness but instead the sublime, perfect happiness which mania can produce. Connected with the perfect marriage is the perfect artist producing sublime art, which the whole community celebrates. By the end of the opera the entire town joins Hans Sachs in celebrating the new art of the new, young artist, Walter von Stolzing. This is hardly realistic comedy but more like a manic high point. There is a dark side as well, for example the riot scene at the end of the second act, with comic chaos onstage, plus the sad quality of the hangover about the prelude to the third act of the opera. And of course we have a comic Wagnerian villain of sorts in Sixtus Beckmesser, the stock figure of the comic pedant, as well as the stock comic figure from commedia dell'arte, the Pantalone, the pompous older man foolishly seeking a young wife. He is even willing to employ theft, as in the first scene of Act III when he steals a copy of Walther's prize song in order to get the young wife that he as an older man is clearly not suitable for. December/May matches usually create comedy—in the Roman comedies of Plautus and Terence as well as in commedia dell'arte, and in Chaucer. It is ironic in many ways that this is exactly the nature of Wagner's marriage to Cosima. That Wagner could create comedy about his own stormy marriage is a tribute to his objectivity as an artist. He reported that it bothered him that when he was walking in Bayreuth with his little son Siegfried, people often thought Wagner was the grandfather rather than the father.

Many critics have previously commented that the pedantic Sixtus Beckmesser is based on the Viennese music critic Edward Hanslick, who was a great friend of Brahms and disliked Wagnerian opera, especially the late ones. In one early version of the opera, Beckmesser is in fact called Hans Lick, but Wagner realized that that was libelous. Though Beckmesser remains nasty and pedantic throughout the opera, he is treated respectfully by the other characters on stage since Wagner clearly wanted him to remain an interesting character and not just a buffoon. Wagner could not resist making his villains often his most interesting and complex characters, and some singers have presented Beckmesser as a comic pedant while others have presented him as a flawed master singer whom Pogner wishes his daughter would marry.

The ungenerous older man (Sixtus Beckmesser) makes a significant contrast with the generous, wise old man (Hans Sachs). These characters appear as intermeshed cycles—like yin and yang in Chinese philosophy. We have seen already that Wagner liked to present two characters as contrasting (but sometimes similar) foils; so too with Beckmesser and Sachs.

Both are famous men in Nuremberg and both are Master Singers, but while Sachs remains generous and sympathetic to new art and new artists like the Knight Walther, Beckmesser remains ungenerous and suspicious of new art forms and new artists. Added to this, he wants to marry a woman who is much younger than he is and who clearly loves another man.

But mania may form part of Wagner's theory of artistic creation as well. Certainly Wagner saw art as often the product of a dream, as the product of the artist's dreaming mind. We have seen that dreams often occur in Wagner's operas, and are often described in his operas, and this familiar situation occurs in this opera as well. But his aesthetic theory of dreams as a force that produces art through the work of the artist is most clearly presented in *Die Meistersinger*.

At the opening of Act III, scene 1, when Walther enters, the following exchange occurs between the young artist (Walther) and the old artist (Hans Sachs):

SACHS:
> Grüss Gott, mein Junker! Rethet ihr noch?
> Ihr wachtet lang, nun schlieft ihr doch?

WALTHER:
> Ein wenig, aber fest und gut.

SACHS:
> So ist euch nun wohl bass zu Mut?

WALTHER:
> Ich hatt' einen wunderschönen Traum.

SACHS:
> Das deutet Gut's: erzählt mir den!

WALTHER:
> Ihn selbst zu denken, wag'ich kaum:
> ich fürcht', ihn mir vergehn zu sehn

SACHS:
> Mein Freund! Das grad' ist Dichters Werk,
> dass er sein Träumen deut' und merk'.
> Glaubt mir, des Menschen wahrster Wahn
> wird ihn im Traume aufgetan—
> all' Dichtkunst und Poeterei
> ist nichts also Wahrtraudeuterei,
> Was gilt's, es gab der Traum euch ein,
> wie heut ihr sollet Meister sein?

SACHS:
> God's Greetings, my young knight. Are you rested?
> You were up a while, so have you slept well?

WALTHER:
> A little, but it was a good sleep.

SACHS:
> Do you feel better now?

WALTHER:
> I had the most wonderful dream.

SACHS:
> That sounds good; tell it to me.

WALTHER:
> I hardly think about it.
> I'm afraid I'll forget it.

SACHS:
> My friend! That's what a poet's job is!—
> to remember and interpret his dreams.
> Believe me, the truest fantasies of mankind
> come to him revealed in dreams:
> the whole world of art and writing
> comes from the true interpretation of dreams—
> that dream has inspired you about
> how you can became a master today!

A little bit later in the scene, when Hans Sachs is trying to help Walther to produce a master song so that he can become a Mastersinger and so win Eva's hand in marriage, the following exchange occurs:

WALTHER:
> Wie ich's begänne, wüsst ich kaum.

SACHS:
> Erzählt mir euren Morgentraum

WALTHER:
> Durch euer Regeln gute Lehr
> ist mir's also ob verwischt er wär.

SACHS:
> Grad' nehmt die Dichtkunst zur Hand
> Mancher durch sie das Verlor'ne fand.

6—Die Meistersinger von Nürnberg

WALTHER:
So wär's nicht Traum, doch Dichterei?

SACHS:
'sing Freunde beid', stehn gern sich bei.

WALTHER:
Wie fang' ich nach der Regel an?

SACHS:
Ihr stellt sie selbst und folg ihr dann.
Gedenkt des schönen Traum am Morgen:
Für's andre lasst Hans Sachs nur sorgen.

WALTHER:
"Morgenlich leutend im rosigem Schein,
von Blüt und Duft
geschwellt die Luft
voll aller Wonnen
nie ersonnen
ein Garten lud mich ein,
fast ihm zu sein....

WALTHER:
I hardly know where to begin.

SACHS:
Tell me about your morning dream.

WALTHER:
But your talk about the rules,
it semes to have been forgotten.

SACHS:
Just think of the poetic art you already know:
through it, many have found what they thought they lost.

WALTHER:
So it might not be only a dream, but real poetry.

SACHS:
They're friends and will help each other.

WALTHER:
How can I begin according to the rules?

SACHS:
You can begin it, and then follow through.
Remember your beautiful morning dream,
and Hans Sachs will worry about the rest.

WALTHER:
"Shining in a rosy morning glow,
when the air smells
of flowers and perfume,
and other delights,
never before imagined
a garden invited me in
to be a guest."

In this dialogue between Hans Sachs and Walther von Stolzing we see again that Wagner is dramatizing one aspect of his theory of aesthetics, that art is the result of the artist's dream. The prize song, then, is the product of Walther's dream on the previous night, and what was he dreaming about? A beautiful woman in a garden, Eve in the Garden of Eden, or his Eva Pogner in a garden in Nuremberg. He is hoping to find his primordial woman in Eva, just as Adam found his God-given helpmate in Eve. This Old Testament vision of prelapsarian bliss again indicates that Wagner's comedy is not realistic comedy but instead a product of the manic part of his bi-polar personality. Not many operas include theories of aesthetics, but this one clearly does in this exchange between the wise, generous poet-cobler Sachs and the new artist Walther.

The relationship between Walther and Hans Sachs has been developing throughout the opera and blossoms in this scene. Walther is rather like a young, proud Wagner and Hans like the older, wiser Wagner—both characters can be seen as opposing halves of the composer himself. The cycle of progression from youth to old age is being referred to here since both characters are artists at different points in their individual development.

The allusion to Eve in the Garden of Eden suggests that Walther is Adam, and that he and Eve will find temporary happiness but ultimately be driven out of the garden because of their sins. The allusion further suggests a state of prelapsarian bliss, when man and woman were completely happy and content before evil came into the world. Such a vision of happiness sounds suspiciously like a product of mania—a dream of happiness that is both wonderful and also totally unrealistic in terms of what happiness people can actually achieve on earth.

But this dream, a dream of perfect union with another and of the perfect happiness we all fantasize about at some point in our lives, is what the prize song actually is. And that prize song wins Walther the prize he most seeks: marriage to his Eva Pogner.

The opera itself ends with a manic vision as well: a society united and praising holy German art and their favorite contemporary artist, Hans

Sachs. This too is a wonderful fantasy, one that can never occur in real life. When can all the people in any city agree about who their favorite contemporary artist is? Yet the opera ends with Wagner's manic vision of a united people praising holy German art and its artists.

Is this ending a hymn of praise of only Germany and German nationalism? Is this German chauvinism? Hitler liked to interpret the ending of the opera this way, but the text tells a different truth. As Hans Sachs says in his final monologue:

> Drum sag' ich euch:
> ehrt eure deutschen Meister!
> Dann bannt ihr gute Geister;
> und gebt ihr ihrem Wirken Gunst
> zerging' in Dunst
> das heil'ge röm'sche Reich,
> uns bliebe gleich
> die heil'ge deutsche Kunst!
>
> ---
>
> Therefore I tell you,
> honor your German masters!
> You will thus get good advice;
> and if you give their work your attention,
> then even if the Holy Roman Empire
> were to fall to dust,
> Holy German art
> will still remain.

This passage is perfectly rhymed in couplets to give it added emphasis, and it is repeated exactly by the entire chorus at the end the opera. As Hans Sachs says here, even if all of Germany falls to ruins, what remains holy is holy German art, and (whether German or not) surely we can all praise that achievement. Sachs does not say there is anything uniquely holy about Germans or Germany, but he insists that it is only German art which is important.

Some commentators have argued that the opera is anti–Semitic, but the opera actually argues to an opposite conclusion. Weiner and others have found the ending of the opera to be anti–Semitic because Beckmesser is finally defeated. But is it?

In some of his anti–Semitic moods, Wagner did declare that one or another of the villains in his operas was really a Jew, but Wagner was also wise enough to keep any such identification out of the operas themselves. Robert Gutmann and other critics have tried to argue that all the villains in Wagnerian opera are really Jews, though neither the texts of these operas nor their music provide any evidence for this interpretation. The issue is further complicated by the fact that we are often uncertrain about the identity of the real villain in a Wagnerian opera—is it Alberich or Wotan? Is it Friedrich or Lohengrin? The whole issue of good and evil remains often ambiguous in Wagnerian opera, and for this among many reasons, they remain so widely popular, since the same issue presents confusion in life. Wagnerian opera reflects that human confusion. Is Beckmesser the villain of the piece? Other characters in the opera treat him not as a villain but instead as one of the most honored of the master singers in the guild.

In one of his anti-Semitic moods, Wagner named Beckmesser as a Jew, and as the villain of *Die Meistersinger*. First of all, it is debatable whether indeed he is the villain of the piece (or is the power of the Mastersingers' guild Wagner's real target here?) since many productions of this opera have presented Beckmesser in a very sympathetic light. Second, did Wagner plant any clear evidence in this opera to indicate that Beckmesser is a Jew? To start with the name, Sixtus Beckmesser is a thoroughly German name. What if Wagner had given him the name Harvey Finkelstein? Both names have the same number of syllables so Wagner could have easily done this without having to change a note of the opera. Next, is there anything in the music that would indicate that Beckmesser is Jewish? Some have argued that the sing-song quality of some of Beckmesser's music is a parody of rabbinical music, but that sing-song quality can also be found in the Gregorian chants of the Catholic liturgy. No musicologist has ever proved that rabbinical or Jewish folk music exists in the score. Hans Vaget has suggested that the "Jew in the Brambles" story from the Grimm brothers is planted in the opera to connect Beckmesser with Jewishness. Assuming such an allusion is actually operative, which is debatable, no contemporary audience today would find such a connection or understand such an allusion. In fact, I believe that no audience in Wagner's time would have understood such an allusion either, since no such observation appeared in contemporary reviews of the opera. Even most literary scholars of the Grimms' works would probably miss such an alleged allusion.

Here, it is instructive to contrast *Die Meistersinger* with Shakespeare's *The Merchant of Venice* on the issue of anti-Semitism. Shakespeare's Shylock is everywhere identified as a Jew in the play, and he has a daughter called Jessica. Virtually every other character in the play calls him a Jew, as he himself does. So there is no confusion about the play's anti-Semitism, which becomes graphic when Shylock demands a pround of his adversary's flesh as part of the contract, and he goes to court to get his pound of flesh.

To take another example, in 1994 in London's Palladium Theater, Cameron Mackintosh's very successful production of the popular musical *Oliver* appeared. In that production, virtually every time the villain Fagin appeared on stage, a clarinetist in the orchestra would play some Klezmer music. This caused the audience to laugh because the orchestra was clearly using the Klezmer music to show that Fagin was a Jew. Klezmer music certainly existed in Wagner's time, and other Jewish folk music as well. So, given his opportunity, does Wagner ever do this in his orchestration of *Die Meistersinger*? He does not, even though if he had wanted his audience to perceive that Beckmesser is supposed to be Jewish, Wagner could easily have added some Klezmer music to Beckmesser's onstage music. Yet Wagner does not do this. Beckmesser remains an outsider on some level; for example, Harry Kupfer's famous production of the opera in Berlin in 2000 suggested that the character was homosexual.

Clearly neither the orchestration of the music—nor for that matter, the text or the character's name—indicates in any way that the character is Jewish. In fact, in 16th century Nurenberg, if Beckmesser had been Jewish he could not have been a member of one of its guilds and he would not have been allowed to marry the daughter of a guildmember. The fact that Beckmesser is in fact a highly honored member of the Mastersinger's guild and would be eligible to marry Eva Pogner proves that he is a Christian. Father Pogner never voices any objection at the idea of his daughter marrying Beckmesser, and instead he seems to encourage the match.

Several commentators on manic/depressive or bipolar illness have said that part of the disease is a paranoia connected with the manic phase. I believe this to be the source of Wagner's unfortunate anti–Semitism—simply, he picked up a popular form of the paranoia in German culture at the time. But he was smart enough as a writer and a composer to make very sure that his paranoid anti–Semitism did not appear in any of his librettos or in any of his scores. I think that on some level Wagner knew that his anti–Semitism was a sign of ignorance, so he kept it out of his operas, though he unfortunately let it appear in his conversation, correspondence, and his essays.

Of course an anti–Semite like Adolf Hitler could be expected to capitalize on Wagner's anti–Semitism. Hitler was a brutal thug who wanted to give his movement some intellectual and artistic status, so his attempts to connect Wagner's operas with National Socialism became a natural result. Hitler liked to say that Wagner represented the essence of National Socialism, but if Wagner had been alive, how would Hitler have treated him? Other artists in Germany during the Third Reich were treated to subjugation and a strict censorship of their creative output. Could one imagine an artist like Wagner submitting to that kind of censorship? I suggest that if Wagner had been alive during the Third Reich he would have either fled or ended in a concentration camp, where he might have perished. While he agreed with National Socialism about the sad topic of anti-Semitism, Wagner clearly detested the expansionism and militarism represented by Bismarck and other Prussian junkers during his own lifetime. In February of 1876 Wagner wrote to his friend Emil Heckel from Bayreuth: "The world, and more especially 'Germania,' is becoming increasingly repugnant to me!" (Wagner, Letters, 853).

That Wagner's unfortunate mania sometimes produced his virulent anti-Semitism is a sad and embarrassing fact for all who love Wagnerian opera. But *Die Meistersinger von Nürnberg*, a wonderful product of Wagner's manic periods, does not contain any anti-Semitism; so it is an uncontaminated joy to behold and to listen to. Wagner's mania, despite the occasional bouts of paranoia, provided the greatest comedy in the history of German opera, and that comedy includes many references to both the Old Testament and the New Testament—the Jewish and Christian parts of the Bible. When Walther (a Christian name) wins his Eva (the great heroine of the Old Testament and a Jewish name) and receives the medal which makes him a member of the Meistersinger's guild, that medal has on it a picture of King David from the Old Testament. King David was of course one of the great musicians of the Old Testament, and it is interesting that Wagner uses this Jewish figure as a symbol for the Mastersingers' guild. The mania in the opera has produced the full reconciliation of male and female, society and the artist, old art and new art, and Old Testament and New Testament. At its premiere on June 21, 1868—Johannistag—in Munich, the audience certainly had something to cheer about at the end, and Wagner felt the joy of his most successful premiere.

Chapter 7

The *Ring* Cycle: Suicide as Threat and Triumph

The *Ring* cycle certainly remains Wagner's masterpiece, and it occupied him for almost thirty years. As was usual with him, the libretto took longer to compose than the music, the reason being that when Wagner wrote his libretto he clearly already had the music in his mind. In 1848 Wagner began with *Siegfrieds Tod*, which later became the basis for *Götterdämmerung*. Feeling that the viewer of his opera would have to know something of the youth of his hero Siegfried, Wagner wrote in 1851 *Der Junge Siegfried*, which became the basis for *Siegfried*. In 1852 the texts for *Rheingold* and *Die Walküre* were written, and the earlier texts were changed into *Siegfried* and *Götterdämmerung*.

Wagner privately printed the complete text for *Der Ring des Nibelungen* in 1853, and he then began composing *Rheingold*. By the next year, 1854, Wagner had completed scoring *Rheingold* and then began composing *Die Walküre*. By 1856 Wagner had finished composing *Walküre* and began composing *Siegfried*, though (as in the previous operas) making some changes in the printed text of the *Ring* and in the final version set to music. In 1857, after having composed the first two acts of *Siegfried*, Wagner left the project temporarily and instead began composing the first act of *Tristan und Isolde*. In 1867 Wagner again interrupted the *Ring* project to begin work on *Die Meistersinger*. After that opera had its successful premiere in Munich in 1868, Wagner returned to the third act of *Siegfried*. By the next year Wagner had completed *Siegfried* and began composing *Götterdämmerung*; also in 1869 *Das Rheingold* was first staged in Munich, despite Wagner's objections. In 1870, while Wagner was working on the final opera of the tetralogy, *Die Walküre* had its premiere in Munich, also over Wagner's objections. By 1874 Wagner had completed composing the final opera, and the entire tetralogy was finally staged within one week, as he intended, in his own specially-designed theater at Bayreuth in 1876. An examination of the text of the four operas indicates that Wagner both repeated elements of his earlier literary style and developed some new techniques for this new work.

The *Ring* cycle, that vast tetralogy of operas (or music-dramas, as Wagner liked to call them), uses suicide in several important ways and it becomes a major theme in the entire work. In addition, Wagner developed a distinctive meter and style for the libretto. As many other commentators have pointed out, Wagner used a metered verse characterized by *Stabreim*—or alliteration in English. The heavily alliterated verse that Wagner used in his *Ring* librettos was designed as a consciously antiquated form to reflect the poetical style of old Germanic poetry—the early medieval period of the *Ring* cycle. An equivalent in English is the heavily alliterated verse style of *Beowulf*; this form was clearly Germanic since it was also used in the poetic Eddas. Another English equivalent would be several Victorian poets who were so fond of medieval literature that they wrote a consciously antiquated poetical style to reflect the medieval period, which became their subject matter. Even earlier, in the Romantic period, Keats used the old Spenserian stanza for his "The Eve of St. Agnes"—to reflect the period of the poem rather than the period in which the poem was written. Tennyson did this as well in his *Idylls of the King* and "The Lady of Shallott"—using medieval rather than Victorian poetical forms. Clearly there was a tradition in both English and German of using older poetical forms in the nineteenth century to reflect the literature of earlier periods, and Wagner used this form of medievalism as the basic style for his text in the *Ring* cycle.

As we have seen earlier, Wagner was fond of the repetition of key words in his librettos to emphasize key ideas. He created a verbal equivalent of his musical leitmotiv system by the repetition of words and images to reflect some of the major ideas in each of his four *Ring* librettos. "Schmach" (shame) and "Liebe" (love), for example, are repeated often in *Die Walküre*, in addition to repetitions of key images. Light and darkness, which we saw Wagner use very often in his libretto for *Tristan und Isolde*, also appear in the *Ring* cycle, often with symbolic meanings. The use of these cycles again connects the *Ring* with Vico's concept of the cycles of nature which control our lives. Wagner uses irregular line lengths in these four librettos, but usually the lines are short, with six syllables, generally

7—The *Ring* Cycle

iambic trimeter but often varied. Wagner was clearly imitating the Old High German poetic forms like those in the *Nibelungenlied*.

One of the central concerns of the tetralogy is suicide. Suicide does not appear in *Das Rheingold* or *Siegfried*, but it appears significantly in *Die Walküre* and especially *Die Götterdämmerung*. In these two of the *Ring* operas suicide appears as a major subject, so clearly its treatment deserves close attention.

The subject of suicide first appears in the second act of *Die Walküre*, during Wotan's famous dialogue with his daughter Brünnhilde. As he confesses to his favorite Walküre daughter:

> Ich beruhte Alberich's Ring
> gierig heilt ich das Gold!
> Der Fluch, den ich floh,
> nicht flieht er nun mich:—
> was ich liebge, muss ich verlassen,
> morden, wen je ich minne,
> trugend verrathen
> wer mir traut!
> Fahre denn him,
> herrische Pracht,
> göttlichten Prunkes
> prahlende Schmacht!
> Zusammen breche
> was ich gebaut!
> auf geb ich mein Werk:
> nur eines will ich noch:
> das Ende—
> das Ende!—
> Und für das Ende
> sorgt Alberich!

> I once held Alberich's ring,
> greedily grasped the gold!
> The curse that I fled
> won't flee from me now:—
> what I love I must leave,
> murder him whom I cherish
> and falsely betray
> him who trusts me!—
> Farewell, then,
> godly power!
> divine show's
> resplendent shame!
> Let all I built

> now fall in ruins!
> I give up my work!
> One thing only do I crave:
> the end!
> the end!
> And Alberich will accomplish
> that end!

Wotan yearns for the end of his suffering, the end of his struggles with Alberich over the gold, and yet what he seems to want most is his own death. In calling for the end, Wotan seems to be yearning for his own annihilation even if that means leaving Alberich in control of the Ring.

This same suicidal quality appears in his son Siegmund during the same act of *Die Walküre*, specifically during the "Todesverkundigungmusik"—or the Death Announcement music. As Brünnhilde tells Siegmund when she appears to him:

> Nur Todegeweihten
> taugt mein Anblick:
> wer mich erschaut,
> der scheidet vom Lebens-Licht,
> Auf der Walstatt allein
> erschein'ich Edlen:
> wer mich gewahrt,
> zur Wal kor ich ihn mir.
>
> ---
>
> Only the death-doomed
> are allowed to look on me—
> he who sees me
> leaves the light of life.
> In battle only
> I appear to heroes:
> he who perceives me
> I've picked as one dead.

This passage indicates the deadly nature of Brünnhilde's task: she is announcing to Siegmund that he must now leave life and his wife and sister Sieglinde to join the Valkyrie and the other heroes in Valhalla. When he refuses to leave Sieglinde, Brünnhilde insists that (because he has seen her) he must now go to Valhalla. Siegmund then threatens to commit suicide.

> Diess Schwert—
> das dem Treuen ein Trugvoller schuf:
> diess Schwert

Das Rheingold: James Morris as Wotan, Siegfried Jerusalem as Loge.

> das feig vor dem Feind mich verrath:—
> frommt es nicht gegen den Feind,
> so fromm'es denn wider den Freund!
> Zwei Leben
> lachen dir hier:—

> nimm sie, Nothung,
> neidischer Stahlt!
> Nimm sie mit einem Streich!

> This sword—
> which a traitor gave to an honest man:
> this sword
> which betrays me, alas, to my enemy,
> then let it strike against a friend!
> Two lives
> laugh at you here—
> take them, Nothung,
> useful steel!
> Take them at a stroke!

What Siegmund threatens to do here is first to kill Sieglinde, and then to kill himself. Some critics have suggested that Siegmund is threatening to kill Sieglinde and her unborn child, but he is not sure she is pregnant—in fact, she herself will not find this out until the next act. Instead, Siegmund threatens to kill Sieglinde and then to commit suicide. And the threat works very well, since Brünnhilde promises to help him in his upcoming battle with Hunding instead of following her orders from Wotan to let Siegmund die.

His sister Sieglinde also becomes suicidal during the next act, when she stands with Brünnhilde and her sister Valkyries as Wotan is approaching. As she says to Brünnhilde:

> Nicht sehre dich Sorge um mich:
> enzig taugt mir der Tod!
> Wer heiss dich Maid
> dem Harst mich entführen?
> Im Sturm dort hätt' ich
> den Streich empfah'n
> von derselben Waffe,
> der Siegmund fiel:
> das Ende fand ich
> verreint mit ihm!
> Fern vom Siegmund—
> Siegmund, vor dir!
> O deckte mich Tod,
> dass ich's denke!
> Soll um die Flucht
> dir Maid ich nicht fluchen,
> so höre heilig mein Flehen
> stosse dein Schwert mir in's Herz!

> Don't worry because of me:
> death alone can help me!
> Who told you, o maid,
> to carry me away from this battle?
> In the battle there
> I've been struck
> by the same spear
> which killed Siegmund:
> I've met my end
> united with him!
> Far from Siegmund—
> Siegmund from you!
> Let death come to me
> lest I think of it!
> Before I curse you, maid,
> for saving me,
> hear my holy plea and
> drive your sword into my heart!

Sieglinde, as suicidal as her Wälsung twin Siegmund, wants Brünnhilde to kill her rather than face the future without him. Of course Brünnhilde gives her the will to live (at least temporarily) by telling her that she is pregnant and will soon bear the glorious hero Siegfried.

When Wotan arrives soon afterwards, he vents his fury on his favorite daughter Brünnhilde for disobeying his orders and defending Siegmund instead of Hunding. Wotan threatens to put her into a sleep, saying that whatever man finds her, unprotected, can then have her. By the end of the scene, Brünnhilde acts just as Siegmund had behaved in the previous act, becoming suicidal to get what she wants. She asks that she be surrounded by fire to protect her from cowards, so that only a hero will possess her.

> Diess eine
> musst du erhören!
> Zerknicke dein Kind,
> das dein Knie umfasst;
> zertritt die Traute,
> zertrümm're die Maid:
> ihres Leibes Spur
> zerstore dein Speer:
> doch gieb, Grausamer, nicht
> der grässlichsten Schmach sie pries!
> Auf dein Gebot
> entbrenne ein Feuer:
> den Felsen umglühe
> lodernde Gluth:

> es leck' ihre Zung!
> es fresse ihr Zahn
> den Zagen, der frech sich wagte,
> dem freislichen Felsen zu nah'n!

> This one thing
> you must grant me!
> Kill your child
> who holds your knee,
> trample your favorite
> and dash her to pieces:
> let your spear destroy
> all trace of her body:
> but, merciless god, don't allow her
> the most foul of fates!
> At your order
> let a fire spring up;
> let its hot flames
> encircle her.
> Its tongue shall lick,
> its tooth attack
> any coward who dares to approach
> the fearsome rock in his rashness.

Here we find a powerful plea for self-destruction—suicidal behavior indeed—since Brünnhilde is asking Wotan to destroy her rather than leaving her unprotected. She is threatening suicide if Wotan does not allow her request, and her threat works. Wotan immediately agrees to surround her with fire and so protect her—only the hero who does not know fear will dare to approach his sleeping daughter.

The single *Ring* opera which makes the greatest use of suicide is the grand finale of the tetralogy, *Die Götterdämmerung*, where suicide and suicidal behavior dominate, and in fact the tetralogy ends with an act of suicide. Waltraute appears to her sister Brünnhilde toward the end of the first act, describing the condition of their father Wotan:

> So—sitzt er,
> sagt kein Wort.
> auf hehrem Sitze
> stumm und ernst
> des Speeres Splitter
> fest in der Faust:
> Holda's Apfels
> ruhrt er nicht am:
> Staunen und Bangen
> binden starr die Götter.

> So he sits,
> saying not a word
> silent and solemn
> on his sacred seat,
> with the broken spear
> held tight in his hand:
> Holda's apples
> he does not eat:
> shame and fear
> possess the Gods!

What Waltraute is describing here is clearly suicidal behavior since, if Wotan does not eat the apples of Friea, he will soon grow old and die.

In fact, the suicide of both Brünnhilde and Wotan—as well as of the rest of the gods—is clearly envisioned in the immolation scene that ends the vast tetralogy. As Brünnhilde sings:

> Das Feuer, das mich verbrennt,
> rein'ge vom Fluche den Ring:
> ihr in der Flut
> loset ihn auf,
> und lauter bewarht
> das lichte Gold
> das euch zum Unheil geraubt.—
> Fliegt heim, ihr Raben!
> Raunt es eurem Herren,
> was hier am Rhein ihr gehört!
> an Brünnhilde's Felsen
> fahrt verbeit:
> der dort noch lodert
> weiser Loge nacht Walhall!
> Denn der Götter Ende
> dämmert nun auf:
> so—werf'ich den Brand
> in Walhall's prangende Burg.
> Grane, mein Ross,
> seir mir gegrüsst!
> Weisst du auch, mein Freund,
> wohin ich dich fuhre?
> im Feuer leuchtend
> liegt dort dein Herr,
> Siegfried, mein seliger Held.
> Dem Freunde zu folgen,
> wieherst du freudig?
> Lockt dich zu ihm
> die lachende Lohe?

Fühl' meine Brust auch,
wie sie entbrennt,
helles Feuer
das Herz mir erfasst:
ihm zu umschlingen,
umschlossen von ihm,
in mächtigster Minne
verhählt ihm zu sein
Heiajaho! Grane!
Grüss deinen Herren!
Siegfried! Siegfried! Sieh!
Selig grüsst dich dien Weib!

Let the fire that destroys me
clean the ring of its curse:
in the waters
let it dissolve
and safely protect
the shining, pure gold
that was stolen to your grief—
Fly home, ravens!
Whisper to your lord
what you overheard here by the Rhine!
Fly past Brünnhilde's rock:
tell Loge, who burns there,
to go to Valhalla!
For the end of the gods
has now come:
so do I throw this torch
into Valhalla's proud castle.
Grane, my horse,
hear my message!
Do you know, my friend,
where I'm directing you now?
Lit by fires,
your lord lies there,
Siegfried, my blessed hero.
You whinny with joy
to approach your friend?
Does the laughing fire
take you to him?
Feel how the flames
burn in my breast,
bright fires
size my heart:
to clasp him to me
while held in his arms

> and in greatest love
> to be wedded to him!
> Heiyaho! Grane!
> Greet your lord!
> Siegfried! Siegfried, See!
> In bliss your wife greets you!

What we have here is a double suicide, for Brünnhilde not only kills herself by throwing herself into Siegfried's funeral pyre. She is also killing Wotan, who obviously wishes this death as well. Brünnhilde's final vision, like Isolde's final vision at the end of *Tristan und Isolde*, is a fantasy, a daydream of her lover alive and her joining him. So the *Ring* ends in sacrificial and exalted suicide. Does Wagner suggest here that the greatest happiness can occur, in some situations, only in suicide—especially in a death pact with a person one loves? Both Brünnhilde and Wotan commit suicide, and for Brünnhilde this ends with her vision of being reunited with Siegfried. But here, unlike in the end of *Der Fliegende Holländer*, there is no promise of an afterlife—only the exaltation of that final vision of being united with the beloved. And exaltation remains clearly the final vision, the final sounds, and the final emotion of the *Ring* cycle.

But is this great tetralogy really a tragedy if its ending is so happily triumphant? In these four librettos, Wagner uses comic relief—something which we connect with Shakespearean tragedy and which Wagner has only rarely attempted before. In his theoretical writing, Wagner always exalted Greek tragedy, which certainly does not use comic relief but instead emphasizes the value of the elegiac tragic tone. Wagner, however, abandons his theory to use comic relief in his *Ring* cycle, and Cosima repeatedly emphasizes her husband's love of Shakespeare in her memoirs. Cosima wrote in her diary for July 28, 1881:

> Our morning conversation revolves around *A Midsummer Night's Dream*, and we find ourselves still laughing heartily at Bottom's "Not a word of me," which shows him to be a complete original, a being such as only Nature and Shakespeare can bring forth. And how individual all his comedies are, whereas in Calderon the characters are always the same! We surrender entirely to the magic of Oberon and Titania in our memories. R. works [Cosima Wagner 434].

It is interesting that a few days after that, when Cosima is playing the piano for her husband, he comments negatively on the overly literal labeling of the leitmotivs in editions of his works. Her entry of August 1, 1881, reads: "I play excerpts from *Götterdämmerung*, arranged for piano duet, with Loldi. R. says he is pleased with the work. Unfortunately in this edition there are a lot of markings such as 'wanderlust motive,' 'disaster motive,' etc. R. says 'And perhaps people will think all this nonsense is done at my request!'" (Cosima Wagner, Diaries, 435). Clearly Wagner wanted his use of leitmotivs to be seen as subtle and complex and not easily labeled.

Wagner himself wrote of his indebtedness to Shakespeare in his own autobiography. Very early in *Mein Leben* the composer wrote, "One of the main ingredients of my poetic fancy I owed to Shakespeare's mighty diction, emotional and humorous" (Wagner, *My Life*, 27).

Perhaps because of the extended time Wagner had to work on his vast tetralogy, both aspects of his personality—the manic and the depressive—inevitably entered this largest of his operatic works. The French writer Édouard Schuré caught this aspect of Wagner when he met him after the premiere of *Tristan und Isolde* in Munich.

> Oh, what a strange whirl of emotions one felt on peering into this brain. It was, as the poet [Dante] says, *la bufera infernal che mai non resta*. And dominating all these characters, there were two that revealed themselves almost always simultaneously, like the two poles of his nature: Wotan and Siegfried! Yes, on the deepest level of his thinking, Wagner resembled Wotan, this German Jupiter, this Scandinavian Odin whom he created in his own image, a strange god, a philosopher and pessimist, for ever troubled by the end of the world, for ever wandering and brooding on the enigma of all things. But in his impulsiveness he resembled Siegfried more than anyone else, the strong and ingenuous hero, who knows neither fear nor scruples, forging a sword for himself and setting out to conquer the world. The result was the constant union between profound reflection and ebullient spontaneity [Spencer 180–181].

Here Schuré has captured Wagner's bipolar nature, which includes both the suicidal god Wotan and the young hero Siegfried, who does not know fear. Both the tragic and the comic are united in the *Ring* cycle, with comic relief in all four operas. As Wylie Sypher has pointed out, "Perhaps the most important discovery in modern criticism is the perception that comedy and tragedy are somehow akin, or that comedy can tell us many things about our situation even tragedy cannot" (Sypher 93). There could be no better illustration than the totality of the *Ring*.

Nature, the green world, is victorious by the end of the *Ring*, with its representatives, the Rhinemaidens, on stage and in possession of their ring at last, followed by human beings observing Valhalla burning and the dawn of a new day. The green world triumphs over the greedy feuding of a corrupted divinity and a corrupted humanity. To see comedy as more than a vehicle for a belly laugh, to see it in larger social and anthropological terms, is to understand the comedic aspects of the *Ring*. Overtly comic, even laughable, elements of the plot, staging specifications, and especially the various uses of lighting, as well as the music itself, must be seen as part of a whole—a whole that is ultimately a mythic representation of loss, change, and redemption.

Comedy, and especially its relationship to light and darkness, will help us to comprehend the *Ring*. *Das Rheingold*, which preserves the Aristotelian unity of time by occurring within the space of one day, opens in the murky darkness before dawn with the Rhine maidens happily swimming about their treasure. The Rhine maidens seem the very essence of comedy as they swim about their gold singing, blissfully naive in the presence of its power and beauty. This light, happy mood is disturbed by the heavier, darker sounds from the orchestra as Alberich, the creature of darkness and night, appears. As he says in his opening lines:

> Hehe! Ihr nicker!
> Wie seid ihr neidlich,
> neidliches Volk!
> Aus Nibelheims Nacht
> naht' ich mich gern,
> neigtet ihr euch zu mir.
> ---
> Haha! You nixies!
> How graceful you are,
> desirable creatures!
> From Nibelheim's night
> I would gladly approach,
> if you would come down to me.

One of the Rhinedaughters, Flosshilde, says, "Es dämmert und ruft" ("It grows darker and someone is calling"). What attracts this dwarf Alberich from the darkness of Nibelheim is the gold and its glimmer of light.

As Alberich says of the Rhinemaidens, "Wie scheint im Schimmer/ ihr hell und schoen!" ("How you shine in the glimmery light so bright and beautiful!") Just as naturally as man seeks the light and avoids darkness, Alberich tries to capture these bright creatures, and they feign interest in his amorous advances, then laugh and swim away when he approaches. This teasing, cruel nature remains with the Rhinemaidens throughout the *Ring* until they finally taunt Siegfried in the last act of *Götterdämmerung*. Here, however, the Rhinemaidens confront only the ugly dwarf Alberich, yet they enjoy making fun of him for as long as he endures it. For example, the water makes Alberich sneeze, which inspires Woglinde to say,

"Prustend naht; meines Freiers Pracht!" ("Sneezing my wonderful suitor approaches!") Wellgrunde is even nastier, and when she has finally encouraged Alberich to chase her, she says:

>   Bist du verliebt
>   und lüstern nacht Minne?
>   lass' sehn, du Schöner,
>   wie bist du zu schau'n?
>   Pfui! du haariger,
>   hoeckriger Geck!
>   Scharzes, schweiliges
>   Schwefelgezwerg!
>   Such' dir ein Friedel,
>   dem du gefällst!
>   ------------------------
>   Are you a lover
>   and do you crave love's rapture?
>   Let us see what you
>   are like, handsome fellow—
>   Ugh! You hairy,
>   hunchback beau!
>   Black, horny,
>   sulfurous dwarf!
>   Find yourself a sweetheart
>   whom you can please!

Clearly the maidens enjoy provoking this ugly dwarf, and they swim about laughing as he tries to capture them. Their very cruelty makes the dwarf a sympathetic figure who finally seeks power since he will never get love.

The stage brightens as the rising sun strikes the gold and fills the whole scene with its golden light. The Rhinemaidens sing, "Rheingold! Rheingold! Leuchtende Lust,/wie lachst du so hell und hehr!/Glühender Glanz/entgeleisset dir weihlich in Wag!" ("Rhinegold! Rhinegold! Gleaming joy, how bright and gloriously you laugh! Glowing brightness, you brighten the waves!") The gold itself, protected by the Rhinemaidens, here symbolizes the beauty of nature, so that its seizure suggests the rape of nature by forces of greed and corruption. But at this point the gold seems safe, for only he who will renounce love can tap its power, and the Rhinedaughters are sure that Alberich is much too lusty a dwarf ever to make such a sacrifice to gain their beautiful hoard. Yet he fools them and makes just such a sacrifice by the end of the scene. As Alberich says when he steals the gold:

> So buhlt nun im Finstern,
> feuchtes Gezücht!
> Das Licht lösch' ich euch aus....
>
> ---
>
> Then make love in darkness,
> watery brood!
> I extinguish your light.

By the end of this first scene of the opera, Alberich has become the creature of darkness who destroys light, and the laughing Rhine maidens laugh no longer, for he has destroyed the comedy of their existence—but only temporarily. By the end of the tetralogy's last scene we are shown that the theft caused only an interruption in normal life.

The rising sun provides the transition to the second scene, for here the day dawns on the mountainside before Valhalla, which the gods will finally possess. The repeated use of day and night in the lighting directions clearly exemplifies Wagner's use of Vico's natural cycles. This new day will be the most crucial day in Wotan's life, but it begins comically. Dreaming about his beautiful new castle, the chief of all the gods is awakened by his nagging wife. Fricka, utterly incapable of keeping the philandering Wotan by her side, has become in her bitterness the typical shrew of comedy, whose very nagging drives her husband further away. As she tells Wotan, "Auf, aus der Traume/wonnigem Trug!/Erwache, Mann, und erwäge!") ("Arise from the pleasant deception of dreams! Wake, man, and reflect!") With those irritating words Wotan is awakened. This is a light, bright scene with the new castle glowing in the background, for the giants Fasolt and Fafner have finally completed it and are arriving to collect their wage, the goddess Freia. Fasolt tells Wotan, "Sanft schloss/ Schlaf dein Aug:' wir beide bauten/Schlummers bar die Burg.") ("While your eyes were gently closed in sleep, we, sleepless, both built the castle.") Toil, darkness, and sleeplessness are thus linked to the new home of the gods. So far, Alberich, the giants Fasolt and Fafner, and the new castle have been connected with the darkness; however, the gods are usually associated with bright, gleaming light. We first see them with the fresh light of a dawn. Fasolt calls Wotan, "Lichtsohn du!" (You son of light!") But the chief of the glittery race wants to renege on his agreement with the giants, so he summons the crafty Loge to find him a way of getting out of this pact.

As the god of fire, Loge is lightness and brightness, personified here in the flickering figurations of his motif. Because of his insightful wit and cleverness he functions comically, but his is an evil, self-serving wit that isolates him from the other characters in the *Ring*. He comments in the

Das Rheingold: Mari-Anne Haeggander as Freia, Jan-Hendrik Rootering as Fasolt, Matti Salminen as Fafner.

final scene of the opera that he finds the actions of the gods immoral, but this does not stop him from helping Wotan to trick the giants and to steal the ring from Alberich.

Darkness dominates the third scene of *Das Rheingold*, which is set in Nibelehim. In those murky depths Alberich taunts Mime, flaunting his powers over his own race. Since earlier in the day when Alberich stole the ring, he has immediately enslaved the people around him. The Nibelungs had been happy and carefree, but now they are miserable slaves who have to mine gold for their master, Alberich. He indicates the darkness of his motives when he tries on his new helmet, the Tarnhelm, and says, "Nacht und Nebel—neimand gleich" ("Night and mist—resembling no one"). The orchestral colors darken for his scene, with a more pronounced use of the lower woodwinds and strings. "Nibelheims nacht'gem Land" ("Nibelheim's night-born land"), Wotan calls the place, and it certainly is dark in many different ways. In this scene we also find out that Loge is a cousin of Alberich's, a highly significant relationship because of the similarities it suggests between the two characters. "Den Lichtalben/ lacht jetz Loge; der listige Schelm," ("Loge is hobnobbing with the light-gods now, crafty knave)," says Alberich to his cousin. The word "Nacht" is used repeatedly in this dark scene, which captures the sad enslavement of the dwarves and the haughty and taunting power of Alberich. He has been rejected by the lovely Rhinedaughters, but he can get his revenge on his fellow dwarves in dark Nibelheim.

David Levin and some other commentators on the *Ring* have argued that the Nibelung dwarves (and other dwarves in European literature) are actually meant to be Jews, but there is no evidence in Wagner's text or the music to prove this. The same logic would have to apply as well to all the dwarves in European mythology, from the stories of Hans Christian Andersen to the brothers Grimm and even earlier. Do the dwarves in Walt Disney's film *Snow White and the Seven Dwarves* prove that dear old Walt was anti–Semitic? Hardly. Wagner presents Wotan and Alberich as polar opposites, though similar in some ways, basing this polarity on his own personality.

The fourth and last scene of *Rheingold* is characterized by the general gloom and darkness of a murky twilight. When Donner and Froh clear the clouds away at the end of the scene, we see a sunset in the distance, which tells us that we have come to the end of this fateful day. As Wotan sings at the end of the opera:

> Abendlich strahlt
> der Sonne Auge;
> in prächtiger Glut
> prangt glanzend die Burg.
> In des Morgens Scheine
> mutig erschimmernd,
> lag sie herrenlos,
> hehr verlockend vor mir.

Von Morgan bis Abend,
in Müh und Angst,
nicht wonnig ward sie gewonnen!
es naht die Nacht!

In the evening light
the sun's eye gleams;
in its beautiful glow
the castle shines bright.
In the light of morning
bravely glittering
it stood without a master,
lofty and inviting before me.
Between dawn and sunset
in toil and suffering
it was not happily won!
Night draws on.

With these lines Wagner reminds us of the movement of the sun during this day, which gives a form to this opera. Cycles and cyclical movement clearly provide a structure for Wagner's tetralogy. This sunset also becomes symbolic, for with its waning light the gods pompously parade into Valhalla, which has already been linked for us with darkness and suffering. The intellectual, witty Loge closes the opera with a clever rejoinder to the wailing Rhinemaidens, telling them to bask in the glorious light of the gods. The gods think that their day has ended successfully, for they can now occupy their new home, Valhalla, accompanied by the strains of suitably pompous music. But the sunset in the distance reminds us that this is the beginning of the end for these proud but tainted creatures.

Die Walküre is the most sombre of the *Ring* operas, containing only one scene with any light, witty touches. A misguided production can, of course, add hours of merriment to the work, but this was not Wagner's intention. The lighting effects of this opera are very different from any used in the other three, with repeated moments of fragmented and weak lighting—and this is the cloudiest of the four *Ring* operas as well. The first act opens in Hunding's house as a storm rages outside. The room is dark, for according to Wagner's stage directions only an occasional glimmer from the fire at the hearth lights the scene. Even this flicker finally dies out as the act progresses, but eventually the storm has cleared and moonlight from outside floods the room. Siegmund, by the middle of the first act, notices the flicker of flame from the hearth.

Die Walküre: Peter Hofmann as Siegmund.

Was gliesst dort hell
im glimmerschein?
Welch ein Strahl bricht
aus der Esche Stamm?
Des blinden Auge,

leuchtete ein Blitz;
lustig lacht da der Blick.

What is it glints brightly there
in the gloom?
What ray of light
shines from the ash tree's trunk?
A flash of lightning
strikes the blind man's eyes:
the light sparkles there happily.

The flickering light from the dying fire reveals the sword in the ash tree. After he pulls it out, Siegmund and Sieglinde declare their incestuous love in the beauty of the spring moonlight, which comes flooding even into Hunding's dark hut. As Siegmund tells Sieglinde:

Im Lenzesmond
leuchtest du hell;
hehr umwebt dich
das Wellenhaar;
was micht berückt
errrat' ich nun leicht—
denn wonnig weidet mein Blick.

In the spring moonlight
your face shines radiantly;
framed by your lovely
waving hair;
what bewitched me
now I can see clearly—
as I rapturously feast my eyes.

This beautiful but fragile lighting will repeatedly be connected with these doomed figures and their tragic love. Later, sunlight will be associated with the more forceful Siegfried and Brünnhilde, but for Siegmund and Sieglinde moonlight and firelight are more fitting. This contrasting lighting for contrasting lovers creates yet another polarity in the *Ring*, but (as Vico would undoubtedly point out) both sunlight and moonlight are created by the cycles of nature.

Act II of the opera takes place in a rocky gorge, where Brünnhilde compares Fricka's entrance to a storm, and the storm punctuates this act. More and more clouds darken the stage as Wotan is forced to yield to Fricka's demands that he abandon the Wälsungs and uphold her rights as goddess of the vow of marriage. Even more darkness gathers as Wotan

Die Walküre: Peter Hofmann as Siegmund, Jeannine Altmeyer as Sieglinde.

explains to his favorite daughter, Brünnhilde, the trap that he is in, and then he orders her to announce Siegmund's death to him. When Wotan talks about Alberich, he mentions the fact that the dwarf has begotten a son, and when this happened, Erda had predicted that the downfall of the gods would soon follow. In the next scene, with the incestuous lovers returning, the only light they can see is the light in each other's eyes, along with occasional flashes of lightning that frighten Sieglinde. By the end of this act, when Siegmund is finally killed by Hunding, who is in turn killed by Wotan, the stage is engulfed in darkness. We see the action through a series of lightning flashes, our only source of light in the stormy gloom. Thunder and lightning end this act as Wotan rages at his disobedient daughter.

The last act of *Die Walküre* also uses storms, storm clouds, and occasional flashes of lightning to accompany the general murkiness and moral cloudiness of the action on stage. For the ride of the Valkyries there are again sudden flashes of lightning, many threatening passing clouds, and general gloom. But the girls themselves provide the opera with its one bit of comedy, for they often laugh at their horses' nipping each other and engaging in sexual play. Later, the darkness and storm are directly connected with Wotan and his anger when Waltraute sings, "Nachtige zieht es/von Norden heran" ("Darkness is coming from the north"). Then Ortlinde answers: "Wutend steretr/hier der Storm" ("The raging storm is coming this way"). The storm gets more intense until Wotan himself finally appears on the scene, raging at Brünnhilde, and at the other Valkyries for defending her disobedience.

The stage is darkest when Wotan is angriest, but as he softens in his confrontation with Brünnhilde, gradually the clouds clear and the fragmented lightning gives way to a lovely, clear twilight. In this twilight—the only clear, steady light we have seen so far in this opera—Wotan agrees to protect his sleeping daughter with a wall of fire. The act and the opera end with the flickering light accompanied through Loge's flickering fire-music.

This, the least humorous of the four *Ring* operas, ends with a lovely firelight. Weak light, darkness, clouds, and flashes of lightning have suggested the fragmented, morally weak world of *Die Walküre*. A word that recurs frequently is "Schmach," or shame: the shame of Sieglinde, who must submit to Hunding though she does not love him; the shame of Wotan, who must submit to Fricka, though he no longer loves her, and who cannot control his own daughter; and the shame of Siegmund, who must leave his lover and sister in such terrible need. Such pervasive shame requires obscurity and cover, which is precisely what the opera's lighting effects provide. But in the general darkness another repeated word is "Liebe" (Love): Siegmund's love of Sieglinde and Wotan's love for Brünnhilde.

In direct contrast, *Siegfried* is the most comic of the *Ring* operas, but it remains a Wagnerian comedy, and that means that there are smiles

Die Walküre: **Birgit Nilsson as Sieglinde.**

and ideological conflicts rather than belly laughs and slapstick. People have often maintained that Wagner lacked a sense of humor; they are wrong. He had one, but it was Wagnerian, as this masterpiece reveals. The opera includes comic situations, comic lines, comic music, and a happy ending. Too often, however, conductors and directors have approached *Siegfried* with all the grim determination that should be reserved for *Walküre*. In fact, the comic situations and characters in the opera are often dismissed as embarrassing or eliminated, and the result is bad theater for this opera and lack of tonal variety in the whole *Ring*. Now that most opera companies use some form of surtitles, one can hear more audience laughter during many performances of *Siegfried*.

Act I of *Siegfried* takes place in a dark interior, a cave, and the only source of lighting is a low fire burning near an anvil. From the opening of the first act the orchestra sounds very gloomy, with somber and dangerous-sounding bassoons, tubas, violas, cellos, and basses for Fafner and Mime. The first prolonged use of violins occurs when Siegfried makes his entrance; he and his music brighten up the general gloom and he even enters with a bear and chases Mime around the cave with it, laughing at his practical joke. He then complains of not having a decent sword, which establishes the major problem of the first act. Yet the darkness of the cave also suggests Siegfried's lack of knowledge about himself and his ancestry. He sees the animals in the forest with their young and asks Mime about his parents, for he does not believe that Mime is his real father, but the dwarf avoids most of his questions and just keeps reminding the boy of all that has been done for him.

Mime uses gratitude on Siegfried in the way that most people use a hammer. He is the stereotypical over-possessive parent when he nags at the boy, cooks soups for him, then reminds him of all he has done for him. Mime tells him that his mother died giving birth to him, and then sings a little refrain over and over about "the helpless orphan born in the woods" to remind him of his debt of gratitude. Mime knows how to make guilt work to benefit himself. He is also sardonically comic in his silly and inept attempts to teach the boy fear by conjuring up the dark, dense forest and the big teeth of Fafner. But with Mime's plan to chop the naive boy's head off after he gets the ring, we can see the real evil in the old dwarf.

To kill a dragon Siegfried needs a sword, and his desire to find it in Act I is connected with his patrimony, for the broken fragments of Nothung, which Mime finally gives him, originally composed the sword of his father Siegmund. Freudian and phallic implications aside, Nothung provides a tangible connection between Siegfried and the parents he has never known. The solemn-sounding brasses that announce the arrival of the Wanderer, Wotan, on the scene also connect to Siegfried's ancestry, since the audience knows (unlike Siegfried) that Wotan is his grandfather. Here, the Wanderer's confrontation with the suspicious and nasty old Mime is organized around three questions that they ask each other, and then bet their heads on, but even here there is comedy. When the Wanderer first enters the cave, Mime tells him to live up to his reputation and keep on wandering. Wotan himself ironically addresses Mime as "wise smith," "wily dwarf," and "honest dwarf," all to comic effect. But the dialogue between the two characters has serious functions as well, for Wotan's three answers to Mime's questions about the races that inhabit the world are used to structure the entire opera.

Wotan describes the world of the *Ring* as having three major segments. The first, Nibelheim, is the land of the elves and darkness, ruled by "Schwarz-Alberich" (Dark-Alberich). The setting for Act I of *Siegfried* strongly suggests Nibelheim. Wotan says that the second part of creation is Riesenheim, ruled by Fafner, and it exists on the surface of the earth. Act II of *Siegfried* takes place on this plane, with a dense forest for the setting and with the shady and splotchy lighting typical of a forest. In the bright heights, on the other hand, live the gods, ruled by "Licht-Alberich" (Light-Alberich, or Wotan). Most of the last act takes place on the top of Brünnhilde's rock and in the full blaze of sunlight, at least according to Wagner's stage directions if not in some productions. The opera, then, as outlined by Wotan himself in his responses to Mime's questions, moves from darkness to light. While the variations become more subtle within each act, this is the overall pattern, and the contrast between Licht-Alberich and Schwarz-Alberich described by Wotan creates another Wagnerian polarity here.

This pattern of contrasting lighting is sustained in the middle of the first act when Mime curses the light ("Verfluchtes Licht!"). Being a creature of caves and caverns, he is naturally more comfortable in the darkness, which is symbolic as well of his character and his evil designs on Siegfried's life. The general darkness of this Mime-dominated act is eliminated only during the Forging Music at the end. Siegfried is angry at Mime's inept attempts at forging and decides to act for himself. His effort to repair his father's shattered sword, Nothung (literally, "Found in Need"), creates the only bright passage in this dark act. The music here employs the motif associated with Loge, god of fire, for Siegfried must build a large fire to have enough heat to reforge the sword, and it is also significant that he uses wood from an ash tree. Wotan's spear is ash. Siegfried's new sword is forged symbolically with the remains of the old order of the gods. With Nothung Siegfried has established a tie with his mysterious past, acquired some new knowledge about his parents, and created a weapon for asserting and defending himself.

The second act of *Siegfried* takes place in Riesenheim, in the depths of a dense forest, according to Wagner's stage directions. The act opens in "dark night" and the music helps create this ominous darkness with sounds suggesting the presence of the dangerous dragon Fafner. The ensuing confrontation between Alberich and Wotan occurs in almost total darkness, a lighting scheme that tends to equate these two characters for the audience. Both are after the ring and both want to use Siegfried for their own purposes. Wotan's motives center on the survival of the gods and the defense of his moral and legal system, while Alberich's motives are more selfishly evil and greedy; but both want to use Siegfried, and the blackness of the scene suggests Wagner's dark opinion of their motives.

With the dawn, Siegfried and Mime enter. The light in the middle of a dense forest is alternately shady and sunny and this is reflected in the often undulating Forest Murmurs music. As Siegfried wonders about his past, his parents, and his future, the gently shimmering music suggests the delicate forest light and various bird sounds. Now that Siegfried is alone, the tone in the act brightens. His natural curiosity about the birds and the bees becomes naively charming and typically adolescent. He becomes especially comic when he cuts a reed, whittles a rough flute, and tries to imitate the sound of the birds in the forest. The sour, flat notes he produces are musically comic. The audience laughs at the silly music written for the English horn, and regards the heroic "Dummer," Siegfried,

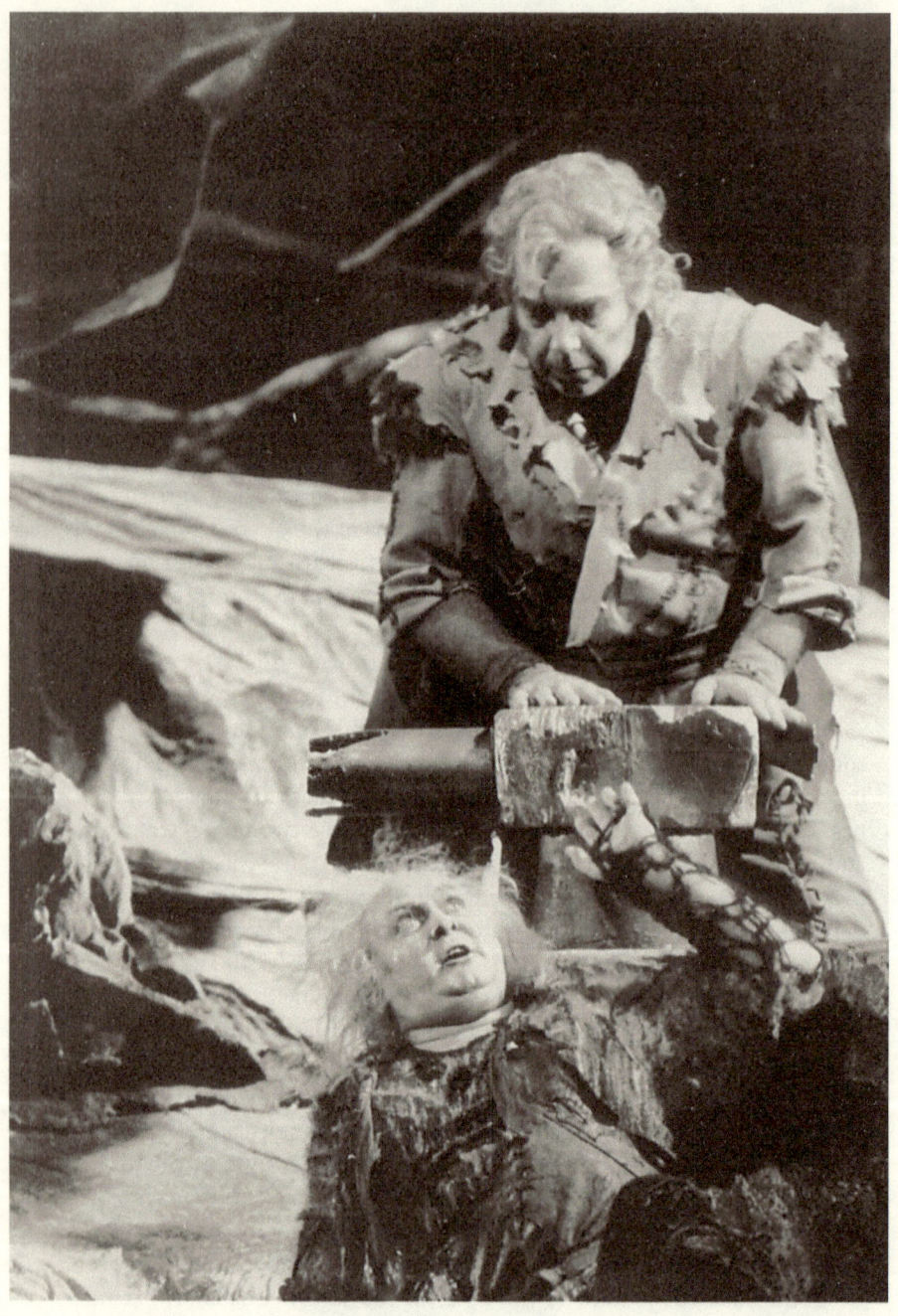

Siegfried: Wolfgang Neumann as Siegfried, Horst Hiestermann as Mime.

with amusement. Significantly, all the other characters in the opera address him as "Kind" (child) or "Knabe" (boy). He is charmingly adolescent here, though some of the less pleasant aspects of adolescence like impatience and impetuosity appear in other parts of the score.

The music sounds fatally dangerous after the Forest Murmurs scene and during the major confrontation of this act, the fight between Siegfried and Fafner. Yet who can take it seriously? The fairy-tale quality of the scene makes most members of the audience smile, and as the dragon's roars become more ferocious, the fun grows. By the end of the fight Fafner has become mortally wounded, but he can still be comically perceptive about Siegfried. "Who gave you this idea, for it couldn't have come from your head?" the dragon asks. Mime is also unintentionally comic when he becomes so excited by the immediate presence of the ring and the power of the Tarnhelm that he can not help chattering too loudly about his eagerness to kill the stupid boy. Once Siegfried has killed the two immediate threats to his life, Fafner and Mime, the orchestral tone brightens again. The forest bird promises the boy the companion he has been seeking throughout the opera who will relieve his loneliness. The forest bird describes Brünnhilde as perched atop a fiery rock and declares that only he who does not know fear can win her. Significantly, she is immediately associated with light.

Like Act II, Act III begins with a stormy night just before the dawn, and with Wotan on stage. Once again we see him in a darkness that must soon give way to dawn, an optimistic light that is often connected with Siegfried in this opera. The old generation must give way to the impetuous and often careless new generation just as surely as day conquers night, or so Wagner is telling us in the opera's lighting. But here at the beginning of this last act the initial confrontation is between Wotan and Erda and, except for her bluish glow, it is a murky scene. Wotan is at his most pathetic here in his noble but anxiety-ridden attempts to avoid his certain fate. The all-wise Erda is sleepy and as unconcerned as any other impersonal force of nature, and thus she provides a dramatically effective foil for Wotan's anxiety. Erda wants to go back to sleep and keeps putting Wotan off, but she is finally angered enough by his persistence to tell him that he is a liar. In fact, the cycle of waking and sleeping occurs here and elsewhere in Wagner's *Ring* cycle, for the cycle of sleeping and waking governs much of our lives. Wotan counterattacks by telling Erda that she is not all-wise since she can not help him to avoid his doom. In the monologue that follows, Wotan comes to realize the hopelessness of his situation and to accept it with resignation. He now knows that his reign and that of the gods has ended. Siegfried represents the new order, and not even Erda can help Wotan avoid his destruction. With the approaching dawn the boy himself enters, following the forest bird, which flies off at the sight of Wotan's fierce ravens.

The dialogue between Wotan and Siegfried becomes a musical and dramatic conflict of the generations. Siegfried is tired of listening to old men and wants to get to the sleeping Brünnhilde, but Wotan wants the respect due his age and position and he is reluctant to lose control of his daughter, even though he knows that his loss is inevitable. Though Wotan calls Siegfried and the Wälsungs "deine lichte Art" ("Your radiant kind"), he is angered by the boy's impatience and lack of understanding. Hence he tries to block the boy's way to the sleeping girl. In the ensuing fight Siegfried's sword Nothung breaks Wotan's ash spear, and the old generation of the world's rulers is defeated by the new. Wotan never again appears onstage in the *Ring*, though his daughters Brünnhilde and Waltraute do refer to him in his absence.

After this final conflict of the opera, all becomes bright and radiant. Fire music, appropriately, describes Siegfried's journey through the flames to reach Brünnhilde. The act, like the entire opera, has moved from darkness to light—another one of Vico's patterns. As Siegfried steps onto the top of the mountain, the scene is bathed in brightness and the audience gets its first view of total sunlight—it does, at least, in Wagner's stage directions. Siegfried and Brünnhilde, and their relationship, glow with sunlight, while, as we have seen, various shades of murky grays represent the other characters in the opera.

Siegfried's description of what he sees as he comes onto the top of the mountain reinforces the message expressed by the many violin crescendi and the stage picture in any good production: radiant sunlight and the sleeping maiden. As a goddess, albeit an ex-goddess, she dwells in the domain of light and air that Wotan had described in the first act. Here there are Freudian overtones as well, for when Siegfried first sees Brünnhilde's body he is afraid. It is she and her sexuality, then, that have finally taught him the fear that neither Mime, Fafner, nor Wotan could teach him. The boy calls out to his mother to calm his rising fears; Wagner, even earlier than Freud, combines newly experienced sexuality with the figure of the mother. Yet Siegfried's boyish fear of a woman's body is so typical that it is comic. Wagner cleverly indicates this with the marvelous naiveté of Siegfried's response when he first removes Brünnhilde's shield—"That is no man!" he says.

As anyone could have predicted, curiosity and physical attraction overcome fear, for Siegfried kisses the sleeping maiden. As she awakens (once again Wagner uses the cycle of sleeping and waking), the first thing she says is "Heil dir, Sonne! Heil dir, Licht! Heil dir, leutender tag!" ("Hail to you, sun! Hail to you, light! Hail to you, shining day!") In the first scene of this act Erda is awakened by Wotan, and now her daughter Brünnhilde is awakened by Siegfried—sleeping and waking become one of the many natural cycles in this tetralogy. The union of Siegfried and light is established here too, for he has become a sun god for her and, just as surely, he gets a first glimpse of total sunlight in the opera with her. What, then, do Brünnhilde and the light symbolize? For him the woman and the light are basically love and knowledge. She immediately loves him, as a result of knowing his parents and of Wotan's spell in the last scene of *Die Walküre*; and the love is of course mutual. The boy has been lonely and seeking a companion for most of the opera, and here, at last, he has found her; but she also represents knowledge. As a child of Wotan and Erda, Brünnhilde has the wisdom that Siegfried knows he lacks in himself. She tells him about his past and his dead parents, which he has been curious about since the beginning of the opera. Potentially, then, presented here is the ideal matching of active energy and wisdom.

At first Brünnhilde, like a typical nineteenth-century virgin, fears the loss of her virginity; she is also consciously aware of her new position as defenseless woman rather than as a goddess. She asks Siegfried to love her but not to touch her, but he is too aroused to be satisfied with something so platonic. "Wake up! Wake up and see the sunlight," he pleads. The woman in her, luckily for him, overcomes the chaste goddess and she becomes inflamed with love's sexual passion, as he already is. The music at this point, with all its mounting crescendi and fast rhythms, is reminiscent of the *Liebesnacht* in *Tristan und Isolde*, and the opera ends with a glorious duet for the lovers that affirms all that the light on stage at this time symbolizes. The final two lines of the opera summarize the lovers' emotions: "Leuchtende Liebe, Lachtender Tod!" ("Shining love, laughing death"). Their radiant new love will defy even death, they sing, as the primordial life force of the green world is reaffirmed in this brightly lit final scene. But the mention of death and its laughing defiance seems vaguely ominous for the future, despite the triumphant, happy present. Siegfried has at last found all that he has sought in this opera, and he shows that he can even laugh at death, but his actions contain the seeds of a sad future and the suggestion of a bipolar cycle of life and death. Here at *Siegfried*'s finale, we have come to the core of Wagner's theory of comedy. To make a joke or get a laugh was never enough for Wagner. He did want his audience to smile and occasionally to laugh—but only within the scope of larger ideological conflicts between good and evil, youth and old age, hate and love, naiveté and wisdom, life and death, and—between darkness and light. What we have here is bipolar comic relief.

Siegfried: **Hildegard Behrens as Brünnhilde.**

Götterdämmerung provides the culmination of the *Ring* in more than one way, including as it does the various comic elements and lighting effects already noticed in the other *Ring* operas. The prologue to the first act of this opera begins with the darkness before dawn, a lighting effect that Wagner is especially fond of because it enables him to suggest both darkness and imminent new light. The darkness is, of course, entirely suitable for the Norns scene, for they predict the destruction of the gods, but with the first glimmers of the new day we see the happy lovers Siegfried and Brünnhilde. The light of day returns the Norns to Mother Earth, for they remain most content in her slumbering darkness, but Siegfried and Brünnhilde, while singing their love music together, refer often to light. Dawn and light are here repeatedly connected with the couple's love, for, unlike Hagen and Alberich, they are the forebearers of a radiant new race.

Each of the three acts of this monumental opera preserves a unity of time, for each of them occurs during a single day—Wagner being careful to indicate the progression of the sun during every act. By the end of the prologue to *Götterdämmerung*, the sun rises and, as the action of the first act proceeds, the sun continues to climb in the sky. The lightning and thunder often associated with the gods' stormy existence dominate the stage briefly during the second scene of this act when Brünnhilde is visited by her Valkyrie sister Waltraute. In contrast to the dark unhappiness of the gods, Brünnhilde sings of the brightness of her love for Siegfried and tells her sister that she will never give up the token of that love, the ring. But by the end of this scene twilight has fallen and in the gathering darkness Siegfried comes to the rock and, transformed by the Tarnhelm into the shape of Gunther, captures Brünnhilde. We know by her speech that she does not recognize him. "Wer bist du, Schrecklicher? Stammst du von Menchen? Kommst du von Helias Nachichtem Heer?" ("Who are you, terrible creature? Are you a man? Do you spring from Hell's night-born race?") Thus Brünnhilde associates trickery, deceit, and evil with the dark powers of the night, while for her Siegfried remains a sun god. Yet across their happiness a fatal shadow has fallen and by the end of this first act of *Götterdämmerung* total darkness has enveloped the stage.

Act II of this opera, like the prologue of Act I, begins with the predawn darkness. In this murk Alberich appears before his son Hagen, reminding him of the rightness of his cause, the power of the ring, and, most of all, of his determination to possess the ring once again. The lack of bright lighting on stage is reflected in Alberich's language.

> die wir bekämpfen
> mit nachtigem Krieg
> schon gibt ihnen Not unser Neid.
>
> ---
>
> Those whom we fight
> with the forces of darkness
> already our envy gives them grief.

As the dawn approaches, Alberich must leave, warning his son to remain true to him. It is interesting how frequently Alberich repeats the phrase "Mein Sohn" ("My son"), implying that Hagen has a duty to his father. Alberich intends to use this duty, of course, to ensure his own ultimate possession of the ring and not out of any paternal affection. But with the dawn Siegfried returns, and the dawn motif takes on a significance that is similar to that of the nature motif, for light and nature are permanent elements that can survive the total destruction at the end of the opera.

The second act of this opera uses the very dramatic situation of a ruined wedding party, just as the second act of *Lohengrin* did. Brünnhilde cannot believe her eyes when she sees her husband Siegfried eagerly awaiting a marriage to Gutrune. As she expresses it, "Mir schwendet das Licht" ("I am losing the light"), for indeed the light has gone from her life. Siegfried's response to her charges is: "Gunther, dein Weibe is übel! Erwache, Frau! Hier steht dein Gatte." ("Gunther, your wife has become sick! Awake, lady! Here is your husband.") That Siegfried should awaken her to this sham marriage is an ironic reversal of his earlier action in awakening her during the last act of *Siegfried*. As the sun sets at the end of this act, the gathering darkness conceals Brünnhilde, Gunther, and Hagen, all plotting Siegfried's death. The trombones accompany Hagen's fatal blast as he calls for Siegfried's death, and henceforth the harsher qualities of the brass will be used more and more frequently as the opera moves ahead.

The final act of what has been called the greatest of Wagner's tragedies begins comically. The Rhinemaidens, foolish teases that they are, bewail the loss of their gold, but they do a lot of laughing as well. They begin the act by singing about the brightness of the sunlight and the sad lack of it in the murky depths of the Rhine since their gold was stolen.

> Frau Sonne
> sendet lichte Strahlen:
> Nacht liegt in der Tiefe:
> einst war sie hell,
> da heil und hehr
> des Vaters Gold noch in ihr Glänzte.
> Rheingold!
> klares Gold!
> wie hell du einstens strahltest,
> hehrer Stern der Tiefe!
>
> ———————————
>
> Lady Sun
> spread beams of light;
> in the depths it is night:

Götterdämmerung: Hildegarde Behrens as Brünnhilde, Siegfried Jerusalem as Siegfried.

> once it was bright there,
> when, safe and beautiful,
> our father's gold glittered there still.
> Rhinegold!
> Pure gold!
> How brightly once you did shine,
> resplendent star of the deep!

When Siegfried arrives, the girls immediately tease him cruelly with questions like

> Was schiltst du so in den Grund?
> ...
> Welchen Alben bist du gram?
> ...
> Hat dich ein Nicker geneckt?
> ———
> What are you grumbling about?
> ...
> What elf has annoyed you?
> ...
> Has a Nixie been fooling you?

The girls laugh at his inadequate attempts to answer all their absurd questions seriously, but then they ask for the return of their ring. Siegfried answers:

> Verzeht' ich an euch mein Gut,
> das zürnte mir wohl mein Weib.
> ———
> If I wasted my goods on you,
> my wife would be angry with me.

The Rhinemaidens quickly respond:

> Sie ist wohl schlimm?
> Sie schlägt dich wohl?
> Ihre Hand fühlt schon der Held!
> ———
> Is she bad-tempered?
> Does she beat you?
> The hero can feel her hand already!

Thus these teasing Rhinedaughters make fun of the great hero who is fearful of his wife, and they then go on to taunt him for being a miser.

Just when Siegfried seems most inclined to give them the ring, they explain the curse on it, linking the ring with darkness and death. They tell him that if he does not give them the ring he will die that night, but here Siegfried's pride and naiveté become painfully apparent. He insists that he is not afraid of their threats, just as he would not give in to their teasing. So they swim off humming their motif, sure that they will get their ring back by the end of the day. Their final comments become teasing once again as they call him a fool, laugh at him, and then swim away.

While Siegfried's refusal to be intimidated by these comic, silly girls is understandable, they remain nevertheless right about what is going to happen to him by the end of the day, and the comic relief early in the act is soon replaced by tragedy. Hagen arrives, and Siegfried shows himself to be generally witty and humorous. When he mixes a drink for himself in his horn, he spills some by accident and then says that it will bring refreshment to Mother Earth. When Hagen asks him if he can still understand the songs of birds, he responds, "Seit Frauen ich singe hörte, vergass ich der Voglein ganz." ("Since I heard women singing, I have quite forgotten the birds.") Suddenly, though, as the sun slowly sets in the background, Hagen plunges his spear into Siegfried's back. Significantly, Siegfried's dying words are not of revenge or betrayal; instead, he sings of the beautiful light that comes from Brünnhilde's loving eyes. As he dies, he affirms the beauty of love and light instead of the horrors of death, betrayal, and darkness.

In the second scene of the third act, set in the hall of the Gibichungs, Wagner dramatically portrays Gutrune's fears of her bad dreams and of the general darkness. Here she becomes an interesting contrast to Brünnhilde; while Gutrune has always been the passive female who is the puppet of the men around her (her brother Gunther and her half-brother Hagen), Brünnhilde initiates action. Wagner portrays the women as polar opposites. During this murky night, Hagen arrives and kills his half-brother, Gunther, but very quickly Brünnhilde assumes a dominant role, singing the famous immolation scene to bring the tetralogy to its glorious finale. As Carolyn Abbate has pointed out, "Brünnhilde is, then, at once a commanding prophetic voice and a unique listening ear. In her operatic form, both elements are greatly multiplied.... The commanding prophecy and the sibylline ear are finally brought together at the end of *Götterdämmerung*" (Abbate 215).

In the gloom, the flickering firelight brightens as Brünnhilde ignites Siegfried's funeral pyre. From the beginning of her oration, what she remembers most about Siegfried is his radiance. This is a funeral oration, but it remains a joyful one, which ends happily for her. As she sings before she leaps into the flames:

> Ihr zu umschlingen,
> umschlossen von ihm,
> in mächtigster Minne
> vermählt ihm zu sein!
> Hei-a-ja-jo! Grane!
> Grüss deinen Herren!
> Siegfried! Siegfried! Sieh!
> selig grüsst dich dien Weib!

> To clasp him to me,
> to be held in his arms,
> to be united with him
> through the power of love!
> Hei-a-yo-ho! Grane!
> Greet your lord!
> Siegfried! Siegfried! See!
> Your wife greets you joyfully.

Brünnhilde imagines herself joined again with her light-bearing hero, happy and safe in his arms. This is not tragedy, but comedy, for great evil has been purged from the world through her triumphant suicide. By the end of the opera, however, we are again engulfed in that fertile pre-dawn darkness with which the whole tetralogy opened. A new and better day will dawn, for the evil in this world has been purged and the green promise of new life has been preserved. Wagner has shown us the powers of evil and corruption, but his final scene in the *Ring* restores nature's purity and innocence through eroticized suicide—here of Brünnhilde and Wotan—but also a stark reminder of what we saw at the ends of *The Flying Dutchman* and *Tristan und Isolde*. This familiar operatic statement fulfills Wagner's sense of an appropriate end.

Hagen's final grab for the ring is unsuccessful, for the Rhinemaidens are on stage again to pull him down into the depths and to laugh, as they generally do, at his death from greed. They are happy because they have their ring back and the world has been saved—the green, sunny, and essentially innocent world that had been threatened for so long by evil and darkness. The redemption motif ends the opera with tones of fulfillment, restoration, and peace.

The enduring ring in this vast tetralogy becomes the ultimately victorious ring that the earth makes around the sun. The sun god is dead, but the radiant sun endures, implying that finally the *Ring* is a bipolar totality that includes cycles of both tragedy and comedy, both light and darkness, both mania and depression. This larger theme reflects Giambattista Vico's famous theories about the eternal cycles of nature and the possibility of the merged polarities which can govern our lives.

Götterdämmerung: Matti Salminen as Hagen.

Chapter 8

Parsifal: Beyond Polarity

Parsifal was the father of Lohengrin, and Wagner had been thinking about this father at least since *Lohengrin* was first staged in 1850. As a start, he wrote a prose sketch for *Parsifal* in 1857, and worked on the opera again in 1865 and 1877, when he completed the libretto. Also in 1877 he began composition of the score, which he finished in 1882 in time for the premiere of the work at Bayreuth in his own theater. By that date, he had been developing the idea for this, his final opera, for over thirty years. Wagner had the acoustics of his famous theater, which he himself designed, in mind when he wrote the music for *Parsifal*, a "sacred festival drama" he wanted performed only at Bayreuth. Also in 1880 Wagner wrote an important essay called "Religion and Art." The Metropolitan Opera caused a world-wide scandal by staging their own production outside Bayreuth—on Dec. 24, 1903—when the opera was still protected by European copyright laws. Once the European copyright expired on Dec. 31, 1913, other opera houses produced the opera, despite Wagner's wish that the opera be performed only at his theater at Bayreuth.

When he finished composing his *Parsifal*, Wagner was an old man, and not surprisingly the opera is certainly death-ridden. Wagner was sixty-nine years old when the opera was first performed, but he would not survive to reach his seventieth year. *Parsifal* had its premiere at Bayreuth on July 26, 1882, and Wagner died the following winter—on February 13, 1883—in Venice. In fact, a thematic yearning for death and for release from pain remains one of the most poignant and effective aspects of this complex work. Amfortas's wound, the wound that will never heal until the end of the opera thanks to Parsifal's retrieval of the magic spear, remains a haunting image for most of the audience. One of the reasons it is so haunting is that everybody has a wound that will not heal. We all have some psychological wound or scar which remains unhealed in our lives — at least according to Freud and other psychologists.

The plot reflects these themes of pain and death. Already in Act I Amfortas's father Titurel, though calling for the Grail and its salvation, lies in his coffin, and he is dead by Act III. When Titurel asks his son Amfortas to reveal the Grail in all its radiance, Amfortas responds:

> Wehe! Wehe mir der Qual!
> Mein Vater, oh!
> Noch einmal verrichte du das Amt!
> Lebe, leb' und lass mich sterben.
> ------
> Alas, alas for my pain!
> My father, oh!
> Once again perform this duty yourself!
> Live, live, and let me die!

The longing for death, and the suicidal impulse that is a logical extension of this longing, haunts this final and perhaps most moving of Wagner's operas. Was this tone the product of Wagner's disease-ridden final years when he was suffering from painful angina attacks and knew his heart could stop at any time? Was Wagner's suicidal depression the result of all the pain connected with a damaged heart, which Wagner had for the last five years of his life? Was the suicidal quality of this final opera the culmination of the suicidal impulses we had seen in Wagnerian opera since his first mature work, *The Flying Dutchman*? We have already noted that in his correspondence Wagner often showed himself to be suicidal in his own life, and this final opera tells us something more about the suicidal personality of the composer, as well as about the great pain of his final years.

Wagner, as we have seen, suffered from severe, suicidal depression. Of course, it is hardly unusual for depressives to be suicidal, so Wagner's concern with death can be understood in a larger context. In many ways the yearning for death also connects well with Christianity which has been called by many, including Friedrich Nietzsche, a death-ridden religion in which the aim of human life is seen as preparation for the afterlife. If one is convinced that the afterlife to come will include eternal bliss, certainly it makes sense as well to long for a speedy death to get to that wonderful afterlife. But Wagner remained throughout his life not a traditional Christian but a questioner and doubter.

Wagner once declared that the height of wisdom was learning to desire the inevitable. Is it then the height of wisdom to yearn for death, since that is the ultimately inevitability? On January 25, 1854, Wagner wrote to his old Dresden friend August Roeckel:

> Wotan rises to the tragic heights of *willing* his own destruction. This is all that we need to learn from the history of mankind: *to will what is necessary* and to bring it about ourselves. The final creative product of this supreme, self-destructive will is a *fearless* human being, one who never ceases to *love*" [Wagner, Selected Letters, 307].

Wotan, in his monologue in Act II of *Die Walküre*, expresses the suicidal thought of wishing for his own death. *Parsifal* also supports the validity of that same logic, and perhaps the source of that wisdom was Wagner's own experiences with suicidal depression—the dark half of the polar opposites he was forced to live with throughout his life.

In fact, the wound that will not heal certainly remains one of the central images in this complex but fascinating final work of Wagner's genius. Allied to this unyielding problem is a reawakened yearning for death, which we see again in this opera. Just as Wotan reaches the tragic and wise height of wishing for his own death, so that very wish permeates Wagner's final opera, *Parsifal*.

Almost as a signal, Kundry begins the opera with a complaint, and when she enters in the beginning of the second act she cries out. But in the third act, when she sings only four notes—"dienen, dienen" are the words—she finds some kind of peace in death. This is another one of Wagner's mysterious and unexplained deaths since the stage directions do not detail the cause of her sudden death. She seems happy and fulfilled at the end of this mysterious opera, though her peace comes only at the end of her life and in death. But by the end of the opera she has found peace and some kind of redemption.

Parsifal himself survives and he presents the Grail to all the knights at the end of the opera. His bringing together the Grail and the Spear in the Temple of the Grail seems to symbolize some sort of reunification and fulfillment, which the important characters in this opera clearly have been seeking.

Wagner described this work as a "stage dedication festival play" (Buhnenweihfestspiel). The fact that he takes a quasi-religious situation and presents it in a new kind of theater—that which he designed and had built at Bayreuth—suggests that he has invented a new kind of opera that is not really opera at all. I think that what Wagner was introducing was a new kind of religion, based on art, in this case, music-drama. Wagner was not a church-goer or a believer in any organized religion, and he sometimes claimed to be an atheist. What he was saying in this opera was that the opera house had become the modern temple for a new kind of religion, the religion of art. Here Wagner anticipates the wholesale rejection of standard organized religions that would occur in the twentieth century. Instead of a conventional God, Wagner argues that people should worship art and the arts of opera and music, especially his own operas, or music-dramas as he preferred to call them. Wagnerian egomania aside, the vision of art as a religion also had other adherents at the time, since fewer and fewer intellectuals and artists by the end of the nineteenth century found that they could believe in any organized religion, or indeed even in the existence of any god.

The opera house as religious substitute sounds grotesque and irreligious to a conventionally religious person, but for a modern agnostic or atheist, art can offer the kind of holy passion that religion used to be able to provide—but which it no longer offers many people. The idea of theatrical art as religion, however, is not uniquely modern; it points back to ancient Greece, where an altar to the Greek god Dionysos was kept onstage during dramatic performances. As Oscar Brockett described the origins of Greek Drama:

> The worship of Dionysus probably originated in the Near East and was later imported into Greece perhaps as early as the thirteenth century B.C.... The Greeks honored each of their gods through one or more annual festivals. In Attica, where Athens was the principal town, four festivals were held each year in honor of Dionysus, and it was at one of these—the City Dionysia—that drama was first presented [Brockett 18].

Brockett also points out that "music was an integral part of Greek drama. It accompanied the passages of recitative and was an inseparable part of the choral odes. Only rarely was it used apart from words, and then only for special effect" (Brockett 3). Here Brockett suggests that the performance of drama in ancient Greece would seem like opera to a modern audience because it had such a large musical component, especially when the music connected with the words the actors were speaking.

In terms of its text, *Parsifal* is one of the most rhymed and musical of Wagner's libretti, second only to *Die Meistersinger* in that respect. But while Wagner uses rhymes for most of the characters and the choruses in the opera, the quality of the poetical language is sharply different for Kundry's first lines:

> Hier! Nimm du! Balsam...
> ...
> Von wieter her als du denken kannst.

> Hilft der Balsam nicht,
> Arabia birgt
> dann nichts mehr zu seinem Heil.
> Fragt nicht weiter
> Ich bin müde.
>
> ---
>
> Here! Take this—balsam
> ...
> From further away than you can think.
> If the Balsam does not help
> then Arabia has
> nothing more to help him.—
> Ask no more.
> I am tired.

Notice that there is absolutely no rhyme in these lines. Also, Wagner does not use a regular line length; instead, the lengths of the lines vary. The lines seem to use basically iambic feet, but the meter often varies within the line (the remainder of the libretto is primarily in iambic tetrameter and pentameter). Perhaps Wagner wants here, in his final libretto, to use the language and poetry of normal conversation for Kundry, marking her character as different from the others on stage. In any case, her language sounds simple and direct in this most complex and symbolically suggestive of Wagner's operas.

Gurnemanz and the rest of the knights of the Grail are assigned a much more musical and rhymed verse. For example, in the following speech, we clearly see that Gurnemanz's language has extensive rhyming. Here Gurnemanz attempts to answer the young knights' questions about Titurel and Klingsor:

> Titurel, der fromme Held
> der kann't ihn wohl
> Denn ihm, da wilder Feinde List und Macht
> des reinen Glaubens Reich bedrohten,
> ihm neigten sich in heilig ernster Nacht
> deinst des Heilands selige Boten
> daraus der trank beim letzten Liebesmahle
> das Weihgefäss, die heilig edle Schale,
> darein am Kreuz sein göttlich Blut auch Floss
> dazu den Lanze Speer, der dies vergoss
> der Zeugengüter höchstes Wundergut
> das gaben sie in unsres Königs Hut.

Opposite: Parsifal: **Jon Vickers as Parsifal.**

> Titurel, the famous hero,
> knew him well.
> For him, when fierce foes' magic and might
> threatened the place of true faith,
> help arrived one holy night in the form of
> the holy vessel, the sacred Holy Cup
> from which He drank at the last love feast
> in which too His divine blood came from the Cross
> and with it the same Spear which caused the blood to flow,
> the supremely rich bounty of these holy witnesses
> came into our king's possession.

This is one of the most rhymed parts of Wagner's libretto for *Parsifal*, but even here the rhyme is not wholly regular, as it is in many passages from the more conservative *Meistersinger*. This marked irregularity of the rhymes makes their appearance seem all the more unusual, given the occasionally prose-like and conversational tone of this most unusual of Wagner's librettos.

Here in his final opera Wagner seems to be creating a new kind of conversational poetry for Kundry's lines. As a creative personality, Wagner could not do the same kind of opera over and over. Even in the librettos, each opera has a unique poetical style and a unique musical language, as many musicologists have observed. Wagner seems to be prefiguring in his text for Kundry the modern, conversational poetry of the twentieth century, when modern poets like E. E. Cummings and W. H. Auden would reject the meters and rhymes of traditional poetry—although traditional meter and rhyme does characterize the poetry of the rest of the characters in *Parsifal*. Clearly Wagner, in addition to music, made creative use of both language and poetical form to add to the uniqueness of this final opera. Yet aside from these novel contributions, other questions remain to be asked about *Parsifal*.

Does bipolar illness appear in this opera, as we have seen it in so many of the other operas? Certainly suicidal depression enters the opera, especially in the form of Amfortas's and Kundry's suffering and grief. The suffering caused by the wound that will not heal is a recurrent theme and image in this final opera, with the implication that death alone brings relief from suffering. In such a situation, is it not logical to kill oneself?

As Amfortas says in the final act of the opera as he gazes on the corpse of his father Titurel:

> Ja, Wehe! Wehe! Weh' über mich!
> So ruf ich willig mit euch.

Williger nahm' ich von euch den Tod,
Der Sünde milderste Sühne!
Mein Vater!
Hochgesegneter der Helden!
Du Reinster, dem einst die Engel sich neigten:
Der einzig ich sterben wollt,
dir—gab ich den Tod!
O der du jetzt in Göttlichem Glanz
den Erlöser selbst erschaust
erflehe von ihm das sein heliges Blut,
wenn noch einmal heut sein Segen
die Brüder soll erquicken,
wie ihnen neues Leben
mir endlich spende den Tod!
Tod! Sterben!
Einzige Gnade!
Die schreckliche Wunde, das Gift, ersterbe,
das es zernagt, erstarre das Herz!
Mein Vater! Dich ruf' ich,
rufe du ihm es zu:
Erlöser, gib meinem Sohne Ruh!

Ah, alas, alas, alas to me,
Thus I willingly weep with you.
Even more willing would I accept death from you,
the mildest atonement for sin.
My father!
Most holy of heroes!
More pure, to whom an angel bowed:
I, who alone longed to die,
to you brought death!
O you who is in holy radiance
do behold the redeemer's presence,
entreat of him that his holy blood,
if again today his holiness
will revive these my brethren,
as it gives them new life
may at least grant me only death!
Death! To die!
Sublime mercy!
Take from me the ugly wound, the poison,
And stop the heart it eats at.
My father! As I call you,
I beg you to ask him:
"Redeemer, give my son peace."

The peace that Amfortas is praying for is the peace of death. The longing for death, a suicidal longing certainly, remains clearly and repeatedly present in the character of Amfortas. His repeated pleas for death probably reflect Wagner's most profound and deepest depressions as he too longed for death, which seemed the only recourse for his suffering. Here in his final opera the suicidal mind is presented in perhaps its most painful and also its most beautiful form. The melodies and harmonies which accompany Amfortas's words quoted above reflect a new kind of musical beauty for Wagnerian opera.

Although the balsam that Kundry brings Amfortas in the first scene of the opera fails to relieve his pain and suffering, in the final scene Parsifal brings a balsam in the form of the reunited grail and spear, and this finally brings relief to Amfortas. So the opera ends with relief from suffering for Amfortas, the old suicidal sufferer. And within a year after the opera's premiere, Wagner would also experience relief from his suffering in his death in Venice. Clearly the depressive side of bipolar illness shows itself in this opera, but is there mania in the opera as well?

Certainly the appearance of the Flower Maidens and their happy, erotic music in the second act of *Parsifal* provides a form of mania and manic happiness for the opera, but with it comes the powerful Kundry, who seems to represent the spirit of Dionysus and all his sexual excesses. Just as the manic phase can lead to destruction, so too can Kundry, whose fatal kiss at the end of the act will bring destruction to the Grail brotherhood unless Parsifal resists it. Fortunately, he does resist it, so that we get a third act which brings greater happiness, fulfillment, and even redemption.

If the second act with its Magic Garden is the polar opposite of the first act's Temple of the Grail, the self-castrating villain Klingsor, himself once a Knight of the Grail, is the polar opposite of the wounded leader of the Grail Brotherhood, Amfortas. Here too the Manichean vision of the medieval world appears, with the powers of good and the powers of evil equally potent, acting always in opposition, polar opposites, with neither more powerful than the other. One can understand why the Catholic Church would dismiss this belief as a heresy, since it denies the omnipotence of God, but for Wagnerian opera Manicheanism provides a polarity of equally powerful but opposing sides, which Wagner found attractive because such an opposition reflected the structure of his own bipolar personality.

Part of that personality combined inherent sexuality with the figure of the mother, a combination which we have also seen in *The Flying Dutchman*, *Tristan und Isolde*, and the *Ring* cycle. Kundry in the second act provides Parsifal with the name he has lacked so far in this opera; she tells

Parsifal: **Placido Domingo as Parsifal.**

him his name, and who his father and mother were, often in the rhythms of a lullaby. As Kundry talks of his parents, she also introduces Parsifal to the idea of love:

    Die Liebe lerne kennen,
    Die Gamuret umschloss,

Als Herzeleid's Entbrennen
Ihn sengend überfloss!
Die Leib und Leben einst dir gegeben,
Der Tod und Torheit weichen muss,
Sie beut dir heut' als Muttersegens
letzten Gruss.
Der Liebe ersten Kuss!

Learn to recognize love
that surrounded Gamuret,
When Herzeleide's hot passion
embraced him!
She who gave you a body and a life,
And before whom death and folly must avoid,
She gives you today, as the last
farewell of a mother's blessing,
Love's first kiss!

The kiss Kundry offers in the name of Parsifal's mother is really an attempt to help Klingsor destroy him, and we have seen that often in Wagnerian opera sexuality remains connected with maternity. Perhaps it is significant that by the end of the act Parsifal has resisted this fatal kiss, captured Klingsor's spear, and destroyed his kingdom.

If Acts I and II are polar opposites, reconciliation becomes the goal of Act III—rather like Hegel's format of thesis, antithesis, and synthesis. Yet some critics have denied that the opera leads to reconciliation. For example, the critic John Gutman has argued that the opera *Parsifal* is really about racial purity, but there is no evidence for racial bias in the text or music of the opera. Gutman bases his argument on some articles on race that Wagner wrote which appeared in the *Bayreuther Blatter*, his house organ in Bayreuth. There is certainly no evidence for this in the text of this opera, but since some critics want to believe that all Wagner's operas are anti-Semitic so this view will always have its adherents. There certainly is a Grail Brotherhood in the opera, but the characters never talk about racism or anti-Semitism or even anti-Arab feelings. Instead, the main characters all describe a yearning for peace, enlightenment, reconciliation, and the end of pain.

But what, ultimately, is the meaning of *Parsifal*? Many critics of Wagner and opera in general have written about this topic, but what is one left with after viewing the last act, the last scene, in terms of the meaning of this highly symbolic and most enigmatic of Wagner's works?

One thing that remains different about this opera is its lack of the natural cycles we have found in so many of Wagner's earlier works. The stage directions of Act I do call for a daybreak, the dawn of a new day, but Wagner does not indicate when that day ends. Act II begins with Klingsor awakening Kundry, just as the last act of *Siegfried* began with Wotan awakening Erda, so the cycle of sleeping and waking occurs here. The stage directions for Act III say that the scene is set in the spring, in time for the Good Friday music and the Easter season, but Wagner's use of Vico's cycles of nature is fragmentary here, suggesting that the composer was searching for something beyond the entrapment of cyclical progressions. *Parsifal* represents a new desire to get beyond polarity and find some form of unifying oneness in life, some form of enlightenment.

Nietzsche felt that the meaning of *Parsifal* revolved around Wagner's return to Christianity and his obsession with death. Nietzsche also believed that the world needed a life-asserting and life-worshipping philosophy such as his own; it did not require Wagner's obsession with death. Of course Nietzsche's response may have been egocentric, but I think he was right on several levels.

Certainly one of the things Wagner does in this work is create a religious atmosphere. There are many religious words and references in the libretto: the grail, the cross, the spear, celestial voices in a temple, references to a redeemer, the Good Friday music, and the ending of the first and last acts in a Temple of the Grail. But despite the religious words and Christian referents, there is no Church in this "sacred dedication stage work." The opera is set in the early medieval period, when medieval Christianity contained a strangely pagan element. The Grail itself is never mentioned in any of the major Christian texts, like the New Testament, but instead exists in medieval stories and legends.

Certainly Christianity is referred to in this opera, but so is Manicheanism and Buddhist enlightenment. There remains, of course, a long tradition of religious works by composers, but these are works that premiered in a church—masses, motets, te deums, stabat maters, etc. They were generally commissioned by a cardinal or bishop for performance in a church, and though some of them are not generally performed there anymore—for example, the Verdi Requiem—the church was their original and intended setting. Wagner could have composed in one of these genres—he could have composed a mass, a te deum, a stabat mater, etc, but he did not. I think that he composed a religious work for a theater, specifically an opera house, suggests that he was not a believer in any organized religion and instead wanted a theater or opera house to become, on some level, a house of worship. If he could not believe in any recognized, organized religion, he could believe in art, especially opera (or music drama, as he would have preferred) as something of religious significance. This could be seen as Wagnerian egomania—the worship of Wagner through his music in the theater he designed (and the only place he wanted *Parsifal* performed). But on a more critical level, *Parsifal*'s religious atmosphere implies that Wagner is suggesting that art is ultimately what many people can believe in—that the audience can experience the greatest spirituality in the theater rather than in a house of worship of any religion.

The ending of *Parsifal* also suggests the reconciliation of opposites, for in the final scene spear and cup are finally reunited. So what do spear and cup symbolize? On a purely Christian level, they are the spear that Christ was attacked with and the cup that held his blood as well as the cup which he last drank from, but is this opera really about Christianity? Some have seen the ending of the opera as a parody of the Catholic mass—containing not the Eucharist but only the external symbols of Christ's suffering. The ending reflects the often comic medieval obsession with relics. Venetians stole the bones of St. Mark from Alexandria, for example, to enhance the religious power of their own city, yet the comic contradiction here is hardly part of the world of *Parsifal*. We have already discussed the belief of medieval Manicheanism in the limited power of God. The early medieval period in particular contained the strange combination of Christianity with other non-Christian religions. Wagner used this very medieval mixture in his *Tannhäuser*, which includes both St. Elisabeth and the Roman goddess Venus.

Wagner was not a church-goer and often made anti-Christian and especially anti-Catholic and anti-Jesuit comments—often more virulent than his notorious anti-Semitic comments. Is *Parsifal* representative of Wagner's desire to believe in Christianity or Catholicism even though he could not? Well, maybe, but I doubt it. On a symbolic level, then, the connection of spear and cup seems to symbolize and to suggest much more than Christian belief. The process of the reconciliation of opposites remains a central symbol of the final scene of *Parsifal*. The opera moves from sickness in Act I (the wounded Amfortas) to health in Act III (the finally healed Amfortas). This movement beyond a sick polarity to a healthy unity is symbolized by the reunion of spear and cup. But what do each of them represent?

On a Freudian level, they clearly represent male and female, making the ending of the opera a kind of fertility rite. Certainly the phallic spear easily symbolizes the male principle while the cup easily suggests the female. Could the ending of *Parsifal* symbolize that the unity of male and female creates the fertility which will continue human life on earth, even though individual lives end? By the end of the opera Titurel is dead (in fact his coffin is on stage), and the young Parsifal has become a kind of sun god—a symbol of human fertility, which sustains human life on

Parsifal: Placido Domingo as Parsifal, Jessye Norman as Kundry.

earth. Or does the combination of male and female symbols suggests a kind of androgynous unity, accepting both the male and female parts of our complex personalities? Is Wagner suggesting here that psychic health and individual enlightenment comes with our accepting both the male and female parts of our total personalities?

Wagner was certainly very interested in Nietzsche's theories of the Apollonian and Dionysian principles in art. The spear could also be seen as a symbol of the lyre of Apollo, and the cup could be seen as a symbol of the wine cup of the god Dionysus. Is the combination of spear and cup, in the Nietzschean sense, a suggestion that the greatest art combines both the formalistic, structural principles of Apollonian art with the emotional, sexual principles of Dionysian art? Is the ending of *Parsifal* a statement of Wagner's desire to connect the two Nietzschean polarities in art and create a unified and greater art? Or can the spear symbolize the active, aggressive life and the cup the passive life? Apollo was also the sun god in Greek mythology, while Bacchus remained connected with darkness; so the combination of this symbolism could suggest a totality beyond the natural cycle of light and dark.

Or do the spear and cup symbolize the yin and yang of Buddhism? Two parts of a unified totality, yin and yang symbolize the female and male principles, the passive and the active principle, Kundry and the wounded Amfortas, depression and mania. Buddhism insists that the Western refusal to see beyond such opposing dualities (good vs. evil, male vs. female, active vs. passive) is naive. There is a greater reality which connects these two apparently opposing forces. The material forces and the spiritual forces are not ultimately in opposition in the Buddhist mind; they form parts of a totality which includes them both. With spear and cup united on the altar of the temple of the Grail in the final scene of *Parsifal*, a healthy unity has been achieved. Duality, especially opposing polar forces, which is a typically Western way of looking at the world, gives way to the greater wisdom of the East. The enlightened one, Buddha or Parsifal, once the young fool who is no longer a fool, combines opposing forces to create the unity and the peace we are all looking for.

On a more personal level, do the cup and spear symbolize the warring manic and depressive halves of Wagner's own bipolar personality? Does the combining of cup and spear at the end of the opera suggest on some level that Wagner desires the healthy, unified personality which can include both his depressive and manic halves? Perhaps the unified whole represents Wagner's hope for a balsam, a medicine, which could heal his own bipolar suffering? Kundy enters in Act I with a healing balsam from the East that fails to heal Amfortas, but Parsifal brings a magical spear which, when joined with the grail cup, does heal him. Can this unity suggest that Wagner yearned for a medicine, a lithium or lithium equivalent (which of course did not exist in the 19th century), something that could "unify" his bipolar suffering and end his pain?

This unity is something we can all desire, since the manic-depressive, bipolar personality is an extreme version of what we all are experiencing. There is an optimistic and a pessimistic side to us all, a manic and depressive side to us all. The manic-depressive, bipolar patient experiences in extreme the up and down cycles that we all experience in life. We all yearn for a peaceful harmony in our lives, a unity which can connect our warring opposites, transcend bipolarity, and even connect us to some peace or even a higher Buddhistic understanding. Schopenhauer described the world as will and idea, eternally divided and in opposition to itself. Freud wrote of the conflicts between super-ego and id, the idealistic part of us and the demanding, realistic, physical parts. If the end of this bipolarity, this dualism, is not God, then certainly it is a "peace which passeth understanding," a peace which can bring some unifying harmony to our lives. That seems to be the peace which emerges with the appearance of Parsifal and the retrieved spear to join with the grail in the final scene of the opera.

Is the connection of cup and spear a symbol of the death which we must all ultimately experience, and which Wagner would experience within a year of the premiere of his final opera? Does the ending of *Parsifal* suggest a yearning for the death which can end all our pain and suffering? The ultimate ending of all our suffering is, of course, death, and Wagner once said that the greatest wisdom was to desire the inevitable. Does that suggest that to be suicidal is the greatest wisdom, for our inevitable ending is death? The ending of *Parsifal* does not seem to suggest any belief in an afterlife. We do not see the soul of Titurel or Kundry ascending into heaven—as we see the souls of the Dutchman and Senta ascending into heaven at the end of *The Flying Dutchman*. Perhaps the peace of death and the comforts of great art remain all that we can hope for—and perhaps this is what Wagner is suggesting.

The final lines of *Parsifal* are:

> Höchsten Heiles Wunder!
> Erlösung dem Erlöser!
>
> ---
>
> Healing's highest wonder!
> Redemption for the Redeemer!

But who is that redeemer? Is it Parsifal, the young fool who has become wise through his own suffering? Is it Amfortas, the sick leader of the Grail Brotherhood who is now finally well again? Is it Christ, who died on the cross for us? Is it the Old Testament God, who can offer us death and an afterlife through our children? Is it Buddha, who can offer us a peace which can harmonize the warring oppositions in us? Or is it the unity that comes from the successful and great work of art, and is the pleasure of that unity and that harmony all we can hope for in this life?

Obviously, the ending of the opera is full of possible meanings, and it is to Wagner's credit that the opera suggests so much. One of the reasons *Parsifal* remains such a fascinating work is that we can never be sure what the ending finally means. The greatest artists realize that a work that is eternally ambiguous and symbolic is ultimately more interesting than a work one can easily comprehend. To understand the opera completely would lead to boredom, while to be eternally curious about what the opera really means makes it eternally fascinating for the viewer. Certainly Wagner knew how to fascinate his audience, which is why *Parsifal*'s complexities remain more suggestive than definitive, more alluringly vague than clear.

The opera also suggests a kind of monastic rejection of the material world, in favor of a holier spirituality, yet here again, Wagner symbolizes and suggests but does not state clearly. He wants to give us something to think about, not something to understand completely and then reject. Wagner's ambiguity also provides directors and designers with many possible approaches for their productions. To be curious but confused, to be interested yet still bewildered, has much to offer composers, theatrical designers, and audiences. But much does remain clear in this final opera of Wagner's, since it does move from sickness to health and from bipolarity to some form of enlightened unity.

Does this work suggest rebirth on any level? Clearly there is no real promise of an afterlife here, but there is a sign of rebirth in its suggestion of a renewed life through health and unity. The opera begins with sickness and duality and ends with unity and health. Parsifal offers Amfortas and the Grail Knights a rebirth not in terms of eternal life but in terms of an enlarged awareness and a renewed enlightenment, rather like what Buddha, the enlightened one, offers to us. This is not Christian rebirth, nor is it racial rebirth. The experiences of the Grail Brotherhood, through the intervention of Parsifal, offers rebirth to all, not just to its members. Perhaps the polar opposites of mania and depression can peacefully coexist in some human condition that encompasses their fierce polarity. Wagner's final opera, *Parsifal*, clearly takes us on a search for exactly that condition.

Chapter 9

Suicide in Opera and Drama

Though suicide has generally been a forbidden topic in the Judeo-Christian tradition, it often appears in theater and as opera. Looking at spoken theater first, certainly suicide occurs in the ancient Greek tradition of theater. Greek tragedy contains a few suicides, specifically the suicide of Haemon, Antigone's lover, in Sophocles' *Antigone*. In *Oedipus Rex* Oedipus's wife Jocasta commits suicide, followed by Oedipus's self-destructive behavior of gouging out his eyes at the end of play. Euripides' *Hippolytus* includes the suicide of Phaedra, the wife of Theseus, whose son Hippolytus she has fallen in love with. In Roman theater, the tragedies of Seneca also include some suicides since his plots often reflect the plots of Greek tragedy. Seneca's tragedies are usually bloodier than the Greek tragedies—for example, in Seneca's *Oedipus* Jocasta's suicide results from her ripping open her womb. The English Renaissance dramatists were greatly influenced by Seneca, and his themes of bloodshed and revenge reappear with great frequency in English tragedies of the Elizabethan and Jacobean periods.

In Shakespeare, suicide also appears on stage, though it is not a frequent occurrence. Suicides occur in the following Shakespearean plays: *Othello, Romeo and Juliet, Julius Caesar, King Lear,* and *Antony and Cleopatra*. Brutus as well as Cassius prove their Roman nobility by committing suicide rather than submitting to the conquering armies of Antony and Octavius. Romeo and Juliet, on the other hand, are portrayed as childlike victims of their families' murderous conflicts, and their suicides seem more like accidents of fate—Shakespeare's proverbial "star-crossed lovers." Othello's suicide adds to his nobility of character since we could not image the play's final scene with Othello being dragged off to prison by order of the Venetian delegation. Hamlet considers suicide, especially in his soliloquy "To Be or Not To Be," and often his behavior seems suicidal as he constantly ignores the royal orders of his uncle. But ultimately he is murdered by Laertes' poisoned sword.

One of King Lear's daughters, Goneril, commits suicide when she can not marry Edmund, Gloucester's bastard son. Gloucester himself attempts suicide by the end of the play but is prevented from doing so by his son Edgar. Cleopatra also commits suicide at the end of *Antony and Cleopatra* to avoid being carried to Rome and paraded as a war trophy. Even before her death, Antony commits suicide by falling on his sword after his defeat at the battle of Actium. Shakespeare often connected suicide with Roman nobility and stoicism, a logical connection given all the suicides in ancient Roman history and in Seneca's tragedies. But in *King Lear* the suicide and suicide attempt reflect the generally bitter tone of one of the last of Shakespeare's greatest tragedies.

There are suggested suicides in several of Shakespeare's plays, though the texts are not absolutely definite on the topic. The deaths of Lady Macbeth and Ophelia seem to have been suicides. In *Timon of Athens*, Timon's death also seems to have been suicide—he was certainly bitter enough by the end of this dark play to do such a deed.

The French classical tragedy of the 17th century includes many suicides in the plays of both Corneille and Racine. The most famous certainly remains Racine's *Phèdre*, this play ending in the suicide of the infamous Queen Phedra. But French classical tragedy includes many suicides despite the fact that France was a Catholic country and the Church considered suicide a grave sin.

In the 19th century spoken theater, suicide often occurs. One thinks immediately of Hedda Gabler's dramatic suicide at the end of Ibsen's *Hedda Gabler*. Hedda's suicide becomes her way of escaping the entrapment of her life; all her earlier attempts at asserting her control have only resulted in her own defeat. Suicides certainly are threatened and occur in the plays of Chekhov. His Uncle Vanya considers suicide, and a suicide of the son of the main female character ends Chekhov's *The Seagull*. Several characters in *The Cherry Orchard* also discuss the possibility of suicide, though none does such a thing.

In the 20th century Samuel Beckett's characters frequently discuss the possibility of voluntarily leaving the sad world of his plays. In *Waiting for Godot* both Vladimir and Estragon (the main characters) mention the possibility of killing themselves, though neither do this since they are afraid of being left alone and without each other's company. But Beckett's generally bleak vision of human existence often suggests that the really intelligent people commit suicide.

On the operatic stage suicides also occur. The theme of "Dido Abbandonata," and her subsequent suicide, occurs in several concert arias—Haydn did a famous version of this scene. The great librettist Metastasio did a libretto of *Didone Abbandonata*, and many composers used this text for their music, among them Albinoni, Porpora, Galuppi, Hasse, Jomelli, Paer, Piccini, and Paisiello. The source of the story is Vergil's *Aeneid*, where the wandering Aeneas, after being forced to leave his native Troy after the loss of the Trojan War, wanders to North Africa, where he falls in love with Queen Dido, whom he abandons for the more pious duty of founding Rome. Queen Dido commits suicide as a result of his departure, one of the most famous deaths in classical literature. Berlioz uses the suicide of Dido in his *Les Troyens* to serve as the ending of Act III—providing a parallel to the joint suicides of Trojan women (as Troy is about to fall to the Greeks) which provides the finale of Act I of that massive opera. Also in French opera, Lakmé commits suicide by eating a poisonous leaf in Delibes' *Lakmé*. In Baroque French opera, Rameau's *Hippolyte et Aricie* includes the suicide of the incestuous stepmother Phedre—as in Racine's earlier version of the story, *Phèdre*.

Bellini's Norma in his opera *Norma* seems suicidal in much of her behavior—continuing her obsession with Pollione despite being a celibate priestess of the Druids and considering even the murder of her own children. At the end, in the final scene of the opera, when Norma is sentenced to death by fire, Pollione voluntarily joins her in death—so that both his suicidal death and the immolation scene at the end of the opera prefigure Brünnhilde's behavior at the funeral of Siegfried at the end of Wagner's *Götterdämmerung*.

Also in the 19th century, Gaetano Donizetti's operas became famous for their mad scenes—especially in *Lucia di Lammermoor* and *Anna Bolena*. The act of suicide does not appear in these operas, though the heroines all die, and Donizetti himself eventually went insane and died in a madhouse in his native Bergamo.

One of the most famous arias in opera, "Suicidio!" from Ponchielli's *La Gioconda*, dramatically reflects the suicidal thoughts of the central character, the ironically named La Gioconda, the Happy One. After the death of her mother and feeling the desperation of her situation in Venice, La Gioconda does seriously consider suicide in this aria, and she acts to end her life just before the opera concludes, when the villain Barnaba attempts to rape her.

In opera, suicide is not a constant event, but it recurs often enough to remain a familiar possibility. Of the five great opera composers, only Wagner, Verdi, and Puccini frequently use the dramatic situation of a suicide—Mozart and Strauss rarely. Certainly Wagner most frequently employs this dramatic situation since there are suicides in *The Flying Dutchman, Tannhäuser, Tristan und Isolde* especially, and the *Ring* cycle, plus the suicidal behavior of Klingsor in *Parsifal*, when he castrates himself. After Wagner, the composer that most frequently dramatizes the situation of suicide is certainly Puccini.

Puccini generates the situation of suicide often in his operas—Madama Butterfly commits suicide in the last act of that opera through the Japanese ritual of harakiri. Tosca commits suicide by throwing herself over the parapet of Castel Sant'Angelo at the end of the third act. Suor Angelica, distraught over the death of her child (as related to her in brutal detail by her aunt), commits suicide by poisoning at the end of *Suor Angelica*. In *Gianni Schicchi* Lauretta's famous aria, "O mio babbino caro" includes a threat of suicide if her father does not help her to marry Rinuccio. Puccini's only operetta, *La Rondine*, ends with Magda leaving her lover, but Puccini did write a version in which she ends the opera by committing suicide, though this ending is rarely used. Liu in *Turandot* commits suicide in the third act of that opera rather than telling Turandot the identity of the unknown prince. Overall, there is substantial evidence that Puccini, like Wagner, suffered from severe depressions, and both composers often include suicides in their operas. Friends often told Puccini that he had a "povera faccia," or sad face, indicative of the depression which saddened much of his life. Perhaps this very depression is what drove him to his many sexual escapades, which his wife Elvira could never overlook. Forbidden sexual activity seems to have been one way of dealing with his chronic depressions and his own suicidal thoughts.

Mozart, on the other hand, rarely uses suicide, though you could argue that Don Giovanni's defiant behavior to the Commendatore at the end of *Don Giovanni* seems very suicidal. Don Giovanni defies the Stone Guest and refuses to repent even as he is being dragged down to hell. In the last act of *Die Zauberflöte* Papageno considers hanging himself because of his many sources of grief, especially his lack of a wife, but the three wise little geni stop him just in time and present him with a Papagena. Even before this incident, Pamina herself also contemplates suicide when she fears that Prince Tamino is going to abandon her, but here too the three wise little geni prevent her from harming herself. These are the only incidents of suicidal behavior in the Mozart operas, and even here both couples—Prince Tamino and Pamina and Papageno and Papagena—celebrate at the end of the opera.

Earlier than Mozart, in the 17th and 18th centuries, Monteverdi and Handel did occasionally use suicide. It is a topic in Monteverdi's *L'incornanazione del Poppea*, when Seneca talks of the pleasures of suicide, and Poppea certainly encourages him to commit suicide since he does not approve of her or of Nerone's obsession with her. Here too, suicide is connected with ancient Roman culture, the tragedies of Seneca, and Roman stoicism. These concerns were pre–Christian, of course, so such behavior could be displayed on stage despite local censorship.

In Verdi, suicide does occur as well, though here suicide seems a character's response to an extreme situation or the result of Verdi's desire for a dramatic ending to a scene or act, and suicide can certainly create a dramatic ending to an opera. Unlike Wagner's figures, here the characters who commit suicide rarely seem innately suicidal. In *Nabucco* Abaigaille poisons herself at the end of the opera because of the failure of her plots. In *Ernani* the main character commits suicide in the final scene because of the necessities of the plot rather than because of his own compulsive personality. Leonora commits suicide at the end of *Il Trovatore* rather than love a man she is being forced to marry. In *La Forza del Destino*, the tenor Carlo also ends as a suicide in the final scene, but in response to the death of his beloved Leonora. In *Don Carlo*, Don Carlo's behavior in repeatedly defying his father the king certainly seems suicidal, though it is his friend Posa who ends up being killed. By the final scene of that opera, Elisabetta yearns only for "la pace del avel" (the peace of the grave), which seems suicidal. Aida commits suicide by joining Radames in his tomb as it is about to be sealed in the final scene of that opera, but Aida had not appeared suicidal before the trial and sentencing of her lover Radames.

In *Rigoletto*, Gilda's behavior in the last act seems very suicidal, when she enters Sparafucile's inn knowing full well that the assassin will kill the next person who enters. In offering her life for that of her faithless lover the Duke, she seems to become a parody of the good Christian—offering herself for the sake of another. Verdi's Otello, like Shakespeare's Othello and Rossini's Otello, commits suicide because of his grief over his murder of his chaste wife Desdemona, whom he has falsely accused of adultery with Cassio. Suicide obviously became fashionable on stage in the nineteenth century, despite the state censorship of the period, in part because of the recurrence of the topic in the then fashionable style of Romanticism. But as we have seen, even before Romanticism, suicide appeared frequently onstage during the periods of the English Renaissance and French classicism.

In Strauss too there is some suicide, but not much. Salome's defiant behavior toward King Herod seems suicidal and does result in her death at the end of the opera. One of Strauss's most depressed and death-obsessed characters, though she never actually commits suicide, remains his Ariadne in *Ariadne auf Naxos*. She is waiting for Theseus to return to her in Act II of the opera, and once she becomes convinced that he has abandoned her, she longs for death. Her great aria in that opera, "Es Gibt ein Reich, Todesland," indicates the suicidal quality of her desire for death. She feels that since Theseus has abandoned her, she should commit suicide, though Zerbinetta predicts that the arrival of a new god would pique her interest in life, which of course is precisely what happens when the god Bacchus appears toward the middle of the last act of that opera.

Also in the twentieth century, Shostakovich's *Lady Macbeth of Mtsensk* ends with the suicide of the central character while she is living in Siberia. Benjamin Britten's operas also include numerous suicides. Peter Grimes commits suicide at the end of the opera *Peter Grimes*, to the relative indifference of his fellow townsfolk. In one of the most harrowing of scenes in the last act of this opera, Captain Balstrode suggests that Peter Grimes's best option is to drown himself, and he does precisely this. Some have argued that this opera is really about pedophilia, and Peter Grimes's involvement with the deaths of his boy apprentices may be symbolic of Britten's own pedophilia. Certainly Gustave von Aschenbach's behavior in *Death in Venice* seems suicidal, since he remains in Venice even after he has been warned that the plague has come to the city; in both Mann's novella and Britten's opera based on it the central character's behavior certainly seems suicidal. And both Peter Grimes's fate and Gustave von Aschenbach's fate remain connected with obsessions with boys. Britten's earlier opera, *The Rape of Lucrece*, ends with Lucrece's suicide after she has been raped by Tarquinius.

It is interesting that, despite the taboo on suicide in Western religions, suicide is often used to ennoble a character, as for example Othello. His suicide in Shakespeare's play is treated in a way sympathetic to many in the East (particularly Japan), who view suicide as a means of preserving one's honor. As Madama Butterfly's sword says in the first act of Puccini's opera, "death with honor to the person who cannot live with honor." For instance, Brutus's suicide in Shakespeare's *Julius Caesar* adds largely to his honor and nobility as a Roman. His act is well understood in Asia, as well as in the West.

Why do opera composers put suicide on stage so often? In the case of Wagner and Puccini, it was undoubtedly because they themselves often thought about ending their own lives in such a way. Their suicidal fantasies provided an important part of their creativity. In the case of Verdi and some of the other composers and dramatists, suicide was used as a very theatrically effective way to end an opera. Unlike Wagner's Tristan or Puccini's Cio Cio San, Verdi's characters don't mention suicide in the first act, even though they might commit suicide in the final act. These and other opera composers put suicide on stage because they sensed that the public was captivated by the topic. Even though most people will not admit that they find suicide fascinating, clearly audiences are attracted to operas that contain suicide, though only if the right composer is doing the composing. The act of suicide certainly captures the attention of most audiences, even if they themselves are not suicidal. The possibility of voluntarily ending one's own life has been thought about by most people at some points in their lives, so seeing such an act on stage becomes strangely absorbing to them. A common human fantasy, probably an escape fantasy for most people, suicide recurs in the history of both spoken theater and opera in the West despite the strictures of both Church and State. Both great dramatists and great opera composers sensed that the act of self-destruction and even the mere thought of suicide remained forceful and dramatic ways to capture an audience's attention. These dramatists and composers also realized that the Christian taboo on suicide was not shared by the rest of the world, and ancient Roman and Far Eastern views of suicide were often used to contrast with the Christian view of this final act of self-destruction.

Chapter 10

Wagner, the Decadents, and the Modern British Novel

Given all the depression and suicidal ideation in Wagner's life, it is amazing that he lived almost seventy years. Both his correspondence and his operas frequently indicate he regarded suicide as the best of options, both for himself and for his operatic characters. That he lived to an old age indicates that he must have had tremendous resilience, though his misapplication of his many medications in the last few months of his life may indicate suicidal intentions on his part at the end, when he knew that his death was approaching. The panic and pain caused by the frequent heart attacks he experienced late in his life must have made his final weeks particularly stressful, when he frequently called for death to come to him and end his suffering. Finally, he may have hastened that end by his own misuse of the drugs prescribed by his doctor. For a figure of such obvious fame, however, death did not bring an end to renown.

As Wagner lay dead in Venice in February of 1883, his influence continued especially strongly in literature all over Europe. Today, he is generally credited as the founder of the Decadent movement in European literature, which reached a high tide of popularity in the 1880s, 1890s, and around the turn of the century, although it continued to exert its influence well into the middle of the twentieth century, and even afterwards. Wagnerian allusions and Wagnerian themes often occur in Decadent literature, especially the themes of death and suicide. A group of European writers at the time saw Wagner as the avant-garde artist who led by pointing to the inevitability of suicide, and they saw to it that his theme appeared often in their writings.

10—Wagner, the Decadents, and the Modern British Novel

At the time Wagner died his works had not entered the standard repertory of any English or American opera house. Already, in an effort to raise funds for Bayreuth, Wagner himself went to London in the spring of 1877, where he conducted a series of eight concerts. Although they failed to make much money for the Bayreuth enterprise, these concerts proved to be critically successful since they earned serious attention and widespread approval among the artistic avant-garde. While Wagner was in London he met George Eliot, her companion George Lewes, and Robert Browning, among other important writers. One of the first results of this attraction between intellectuals and artists and Wagner's operas was the appearance in 1881 of the first book on Wagner in English, Francis Hueffer's *Richard Wagner*. Hueffer, Ford Madox Ford's father, had already left his native Germany, but he remained an ardent Wagnerian all his life and usually summered in Bayreuth, often attending performances there. In addition to writing the pioneering book on the composer in English, he started a periodical entitled, appropriately, *Die Meister*. The journal became popular among many avant-garde writers and musicians and it served to further the cause of Wagner's music throughout Europe and America. In May of 1882 Angelo Neumann staged the entire *Ring* in London, where it proved a popular success.

Even English royalty helped the Wagnerian cause, as noted by Ernest Newman:

> Neumann was very successful with this first production of the *Ring* in London. Thanks to an introduction from the German Crown Prince he managed to get the Prince of Wales (afterwards King Edward VII) to attend no fewer than eleven of the performances. The Prince had been so charmed by the swimming Rhine Maidens that at one performance of the *Rhinegold* he went behind the scenes and expressed a desire to see the apparatus at work; but when he discovered that the occupant of the car was not to be the pretty young Augusta Kraus but one of the male stage hands he turned away with an impatient "What the devil!" [Newman, IV, 673].

With the Prince of Wales' help, then, by 1882 London had seen on stage all the standard Wagnerian operas except for *Parsifal*, which Wagner wanted performed only at his new theater at Bayreuth. With performances available in London and advocates like Francis Hueffer, the operas were becoming popular in England by the end of the nineteenth century.

As the '90s became increasingly Wagnerian in their musical taste, this influence began to show itself in many of the arts in Britain, and in the increasing volume of critical appreciation of the German composer.

In 1898 George Bernard Shaw wrote *The Perfect Wagnerite*, which summarized the complicated plot of the *Ring* and provided a Fabian socialist interpretation that remains today generally sound. Shaw saw the *Ring* as a parable about the corrupting power of money—which causes a loss of both love and life for many of the people who lust after it. Most critics since Shaw have used this basically Marxist interpretation, although changing some of its elements and eliminating most of Shaw's socialist doctrines.

During the Edwardian period in particular, Wagnerian themes appeared in the short stories and novels of some major British writers. Joseph Conrad's first novel, *Almayer's Folly* (1895), includes references to Wagnerian opera and ends with an Immolation scene that imitates the German composer's work. Conrad's story "Freya of the Seven Isles" (1912) also includes allusions to *Tristan und Isolde* and ends with the death of both young lovers. In *Chance* (1913) Conrad uses patterns of imagery and characterization from Wagner's *Der Fliegende Holländer*, and water imagery pervades this novel, as it does the opera.

With *Victory* (1915) Conrad also used Wagnerian patterns to help create a suggestively operatic atmosphere, ending again with the death and suicide of the two lovers. Conrad mentioned his indebtedness to Wagner and Wagner's interest in suicide as the best alternative to some of life's very difficult situations, situations which appear in many of Conrad's tragic novels. Wagner's operas provided Conrad with many examples of the union of music and myth, and thereby helped him to give his own fiction what he called "the magic suggestiveness of music."—especially music from Wagnerian opera.

D. H. Lawrence's early novel *The Trespasser* (1912) has a major character called Siegmund who often quotes Wagnerian opera and who ends the novel by killing himself as a result of a love affair gone wrong. Lawrence's greater novel *Women in Love* (1916) includes even more Wagnerian allusions and ends with the suicide of one of the major characters, Gerald Crich. Lawrence clearly went through an early phase of what can be called Wagnerian decadence, and he used this influence in his writing. Early in his career Lawrence wrote to his friend Blanche Jennings: "I love music. I have been to two or three fine orchestral concerts here [London]. At one I heard Grieg's 'Peer Gynt'—it is very fascinating, if not profound. Surely you know Wagner's operas—*Tannhäuser* and *Lohengrin*. They will run a knowledge of music into your blood better than any criticism" (Lawrence 41). Here too and in a very direct way Lawrence indicates his indebtedness to music and especially Wagnerian opera. Many of these earlier novels by Lawrence included love, love not reciprocated, and subsequent

10—Wagner, the Decadents, and the Modern British Novel 175

suicide, and he indicated that he absorbed many of these provocative themes from Wagnerian opera and its own uses of love and suicide.

Wagnerian patterns also exist in all of James Joyce's major works, and Joyce often combined his use of Wagner with his use of Giambattista Vico, having learned about Vico's cycles primarily through Wagnerian opera. While the mature Joyce was not very affected by Wagner's music, he always remained interested in the operas as mythic dramas. His fiction indicates an increasing use of Wagnerian patterns for a variety of artistic effects. In "A Painful Case" from *Dubliners* Joyce first used Wagnerian material, *Tristan und Isolde*. The references to the opera in that story comment ironically on the sterility of Mr. Duffy and his cautious refusal of Mrs. Sinico's offer of love, and in that story alcohol becomes the magic potion which the lovers drink. In *A Portrait of the Artist as a Young Man* Joyce uses the forest-bird motif from *Siegfried* and uses the musical motif thematically in the novel. Stephen's ash plant in that novel is a reference to Wagner's Wotan and the spear he carries, and thereby dramatizes Stephen's pretentious desire for power and authority. Also, in *Portrait*, the fourth chapter ends with a vision of woman and water, which is the first of an important series of such allusions in Joyce's fiction.

In *Ulysses* the ash plant cane that Stephen carries has Wagnerian overtones, but they are used in a more complex way. In addition to references to Wotan's spear, as in *Portrait*, a new pattern of allusions to Siegmund's and Siegfried's sword Nothung also appears. They suggest Stephen's desire for a means of defense to assert his own generation and his own sexuality; the sword is a phallic symbol of his young manhood. The fact that the ash plant refers to both Wotan's spear and Siegfried's sword helps Joyce imply the novel's generational conflict is cyclical rather than progressive—as in Vico. *Ulysses* also employs the symbolical combination of water and the female principle: in Stephen's vision of his mother as the sea, in the Rhinemaiden allusions in the Sirens chapter of the novel, and finally in the water imagery in Molly Bloom's final soliloquy. Joyce shared Wagner's redemptive view of woman; the symbolical connection of woman with the fertility of water exemplifies this. Also in *Ulysses*, a pattern of allusions to *Der Fliegende Holländer* provides the novel with a counterpart of Homer's *Odyssey* myth. These allusions help Joyce to characterize Bloom's sympathy with the sufferings of the ordinary man.

Finally, in *Finnegans Wake*, the symbolic combination of water with the female principle and redemption figures prominently. Wagner's *Tristan und Isolde* provides a mythic body of allusions in *Wake* and helps Joyce to structure the novel and parody the Tristan myth. But in the process his characters, by their connection with the characters in the opera, have become more mythic. This is especially true of "Mildew Lisa," a name used for HCE's daughter. The Wagnerian pun involved is comic, a pun on the first line of the Liebestod ("Mild und Leise"), but it also reminds the reader of the cycle of love, death, and rebirth.

Finnegans Wake contains many other puns on Wagner's life, theater, and titles that cleverly parody Wagnerolotry. Joyce used Wagnerian patterns for many effects in his fiction, from mythic elevation to mythic parody, but the effects that recur most frequently are comic, varying in subtlety from irony to punning wordplay.

E. M. Forster loved Wagner's operas all his life. He was moved by performances of the complete operas as well as orchestral excerpts at concerts, and for even more performances went to the Wagner Mecca at Bayreuth. What he especially enjoyed in Wagner's music was its specific definition and visual dimension. Forster liked knowing the literal and even verbal equivalents of the music he was hearing, and this of course is one of Wagner's fortes. As a result, Wagner figures significantly in Forster's essay "Not Listening to Music": "With Wagner I always knew where I was; he never let the fancy roam; he ordained that one phrase should recall the ring, another the sword, another the blameless fool and so on; he was as precise in his indications as an oriental dancer. Since he is a great poet, that did not matter" (Forster 128). It is interesting here that Forster regarded Wagner's writing, at least his libretti, as highly as his music.

Wagner's leitmotifs are very useful not only for organizing music but also for giving the texts visual equivalents, and with opera, the text should be as important as the music. But Forster also recognized the literary possibility in this technique. In an interview with the *Paris Review*, he was asked, "Do you have any Wagnerian leitmotif system to help you keep so many themes going at the same time?" Forster responded, "Yes, in a way, and I am certainly interested in music and musical methods" (Cowley 31). We can see this in virtually all of Forster's novels, where Wagner and his operas are directly mentioned.

Howards End is the Forster novel which contains the most Wagnerian allusions, which help to communicate particular meanings and to establish a specifically Edwardian intellectual milieu. Early in the novel Margaret talks heatedly about the confused connections between the arts:

> But, of course, the real villain is Wagner. He has done more than any other man in the nineteenth century towards the muddling of the arts. I do feel that music is in a very serious state just now, though extraordinarily interesting. Every now and then in history there do come these terrible geniuses, like Wagner, who stir up all the wells of thought at once. For a moment it's splendid. Such as splash as never was. But afterwards—

> such a lot of mud; and the wells—as it were, they communicate with each other too easily now, and not one of them will run quite clean. That's what Wagner's done [39-40].

Margaret is perceptive here in recognizing Wagner's immense influence upon a succeeding generation of artists and thinkers.

Later in *Howards End*, one of the most important passages in the book occurs and clearly states its major theme, using an image derived from *Das Rheingold*:

> Margaret greeted her lord with peculiar tenderness on the morrow. Mature as he was, she might yet be able to help him to the building of the rainbow bridge that should connected the prose in us with the passion. Without it we are meaningless fragments, half monks, half beasts: unconnected arches that have never joined into a man. With it love is born, and alights on the highest curve, glowing against the grey, sober against the fire. Happy the man who sees from either aspect the glory of these outspread wings [186].

As Forster says even more clearly later in *Howards End*:

> Only connect! That was the whole of her sermon. Only connect the prose and the passion, and both will be exalted, and human love with be seen at its height. Live in fragments no longer. Only connect, and the beast and the monk, robbed of the isolation that is life to either, will die [186-87].

Clearly here Forster intuited the bipolar quality of much of Wagnerian art and wanted to create a kind of novel which would move beyond polarity into a unified whole.

Wagner's operas also had a pronounced influence upon some of the major novels of Virginia Woolf. *The Voyage Out* (1915), *Jacob's Room* (1922), *The Waves* (1931), and *The Years* (1937) all owe something to Wagnerian opera. These works span most of Woolf's writing career, which implies a prolonged and probably changing influence, and the time gaps between the works also allow for some differences in her uses of the operas. She had a lasting fascination with the person of heroic potential, the influence of such a person upon the ordinary man, the suddenness of death, and the pervasive presence of the dead among the living. All these themes are archetypal rather than social or economic, and they lend themselves to mythic treatment.

Woolf's curiosity abut the artistic uses of myth naturally drew her to Wagner's mythic operas. Since Woolf often went to concerts and operas when she was in London, her lifelong involvement with music would also attract her to the composer, especially given the exalted opinion of his works and the frequency of their performance in London during her most formative years. The combination of myth and music, embodied so consummately in his operas, links two of her special interests.

In 1909 Virginia Woolf wrote a long article for the *London Times*, entitled "Impressions of Bayreuth," describing the Bayreuth festival's season of 1909 for Londoners who were unable to get there. In the process of reporting her reactions to the performances, she demonstrates a profound knowledge of Wagnerian opera and Wagnerian production; this article was written by someone who knew the operas well. She was particularly fascinated by the Bayreuth production of *Parsifal* and says in her article:

> Somehow Wagner has conveyed the desire of the Knights for the Grail in such a way that the intense emotion of human beings is combined with the unearthly nature of the thing they seek. It tears us, as we hear it, as though its wings were sharply edged. Again, feelings of the kind that are equally diffused and felt for one object in common create an impression of largesse and ... of an overwhelming unity. The grail seems to burn through all superincumbences; the music is intimate in a sense that none other is; one is fired with emotion and yet possessed with tranquility at the same time, for the words are continued by the music so that we hardly notice the transition. It may be that those exalted emotions, which belong to the essence of our being, and are rarely expressed, are those that are best translated by music [Woolf 23].

While her discussion of the opera's basic dichotomy of emotional appeals is highly perceptive, the desire to verbalize its effect implies an essentially literary response. Her final comment about music and literature sustains this impression of her as a music-lover with literary interests. Although she was fond of the other operas as well, "Impressions at Bayreuth" indicates that *Parsifal* had a special hold on her emotions, a hold that was reflected in references to the opera in several of her novels. Virginia Woolf, according to most of her biographers, suffered from bipolar illness. She may have sensed the bipolarity in many of Wagner's operas, and that may have been part of her attraction to his works.

In France, Wagner's influence was even more pervasive than in England according to Eugen Weber, despite Wagner's notorious Francophobia. As Weber writes: "Wagner's influence was limited by the anti–German reaction of 1870-71 and affected only narrow avant-garde circles for the next decade or two. After 1885, however, and especially in the 1890s, Wagner became the inspiration and touchstone of everything that was bold and new. The *Revue Wagnerienne*, devoted to his gospel, became one of the advance posts of decadence and symbolism." (Weber 144). In addition, many of the French Symbolist poets like Valéry, Mallarmé, and Gautier wrote for this Wagnerian periodical, and they often used Wagnerian themes in their poetry.

Weber also comments on the increasing frequency of the performances of Wagner's music in France:

> The introduction of ... Wagner himself to a broader public owed a great deal to two musical entrepreneurs of genius: Jules Pasdeloup and Jules-Edouard Juda Colonne. The former started his Sunday "popular concerts" in 1861. The later, once conductor for Pasdeloup, founded his own series in 1873. Here, for the first time, music lovers could actually listen to the great orchestral works so seldom heard by those who lived before the age of the phonograph. And though, in the wake of the Franco-Prussian War, Passdeloup had promised to play no more German music, he soon broke his promise, as did Colonne. When Wagner died, in February 1883, *Le Figaro* noted in passing that fragments of his operas were "now accepted in France and played at the *concert Pasdeloup*." After 1890 Wagner's works seem to have figured in every Sunday program [Weber 144–145].

Along with the music of Wagner came many of the ideas contained in his operas—especially the attraction to suicide, which recurs in the operas and which influenced the intellectual movement that eventually came to be known as Decadence. As an example of such Decadence of the Wagnerian sort, *Axel*, a play by Villiers de l'Isle Adam, gained a special notoriety. Here, the yearning for death is especially prominent among the main characters. As to normal life, says one of the characters in the play, "our servants will see to that for us." Throughout this play the author uses his characters, especially his main character, to give voice to a cultural yearning for death and suicide—a yearning almost as powerful as that voiced by Wagner's Tristan.

Eugen Weber also discusses Wagnerian influences in the French novel *A Rebours*:

> One of the most forceful expressions of this point of view sprang, fully armed, from the pen of a converted Naturalist as early as 1884. Joris-Karl Huysmans, when he wrote *A Rebours*, was a high civil servant, deputy head of that branch of the Surete which kept an eye on anarchist and other subversive activities. The book's conclusion was not that everything was decaying; it was already hopelessly rotten. The aristocracy had been despoiled and cast aside, the clergy was at a low ebb, the bourgeoisie was vile, the people crushed, the crowd turbid and

servile, the arts silly at best. "Collapse society: die, old world!" Des Esseintes cries as the book ends and the tide of human mediocrity surges to the heavens. The disgust with humanity, already striking in the writings of the Naturalists, erupts among the aesthetes of the fin de siecle [Weber 148].

The world-weary despair and longing for death that characterize much of fin de siecle literature, especially Adam and Huysmans, powerfully reflect the depression and suicidal ideation which we have found so frequently in Wagnerian opera. Just as Tristan and Isolde conclude at the end of Wagner's opera that they both will be better off dead, so too these later writers echo this Wagnerian theme, which they revive and amplify to create what became known as the Decadent period in European literature.

In addition to France and Britain, Italy became obsessed with Decadence and the Decadent writers as well. Gabriel D'Annunzio clearly reflected the death-obsessed movement of Decadence in his *Il Trionfo della Morte*, where death is seen as the ultimate triumph and where life is seen as futile and stupid. D'Annunzio claimed to be one of Wagner's pallbearers in Venice, where the composer died in 1883, and in his writings the Italian poet made personal use of many Wagnerian themes, particularly suicide and death, which must be regarded as recurrent Wagnerian obsessions. For example, D'Annunzio often suggests in his work that the human act of playing with death may well be the principal source of enjoyment in life.

In Germany the leading Decadent writer was Thomas Mann, who wrote about Wagner and Wagnerian opera repeatedly, especially in his famous essay *The Suffering and Greatness of Richard Wagner*, where he confesses his debt to the opera composer. Several Wagnerian themes appear throughout Mann's writings, but especially the theme of futility and death. Other critics have noted the connection between *Tristan und Isolde* and Thomas Mann's *Death in Venice*, which is a homosexual variant of the Liebestod theme, with the famous writer Gustav von Aschenbach going to Venice and becoming obsessed with Tadzio, a young boy from Poland. Since Wagner died in Venice, Mann's title is clearly a Wagnerian allusion; and in his novella we have an artistic work about obsessive love and its result, the suicidal death of Gustav at the end of the story. Though he is repeatedly warned about the presence of the plague in Venice, Gustav refuses to leave his beloved Tadzio, though ironically he never speaks a word to him. The final pages of the novella reflect the final fantasy vision of Aschenbach as he imagines the beloved Tadzio in the water and beckoning to him—just as Isolde's Liebestod ends with her vision of Tristan in the water, beckoning to her.

Mann also wrote a famous story called "The Blood of the Wälsungs," which makes use of the incestuous Wagnerian Wälsung brother and sister, Siegmund and Sieglinde. By the end of Mann's story, the sibling relationship becomes incestuous as well. Again, as if to underscore Wagner's perceptive portrayal, Mann's story "Tristan" provides a modern, ironic love story which uses allusions to Wagner's *Tristan und Isolde* for purposes of contrast with a modern absence of a loving relationship.

The last of the great Decadent writers was undoubtedly Samuel Beckett, whose Nobel Prize for Literature in 1962 capped a distinguished career. His chief writings extend the main Decadent themes into mid-century, for in his plays as well as his novels ideas of death and especially suicide play an important role, as the result of a view of life that remains essentially bleak and hopeless. While Beckett never alludes to Wagnerian opera directly, his use of Wagnerian obsessions such as death, suicide, dream-visions, and hopelessness reflect the depressive element in Wagnerian opera.

Beckett's most famous play, *Waiting for Godot*, for example, presents us with an onstage image of two old bums, two old comedians, who are waiting for a Godot who never arrives. They are killing time until time kills them, waiting for Godot, who keeps sending messengers who promise his eventual arrival. "Godot" sounds like a variant of God, and indeed there are numerous religious references in the play. Yet while Godot can be God, he can also be a symbol of something people always want but will never find—demonstrated by the futile waiting throughout the play. One of the few bright spots in Vladimir and Estragon's lives is the thought of suicide. They sometimes become excited about the thought of suicide because they hope death by hanging will give them an erection and an orgasm, things very unusual in their sterile existence of futile waiting. To us, their fascination with death and suicide, and their yearning for some fulfillment, some god, who will never arrive, seem very similar to the roles of Tristan and Isolde in Wagner's opera.

In this later work, however, suicide and death, recurrent themes in the novels and plays of Beckett, become a final endorsement, the last and perhaps most brilliant flowering of the Decadent movement in literature, and of the larger artistic movement which clearly began with Wagnerian opera. To die, even to commit suicide, thus becomes the final act of both desperation and hope. For Beckett as much as for Wagner, suicide stands as the ultimate escape and the only source of comfort for a long-suffering humanity.

Conclusion

Wagner died in Venice on February 13, 1883, and it was appropriate on some level that the composer died in Italy since the country had been such a major source of inspiration for him. After Ludwig II became his patron and he could afford many luxuries thanks to the generous king, Wagner often went to Italy, especially in the winters, when the cold climate in Bayreuth was hard on his heart. Wagner repeatedly wrote in his correspondence how much he enjoyed being in Italy, especially Venice, Naples, and Sicily. Indeed, his daughter Blandine married Count Biagio Gravina, a Sicilian nobleman, and spent most of her life in Sicily. At the Albergo della Palme in Palermo there still exists the Salone Wagner where the composer stayed whenever he was in Palermo.

Wagner also wrote most of the music for *Tristan und Isolde* in Venice, and being surrounded by water undoubtedly added to the undulating quality of most of the music in that opera. Wagner said he got the whole idea for his *Ring* cycle while dreaming on a boat off the coast of Spezia in Italy. He reported that Titian's great painting of the Assumption of the Virgin Mary in Venice inspired him to write the Liebestod at the end of *Tristan und Isolde*. He also wanted the Temple of the Grail in *Parsifal* to be modeled on the beautiful medieval cathedral in Siena, and a garden in Italy inspired his vision of Kundry's garden in Act II of *Parsifal*.

We have seen how much water inspired Wagner and how often water appears in Wagnerian opera, especially *The Flying Dutchman*, *Tristan und Isolde*, and the *Ring* cycle. Wagner often went to spas in Germany to find a water cure for his many health problems, but Germany, except for its north coast, is a land-locked country. While cities like Dresden and Munich

Conclusion

have rivers, to view a great ocean Wagner repeatedly made the journey to Italy.

While in Italy the mighty cycles of the tides of the ocean would have been constant reminders to him of the powerful cycles of nature. Even in Venice Wagner would have been reminded of the oceanic tides as he looked out onto the Grand Canal from his apartment window. The sides of the Venetian canals are marked with water lines from the oceanic tides. Wagner certainly absorbed Vico's theories about the cycles of nature, and the power of those cycles of nature on human existence, from his reading of his favorite German writer, Goethe. Goethe knew Vico's works, and Goethe's own writings reflect Vico's theories about the cycles of nature. Goethe's greatest work, his play *Faust*, begins with angels singing about the cycles of nature, and those very cycles become a dominant theme in his great play.

Photograph of Richard Wagner by Franz Hanfstaengl

An even greater cycle controlled Wagner and his operas, however: the manic-depressive cycle that he was prone to. Those manic highs—when he would dream of his operas conquering the world, when he would dream that his art would save Germany and even save the world, when he would go on lunatic spending binges and end in debt—often ended abruptly. Then he could abruptly experience the depression which left him wishing only for his own speedy death and planning specific ways to hasten that end. Suicide became the most recurrent fascination of his life, often mentioned in both his operas and his correspondence.

The extremism of these cycles even influenced his philosophical thought. As Bryan Magee has pointed out in his excellent book *Wagner and Philosophy*, the two major currents in his philosophical thinking tended to extremism. The young Wagner, influenced by Bakunin and Marx, hoped that with the elimination of the wealthy and powerful classes in Europe a new and perfectly just society could be established. The ideal society, rid of class, the obsession with money, and the yearning for power, could be created in his lifetime. But by the time of Wagner's maturity,

Arthur Schopenhauer's pessimism became the dominant mood in Wagner's philosophical thinking. Schopenhauer suggests that life is so full of frustration and unhappiness that death is to be preferred, and Wagner and his Wotan come to agree with Schopenhauer's depressive view of life's futility. Here too Wagnerian manic-depressive thinking reflected the composer's philosophy—either the manic vision of a dream of a perfect and perfectly attainable society or the depressive dream of a quick departure from the hateful world. The middle-ground, or the Golden Mean of ancient Roman philosophy, had no attraction for Wagner, since his thinking, and his art, were controlled by the extremism of the cyclical mood swings of his manic-depressive personality.

As Richard Wagner lay dead in Venice in the winter of 1883, a death possibly hastened by his own hand, the significant human results soon began to appear. Already for some time, family members and close friends had feared that the widow Cosima would take her own life in her terrible grief over the composer's death. Her former husband von Bülow suspected this and immediately telegrammed her "Soeur, il faut vivre" (Sister, one must live!). Fortunately she did not commit suicide; instead, she lived on until 1930 and acted decisively to establish the Bayreuth Festival as a yearly event—perhaps the most enduring celebration of Richard's continuing fame and stature. At the time of his death, most Wagnerians believed that the whole Bayreuth enterprise would die without the forceful presence of the composer, but Cosima was determined to prove them wrong, and she of course did.

Among a group of close friends was Josef Rubinstein, a young Jewish musician and a homosexual. In 1872, Rubinstein, a complete stranger to the composer, wrote a very sad letter to Richard Wagner that began: "I am a Jew. That says it all!" In that letter Rubinstein described his depressions, desperation, and his attempts to commit suicide. Today, one might think this is exactly the kind of person Wagner would have avoided since Rubinstein was a Russian Jew and clearly a deeply troubled man. But Wagner was so moved by the suffering described by the young man in his letter that the composer invited him to his home, Tribschen, on Lake Lucerne in Switzerland, and then gave him a room. Rubinstein's expertise as a pianist impressed Wagner, who never had mastered the piano himself, so the young man became Wagner's house pianist. In short, Wagner provided this suffering, suicidal young Jew with shelter and a job.

Yet Rubinstein was often difficult to live with, and Cosima and the children sometimes complained about his prickly temperament. For example, he would only accept messages when they came from Wagner himself, and not when they were conveyed through his wife or other family members.

Again when Wagner moved to his Villa Wahnfried in Bayreuth in 1874, a room was made available in the house for Josef Rubinstein, who became part of the Nibelungen Chancellery—a group of young musicians who helped Wagner with copying, transcribing, and producing musical scores. Rubinstein also composed the piano transcriptions for Wagner's *Siegfried Idyll* and for his final opera *Parsifal*. When Wagner went to Italy during the winters, Josef Rubinstein was there as well, acting both as the composer's pianist and as a personal friend. Wagner even wrote to Rubinstein's parents to describe his attempts to help the suicidal but highly talented young man. When Wagner died in Venice in 1883, Rubinstein was there to help the family cope with their grief, but the next year, in September of 1884, he went to Lake Lucerne by Tribschen, where he had first met Wagner, and drowned himself, causing his family and the Wagner family great anguish.

In 1886, Ludwig II of Bavaria, Wagner's most important patron, was deposed as king of Bavaria because of his increasingly erratic behavior. With his sanity in doubt, Ludwig was jailed in one of his castles, Schloss Berg, on Lake Starnberg in the Bavarian Alps. Then, on the morning of June 13, 1886, he was found floating in the lake along with the body of his personal physician. Exactly what happened will never be known, but it is probable that the suicidal, homosexual, and guilt-ridden king committed suicide by drowning himself in the lake, and that his doctor died trying to save him.

In 1882 in London the writer Virginia Woolf was born. She soon became fascinated with Wagnerian opera and even went to Bayreuth, where she wrote reviews of performances for the *London Times*. As a woman, however, she was often suicidal and she suffered from manic-depressive, or bipolar, illness. She was also a lesbian who had apparently Platonic love affairs with several women before and during her marriage to Leonard Woolf. During the height of World War II, during the blitz in London in 1941, she drowned herself in the river Ouse in Sussex.

Certainly a line of suicidal people formed a part of the Wagner circle at the end of the nineteenth century and after, and clearly one of the things that attracted them to Wagnerian opera was the suicidal theme so prevalent there. Some observers say that Wagnerian opera simply encouraged the act of suicide since so many of these operas glorify that act. Others would say that the operas helped these people to endure their personal suffering by knowing that the great composer Wagner shared their problems and suffering and that he used what he felt and knew from his own suffering to create great art. Surely the Wagnerian canon shows us nothing less, for both Wagnerian comedy and Wagnerian tragedy reflect the cycles that balance and control the realities of human life.

Bibliography

Abbate, Carolyn. *Unsung Voices: Opera and Musical Narrative in the Nineteenth Century*. Princeton, N.J.: Princeton University Press, 1991.

_____, and Roger Parker, eds. *Analyzing Opera: Verdi and Wagner*. Berkeley: University of California Press, 1989.

Barondes, Samuel H. *Mood Genes: Hunting for Origins of Mania and Depression*. New York: W. H. Freeman & Co., 1998.

Barth, H. D. Mack, and E. Voss, eds. *Wagner: A Documentary Study*. London: Thames & Hudson, 1975.

Bassett, Peter. *Wagner's Parsifal: The Journey of a Soul*. Adelaide, Australia: Wakefield Press, 2000.

Blunt, Wilfrid. *The Dream King: Ludwig II of Bavaria*. New York: Penguin, 1970.

Boyle, Nicholas. *Goethe: The Poet and the Age. Vol 1. The Poetry of Desire (1749–1790)*. Oxford, England: Oxford University Press, 1991.

Breton, André. *Manifestoes of Surrealism*. Translated from the French by Richard Seaver and Helen R. Lane. Ann Arbor: University of Michigan Press, 1969.

Brockett, Oscar G. *History of the Theatre*. Boston: Allyn and Bacon, 1982.

Buller, Jeffrey L. *Classically Romantic: Classical Form and Meaning in Wagner's "Ring."* Philadelphia: XLIBRIS, 2001.

_____. "Spectacle in the Ring," *The Opera Quarterly*. Vol. 14, No. 4. Summer, 1998. pp. 41–58.

Burbridge, Peter, and Richard Sutton, eds. *The Wagner Companion*. London: Faber, 1979.

Burian, Jarka. *Svoboda: Wagner*. Middletown, Conn.: Wesleyan University Press, 1983.

Chancellor, John. *Wagner*. New York: Granada, 1978.

Chapman-Huston, Desmond. *Ludwig II: The Mad King of Bavaria*. New York: Dorset Press, 1990.

Cicora, Mary A. *Parsifal-Reception in the Bayreuther Blätter*. New York: Peter Lang, 1987.
_____. *Wagner's Ring and German Drama*. Westport, Conn.: Greenwood Press, 1999.
Conrad, Peter. *Romantic Opera and Literary Form*. Berkeley, Calif.: University of California Press, 1977.
_____. *A Song of Love and Death: The Meaning of Opera*. St. Paul, Minn.: Graywolf Press, 1996.
Cooke, Deryck. *I Saw the World End: A Study of Wagner's Ring*. New York: Oxford University Press, 1979.
Corazzol, Adriana Guarnieri. *Tristano, mio Tristano: Gli Scrittori Italiani e il Caso Wagner*. Bologna: Il Mulino, 1988.
Corse, Sandra. *Wagner and the New Consciousness: Language and Love in the Ring*. Cranbury, N.J.: Associated University Presses, 1990.
Cowley, Malcolm, ed. *Writers at Work: The Paris Review Interviews*. New York: Viking Press, 1957.
Culshaw, John. *Reflections on Wagner's Ring*. New York: Viking Press, 1976.
_____. *Ring Resounding*. New York: Viking Press, 1967.
Deathridge, John, and Carl Dahlhaus. *The New Grove Wagner.* in *The New Grove Dictionary of Music and Musicians*. Stanley Sadie, ed. New York: Norton, 1984.
DiGaetani, John Louis. *Richard Wagner and the Modern British Novel*. Cranbury, N.J.: Fairleigh Dickinson University Press, 1978.
_____. *Penetrating Wagner's Ring: An Anthology*. New York: Da Capo Press, 1991.
_____. *Puccini the Thinker*. New York: Peter Lang Press, 2001.
Dreyfus, Laurence. "Herman Levi's Shame and *Parsifal*'s Guilt: A Critique of Essentialism in Biography and Criticism." *Cambridge Opera Journal*. Vol. 6, No. 2 (1999), pp. 125–145.
Eger, Manfred. *Wagner und die Juden: Fakten und Hintergrunde: Eine Dokumentation zur Ausstellung im Richard Wagner Museum Bayreuth*. Bayreuth, Germany: Druckhaus, 1985.
Fischer-Dieskau, Dietrich. *Wagner and Nietzsche*. Translated by Joachim Neugroschel. London: Sidgwick and Jackson, 1976.
Forster, E. M. *Howards End*. New York: Vintage Books, 1921.
_____. *Two Cheers for Democracy*. New York: Harvest Books, 1951.
Freud, Sigmund. *Beyond the Pleasure Principle*. Translated by James Strachey. New York: Norton, 1961.
Frye, Northrop. *Anatomy of Criticism*. New York: Atheneum, 1957.
Furness, Raymond. *Wagner and Literature*. New York: St. Martin's Press, 1982.
Gay, Peter. *Freud: A Life for Our Time*. New York: Norton, 1988.
Glass, Frank W. *The Fertilizing Seed: Wagner's Concept of Poetic Intent*. Ann Arbor, Mich.: UMI Research Press, 1983.
Goethe, Johann Wolfgang von. *Goethe's Faust*. The original German and a new translation and introduction by Walter Kaufmann. New York: Doubleday, 1963.
Goodwin, Donald W., and Samuel B. Guze. *Psychiatric Diagnosis*. New York: Oxford University Press, 1989.
Graham, Ilse. *Goethe: Portrait of an Artist*. New York: Walter de Gruyter, 1977.
Gregor-Dellin, Martin, and Michael von Soden. *Richard Wagner: Leben, Werk, Wirkung*. Dusseldorf: Econ, 1983.

Griffin, Justin. *The Holy Grail: The Legend, the History, the Evidence*. Jefferson, N.C.: McFarland, 2001.
Gutheil, Emil A. *Music and Your Emotions*. New York: Liveright, 1952.
Gutman, Robert W. *Richard Wagner: The Man, His Mind, and His Music*. New York: Harcourt Brace Jovanovich, 1968.
Herzeld, Friedrich. *Das Neue Bayreuth*. Berlin: Rembrandt, 1965.
Holman, J. K. *Wagner's Ring: A Listener's Companion and Concordance*. Portland, Oregon: Amadeus Press, 1996.
Huebner, Steven. *French Opera at the Fin de Siecle: Wagnerism, Nationalism, and Style*. New York: Oxford University Press, 1999.
Inwood, Margaret. *The Influence of Shakespeare on Richard Wagner*. Lewiston, N.Y.: Edwin Mellen, 1999.
Jamison, Kay Redfield. *Night Falls Fast: Understanding Suicide*. New York: Knopf, 1999.
_____. *Touched with Fire: Manic-Depressive Illness and the Artistic Temperament*. New York: Free Press, 1994.
_____. *An Unquiet Mind: A Memoir of Moods and Madness*. New York: Vintage Books, 1996.
Katz, Jacob. *The Darker Side of Genius: Richard Wagner's Anti-Semitism*. Hanover, N.H.: Brandeis University Press, 1986.
_____. *Richard Wagner: Hebrew*. Jerusalem: Markaz Zalman Shazar, 1986.
_____. *Richard Wagner: Vorbote des Antisemitismus*. Konigstein: Judischer Verlag, 1983.
Kesting, Hanjo. *Das Pump-Genie: Richard Wagner und das Geld: Nach Gedruckten und Ungedruckten Quellen*. Frankfurt am Main: Eichborn, 1993.
Köhler, Joachim. *Wagners Hitler: Der Prophet und sein Vollstrecher*. Munich: Blessing, 1997.
_____. *Wagner's Hitler: The Prophet and His Disciple*. Translated and Introduced by Ronald Taylor. Malden, Mass.: Polity Press, 2000.
Kreis, Rudolf. *Nietzsche, Wagner und die Juden*. Wurzburg: Konigshausen & Neumann, 1995.
Large, David C., and William Weber. *Wagnerism in European Culture and Politics*. Ithaca, N.Y.: Cornell University Press, 1984.
Lawrence, D. H. *The Collected Letters of D. H. Lawrence*. Edited by Harry T. Moore. 2 vols. London: Heinemann, 1962.
Lee, M. Owen. *Wagner: The Terrible Man and His Truthful Art*. Toronto: University of Toronto Press, 1999.
_____. *Wagner's Ring: Turning the Sky Around*. New York: Limelight Editions, 1998.
Levin, David J. *Richard Wagner, Fritz Lang, and the Nibelungen: The Dramaturgy of Disavowal*. Princeton, N.J.: Princeton University Press, 1998.
Lilla, Mark. *G. B. Vico: The Making of an Anti-Modern*. Cambridge, Mass.: Harvard University Press, 1993.
Magee, Bryan. *Aspects of Wagner*. New York: Stein and Day, 1969.
_____. *The Philosophy of Schopenhauer*. New York: Oxford University Press, 1983.
_____. *Wagner and Philosophy*. New York: Allen Lane/Penguin Press, 2000.
Mander, Raymond, and Joe Mitchenson. *The Wagner Companion*. New York: Hawthorn Books, 1977.

Manera, Giorgio, and Giuseppe Pugliese. *Wagner in Italia.* Venice: Marsilio, 1982.
Mann, Thomas. "The Suffering and Greatness of Richard Wagner" in *Essays.* Translated by H. T. Lowe-Porter. New York: Vintage, 1957.
Marek, George R. *Cosima Wagner.* New York: Harper & Row, 1981.
Martin, Stoddard. *Wagner to the Wasteland: A Study of the Relationship of Wagner to English Literature.* Totowa, N.J.: Barnes & Noble, 1982.
Mayer, Hans. *Wagner.* Ramburg: Rowohlt Taschenbuch, 1959.
Millington, Barry. "Nuremberg Trial: Is There Anti-Semitism in *Die Meistersinger?*" *Cambridge Opera Journal,* 3, No. 3: 247–260.
_____. *Wagner.* New York: Vintage Books, 1987.
_____, ed. *The Wagner Compendium: A Guide to Wagner's Life and Music.* New York: Schirmer Books, 1992.
_____, and Stewart Spencer, eds. *Wagner in Performance.* New Haven: Yale University Press, 1992.
Minois, Georges. *History of Suicide: Voluntary Death in Western Culture.* Translated by Lydia G. Cochrane. Baltimore: Johns Hopkins University Press, 1999.
Müller, Ulrich, and Peter Wapnewski, eds. *Wagner Handbook.* Cambridge, Mass.: Harvard University Press, 1992.
Nattiez, Jean-Jacques. *Wagner Androgyne: A Study in Interpretation.* Translated by Stewart Spencer. Princeton, N.J.: Princeton University Press, 1993.
Newman, Ernest. *The Life of Richard Wagner.* 4 vols. New York: Cambridge University Press, 1976.
Nietzsche, Friedrich, and Richard Wagner. *The Nietzsche-Wagner Correspondence.* Translated by Caroline V. Kerr. New York: Liveright, 1949.
Osborne, Charles. *Wagner and His World.* New York: Charles Scribner's Sons, 1977.
_____. *The World Theatre of Wagner.* New York: Macmillan, 1982.
Rather, L. J. *The Dream of Self-Destruction: Wagner's Ring and the Modern World.* Baton Rouge: Louisiana State University Press, 1979.
Reinhardt, Hartmut, "Wagner and Schopenhauer" in Ulrich Muller and Peter Wapnewski, eds. *Wagner Handbook.* Translation edited by John Deathridge. Cambridge, Mass.: Harvard University Press, 1992.
Robertson, J. G. *A History of German Literature.* Revised by Edna Purdue. New York: British Book Centre, 1962.
Rose, Paul Lawrence. *Wagner: Race and Revolution.* New Haven: Yale University Press, 1992.
Scholtz, Dieter David. *Richard Wagners Antisemitismus.* Wurzburg: Königshausen and Neumann, 1993.
Schopenhauer, Arthur. *Essays and Aphorisms.* Translated by R. J. Hollingdale. New York: Penguin Books, 1981.
_____. *Philosophical Writings.* Edited by Wolfgang Schirmacher. New York: Continuum, 1996.
Shaw, George Bernard. *The Perfect Wagnerite: A Commentary on the Nibelung's Ring.* New York: Dover, 1967.
Skelton, Geoffrey. *Richard and Cosima Wagner: Biography of a Marriage.* Boston: Houghton Mifflin, 1982.

Spencer, Stewart. *Wagner Remembered.* London: Faber & Faber, 2000.
Spotts, Frederic. *Bayreuth: A History of the Wagner Festival.* New Haven, Conn.: Yale University Press, 1994.
Tanner, Michael. *Wagner.* Princeton, N.J.: Princeton University Press, 1996.
Vaget, Hans Rudolf. "Sixtus Beckmesser—A 'Jew in the Brambles'?" *The Opera Quarterly.* Vol. 12, Number 1, August 1995, 35–45.
Vico, Giambattista. *The Autobiography of Giambattista Vico.* Translated by Max Fixch and Thomas Bergin. Ithaca, N.Y.: Cornell University Press, 1975.
Wagner, Cosima. *Cosima Wagner's Diaries.* Translated by Geoffrey Skelton. New York: Harcourt Brace Jovanovich, 1980.
_____. *Cosima Wagner's Diaries: An Abridgement.* Edited by Geoffrey Skelton. New Haven, Conn.: Yale University Press, 1997.
Wagner, Gottfried. *Twilight of the Wagners: The Unveiling of a Family's Legacy.* English Translation by Della Couling. New York: Picador, 1999.
Wagner, Nike. *The Wagners: The Dramas of a Musical Dynasty.* Translated by Ewald Osers and Michael Downes. Princeton, N.J.: Princeton University Press, 1998.
Wagner, Richard. *The Family Letters of Richard Wagner.* Translated by William Ashton Ellis. Ann Arbor: University of Michigan Press, 1991.
_____. *Der Fliegende Holländer: Romantic Opera in Three Acts.* English Translation by Susan Webb. New York: Metropolitan Opera Guild, 1993.
_____. *The Letters of Richard Wagner to Anton Pusinelli.* Translated by Elbert Lenrow. New York: Vienna House, 1972.
_____. *Lohengrin: Opera in Three Acts.* English Version by Stewart Robb. New York: G. Schirmer, Inc., 1963.
_____. *Die Meistersinger von Nürnberg.* English Translation and Notes by Susan Webb. New York: Metropolitan Opera Guild, 1992.
_____. *My Life.* Translated by Andrew Gray. New York: Da Capo, 1992.
_____. *Opera and Drama.* Translated by William Ashton Ellis. Lincoln: University of Nebraska Press, 1995.
_____. *Parsifal: Music Drama in Three Acts.* Translated by Stewart Robb. New York: G. Schirmer, 1962.
_____. *Religion and Art.* Translated by William Ashton Ellis. Lincoln: University of Nebraska Press, 1994.
_____. *Selected Letters of Richard Wagner.* Translated by Stewart Spencer and Barry Millington. New York: Norton, 1987.
_____. *Tannhäuser: Opera in Three Acts.* English Translation and Notes by Susan Webb. New York: Metropolitan Opera Guild, 1998.
_____. *Three Wagner Essays.* Translated by Robert L. Jacobs. London: Eulenburg Books, 1978.
_____. *Tristan und Isolde.* English version of libretto by Stewart Robb. New York: G. Schirmer, Inc., 1965.
_____. *Wagner on Music and Drama.* Edited by Albert Goldman and Evert Springchorn. New York: Dutton, 1964.
_____. *Wagner's Ring of the Nibelung.* Translated by Stewart Spencer. New York: Thames and Hudson, 1993.
_____, and Franz Liszt. *Correspondence of Wagner and Liszt.* 2 vols. Translated by Francis Hueffer. New York: Greenwood Press, 1969.

Warrack, John, and Ewan West, eds. *The Oxford Dictionary of Opera*. New York: Oxford University Press, 1994.

Watson, Derek. *Richard Wagner: A Biography*. London: Dent, 1979.

Weber, Eugen. *France Fin de Siecle*. Cambridge, Mass.: Harvard University Press, 1986.

Weiner, Marc A. *Richard Wagner and the Anti-Semitic Imagination*. Lincoln: University of Nebraska Press, 1995.

White, Chappell. *An Introduction to the Life and Works of Richard Wagner*. Englewood Cliffs, N.J.: Prentice-Hall, 1967.

Williams, Alastair. "Technology of the Archaid: Wish Images and Phantasmagoria in Wagner." *Cambridge Opera Journal*, Vol 9, No. 1, (1998), 73–87.

Williams, John. *The Life of Goethe: A Critical Biography*. Oxford, England: Blackwell, 1998.

Windell, George G. "Hitler, National Socialism, and Richard Wagner" in DiGaetani, John L., ed., *Penetrating Wagner's Ring: An Anthology*. New York: Da Capo, 1991.

Woolf, Virginia. "Impressions at Bayreuth," ed. by John L. DiGaetani, *Opera News*, 41 (August, 1976), 22–23.

Wright, William. *Born That Way: Genes, Behavior, Personality*. New York: Alfred A. Knopf, 1998.

Wylie, Sypher. *Comedy*. New York: Doubleday & Co., 1956.

Index

Abbate, Carolyn 145
Adam, Villiers de l'Isle 179–80
Altmeyer, Jeannine 131
Andersen, Hans Christian 127
Apel, Theodor 10
Aristotle 123ff
Assumption of the Virgin (Titian) 92, 182
Auden, W. H. 154

Bayreuth Festival 20, 21, 71–72, 96, 112, 148, 150, 158, 160, 173, 176, 178–84
Beckett, Samuel 166ff, 181ff
Beethoven, Ludwig van 57
Behrens, Hildegard 77, 140, 143
Bellini, Vincenzo 167
Berlioz, Hector 7, 167
Boehm, Gottfried von 71
Boyle, Nicholas 4
Brahms, Johannes 102
Breton, André 69–70
Brieg, Werner 37–38
Britten, Benjamin 170
Brockett, Oscar 151
Browning, Robert 173
Bruckner, Anton 7
Buddhism 159–64
Bülow, Hans von 9, 17–20
Bulwer-Lytton, Edward George 22
Burrell, Mrs. 92–93

Calderón de la Barca, Pedro 121
Cassilly, Richard 47, 82
Chaucer, Geoffrey 102
Chekhov, Anton 166
Christianity 149ff, 159–169
Coleridge, Samuel Taylor 56
Colonne, Jules-Edouard 179
Conrad, Joseph 174
Conrad, Peter 64, 74
Corneille, Pierre 166
Cowley, Malcolm 176
Cummings, E. E. 154

Dalí, Salvador 69
D'Annunzio, Gabriele 180
Dante Alighieri 14, 122
decadent writers 179–181ff
Delibes, Léo 167
Disney, Walt 127
Domingo, Placido 61, 157, 161
Donizetti, Gaetano 167
Dowland, John 7

Eckert, Karl 71
Elgar, Edward 7
Eliot, George 173

Die Feen 21
Der Fliegende Holländer 21–36ff
Forster, E. M. 176–77
free association 76–79

Freud, Sigmund 1, 11, 51, 57, 68–70, 74, 80, 92, 134, 138, 149, 160, 163
Fuchs, Hanns 3

Gautier, Théophile 179
Gessendorf, Mechthild 31
Geyer, Ludwig 92–93
Glinka, Mikhail 7
Goethe, Johann Wolfgang von 4, 22, 54, 87, 89, 183
Gozzi, Carlo 21–22, 100
Gravina, Count Biagio 182
Grieg, Edvard 174
Grimm, Jakob and Wilhelm 108, 127
Gutmann, Robert 107–08, 158

Haeggander, Mari-Anne 126
Hagegard, Hakan 50
Handel, George Frideric 7, 169
Hanfstaengl, Franz 8
Hanslick, Edward 102
Haydn, Joseph 167
Heckel, Emil 110
Hegel, Georg 154
Heine, Heinrich 23
Heppner, Ben 97
Hierstermann, Horst 136
Hofmann, Peter 129, 131
Holst, Gustav 7
Hueffer, Francis 173ff
Huysmans, Joris-Karl 179–80

Ibsen, Henrik 166
"Impressions of Bayreuth" (V. Woolf) 178
Ives, Charles 7

Jacobs, Robert 3
Jamison, Kay Redfield 7, 33–34ff
Jerusalem, Siegfried 115, 143
Joyce, James 4, 175–76
Judeo-Christian Tradition 165–71

Keats, John 56–57, 112
Keppler, Friedrich 19
Klemperer, Otto 7
Kupfer, Harry 109

Lawrence, D. H. 174ff
leitmotivs 122
Levin, David 127

Das Liebesverbot (Wagner) 21–22
Liszt, Franz 10–17, 53, 83, 100
lithium 2, 162
Lohengrin 55–72ff
Ludwig I 72
Ludwig II 9, 18, 21, 71–72, 83–84, 182, 185

Mackintosh, Cameron 109
Magee, Bryan 10–11, 183–84
Magritte, Rene 69
Mahler, Gustav 7
Mallarmé, Stephane 179
Manichean heresy 70, 156, 159–60
Mann, Thomas 3, 53, 81, 170, 180–81
Marek, George 81–83
Marton, Eva 66
Marxism 174, 183
Mattila, Karita 97
Die Meistersinger von Nürnberg 94–110ff
Metastasio, Pietro 167
Metropolitan Opera Company 148
Millington, Barry 22–23, 58–59, 95
Monteverdi, Claudio 169
Montez, Lola (Eliza Gilbert) 72
Morris, James 25, 31, 115
Mozart, Wolfgang Amadeus 168
Mueller, Richard 21
Mussorgsky, Modest 7

Nattiez, Jean-Jacques 3
Neumann, Angelo 173
Neumann, Wolfgang 136
Newman, Ernest 8, 9, 19–24, 38–39, 59, 91–95, 173
Nietzsche, Friedrich 3, 74, 149, 159, 162
Nilsson, Birgit 133
Nordau, Max 3
Norman, Jessye 47, 161

Oedipus Complex 3, 41, 73–76
Oliver 109
Osborne, Charles 63–64

Panizza, Oskar 3
Paris Review 176
Parsifal 3, 148–164ff
Pasdeloup, Jules 179ff
Pfistermeister, Franz von 71
Plato 139
Plishka, Paul 31

Index

Ponchielli, Amilcare 167
Puccini, Giacomo 100, 168–71

Rachmaninoff, Sergey 7
Racine, Jean 166
Rameau, Jean-Philippe 167
Reinhardt, Hartmut 74, 91
Revue Wagnerienne 179ff
Rienzi 21ff
Ring cycle (*Das Rheingold, Die Walküre, Siegfried, Die Götterdämmerung*) 110–47ff
Ritter, Julie 8–9
Ritter, Karl 17–19, 81–83
Roeckel, August 21, 71, 150
Roehling, Carl 12
Rootering, Jan-Hendrik 126
Rossini, Gioacchino 7
Rubinstein, Josef 184–85

Salminen, Matti 126, 147
Sandwike, Norway 22
Schopenhauer, Arthur 57, 74, 91, 163, 184
Schroeder-Devrient, Wilhelmine 24
Schubert, Franz 87
Schumann, Robert 7
Schuré, Edouard 122
Scriabin, Alexander 7
Shakespeare, William 22, 39, 64, 94, 98, 100, 108, 122, 165–66, 170
Shaw, George Bernard 174
Shelley, Percy Bysshe 90–91
Shostakovich, Dmitri 170
Sicily 182
Siena, Italy 182
Skelton, Geoffrey 71
Spezia, Italy 55, 68, 182
Stabreim 112
Strauss, Richard 169–70
Surrealism 51–52, 69–70
Sypher, Wylie 122

Tanguy, Yves 69
Tannhäuser 37–54ff
Tchaikovsky, Peter 7
Tennyson, Alfred 112
Tomowa-Sintow, Anna 61
Tribschen (Switzerland) 185
Tristan und Isolde 73–93ff
Troyanos, Tatiana 77

Vaget, Hans 108
Valery, Paul 179
Venice, Italy 73, 76, 92, 148, 156, 160, 166, 167, 170, 172, 180–84
Verdi, Giuseppe 100, 159, 168–71
Vergil 167
Verismo 58
Vickers, Jon 152
Vico, Giambattista 3, 4, 35, 48, 54, 90, 98, 100, 112, 125, 130, 138, 146, 159, 175, 183

Wagner, Carl Friedrich 92
Wagner, Cosima 17–20, 38, 41, 55, 57–58, 67, 70, 81–83, 92, 100, 102, 121–22, 184
Wagner, Johanna 67–68, 92–93
Wagner, Minna 14–15, 22, 73
Wagner, Siegfried 102
Wahnfried (villa, haus) 96–99, 185
Wapnewski, Peter 21
Wartburg Castle 37
Webb, Susan 38
Weber, Eugen 178–80
Weikl, Berndt 101
Weiner, David 107
Wesendonck, Mathilde 13–17, 41, 73–75, 81–83
Wesendonck, Otto 15, 73
Wille, Eliza 16
Wolf, Hugo 7
Woolf, Virginia 177–78, 185
Wulffen, Erich 3

www.ingramcontent.com/pod-product-compliance
Lightning Source LLC
Chambersburg PA
CBHW032101300426
44116CB00007B/842